THE COMPLETE BOOK OF

BIBLE
SECRETS

AND MYSTERIES

J. STEPHEN LANG

Tyndale House Publishers, Inc.
WHEATON, ILLINOIS

Visit Tyndale's exciting Web site at www.tyndale.com

TYNDALE is a registered trademark of Tyndale House Publishers, Inc.

Tyndale's quill logo is a trademark of Tyndale house Publishers, Inc.

The Complete Book of Bible Secrets and Mysteries

Copyright © 2005 by J. Stephen Lang. All rights reserved.

Cover photograph of woman in fabric © by Larry Dale Gordon/Getty Images. All rights reserved.

Cover images of trees, statue, stained glass, woman, blue silhouette, lantern, and gold urn © by Photos.com. All rights reserved.

Designed by Ron Kaufmann

Unless otherwise indicated, Scripture quotations are taken from the Holy Bible, King James Version. In many instances, the author has chosen to modernize an archaic word or phrase.

Library of Congress Cataloging-in-Publication Data

Lang, J. Stephen.
The complete book of Bible secrets and mysteries / J. Stephen Lang.
p. cm.
ISBN 1-4143-0168-5 (pbk.)
1. Bible—Miscellanea. I. Title.
BS612.L25 2005
220—dc22   2004024554

Printed in the United States of America

11   10   09   08   07   06   05
7   6   5   4   3   2   1

CONTENTS

INTRODUCTION

Back in 1988, I published *The Complete Book of Bible Trivia*. When more than 700,000 copies and numerous translations and spin-off products were sold, I became happily aware that readers love that book's hodge-podge of questions and answers about the Bible on a wide variety of topics. Now, for both your entertainment and edification, I have compiled a new collection of questions and answers, all related to the general theme of "Bible secrets and mysteries."

Why this theme? Partly because people seem fascinated by the mysterious and puzzling parts of the Bible, as evidenced by various books that claim to break the "codes" of the Bible. This fascination really isn't new, because people have been trying for centuries to "decode" the Bible—such as figuring out who (or what) is represented by 666, the "number of the beast" in the book of Revelation. We may never know (until the end of time, perhaps) how to decode 666, but this hasn't stopped people from speculating. People also love to speculate about other "coded" passages—such as John 21:11, which mentions that Jesus' disciples caught exactly 153 fish in their net. Was John simply reporting a literal fact (there were 153 fish in that net), or did 153 *mean* something else? Many great minds in Christian history were certain that the number had deep spiritual meaning, but no one can agree on just what it was.

Here's a bit of good news: most of the Bible isn't written in code. Most of it is very literal and very easy to grasp. American humorist Mark Twain stated that while many people were bothered by the parts of the Bible they didn't understand, he was bothered by the parts he *did* understand—such as the command to love our neighbors as ourselves. Twain grasped something that countless "code breakers" miss: The Bible isn't a puzzle to be solved. It is God's revelation to humanity, most of it crystal clear and straightforward, no more puzzling than a Stop sign. "You shall not steal" is no mystery, nor is "You shall not commit adultery." "Blessed are the merciful" is easily grasped, as is "All have sinned and come short of the glory of God." No code breaking necessary, thank you.

Having said that, however, the Bible is still *very* mysterious, for it is brimming over with miracles, with revelations of an awesome and invisible God. There are angels and demons, fire from heaven, dreams sent from God, wondrous escapes, battles in which a small force triumphs over a much larger force, resurrections from the dead, glimpses of heaven, the awesomeness of what the Bible calls God's "glory," the work-ings of the Holy Spirit, curious beasts like the leviathan and Behemoth, and prophecies of things to come, including visions of the final battle between good and evil. Yes, the Bible is really very mysterious, in all the right ways.

PART 1

SOME TRULY PUZZLING THINGS

BIBLE MYSTERIES: THE TOP TEN

The book you are now reading explores the Bible's mysteries and secrets—and tests your knowledge of them. To begin, let's see how familiar you are with ten of the most puzzling things in the Bible, things that leave even the best-read Bible scholars scratching their heads in bewilderment.

1. One of the great puzzles of Genesis is this: Where did _____ get his wife?
2. In Revelation, what is the number of the "beast" who persecutes the saints?
3. What heroic Old Testament saint did God almost kill—just after calling him into service?
4. What book of the Bible refers to a mysterious race known as the Nephilim?
5. According to 1 Peter, where did Jesus go between his burial and resurrection?
6. According to Paul, women will be saved through what?
7. In Genesis 6, who do the "daughters of men" marry and bear children by?
8. What were the "sacred dice" used by Israel's leaders in decision making?
9. According to Jesus, what is the one sin that can never be forgiven?
10. What organ, according to Jesus, is the "lamp of the body"?

BIBLE MYSTERIES: THE TOP TEN (ANSWERS)

1. *Cain, son of Adam and Eve, murderer of his only brother, Abel. Genesis 4:17 refers to Cain's wife, but readers wonder where she came from, seeing that the only people on earth (or at least the only ones mentioned in Genesis) were Adam, Eve, Cain, and Abel. The usual explanation—not that it satisfies everyone—is that Cain's wife was also his sister, a daughter (whose name is not disclosed) of Adam and Eve.*

2. *The number 666, of course. Revelation 13:18 invites readers to "calculate" the number—meaning (we think) decipher the number so as to connect it with a particular person. No one has ever done this satisfactorily. See pages 78–80 for much more about the Beast and his number.*

3. *Moses (Exodus 4:24-26). God has just called Moses to lead the Israelites out of slavery in Egypt, and suddenly, for reasons that are not immediately apparent, the Lord "was about to kill him." Exodus 4:25-26 reveals that God was angry with Moses for not circumcising his son in accordance with God's covenant with Abraham.*

4. *Genesis 6:4. Some translations refer to giants instead of Nephilim. They are called "heroes of old, men of renown," but who or what they were still puzzles readers.*

5. *He "preached to the spirits in prison" (1 Peter 3:19), a phrase that gives Bible interpreters fits. Who were these "spirits," and what "prison" is meant? First Peter 3:20 connects the "spirits" to the time of Noah and the Flood, but this only serves to deepen the mystery for Bible scholars.*

6. *Childbearing, as recorded in 1 Timothy 2:15. This occurs in a passage that says women should be submissive and not have authority over a man, but we really aren't sure what Paul meant by "women will be saved through childbearing," since Christian women, like Christian men, are saved by faith.*

7. *The "sons of God" (Genesis 6:1-2). The identity of these "sons" is as puzzling as the identity of the Nephilim (see question 4). Some Bible scholars say that the passage refers to angels fathering children by human women, although this explanation doesn't satisfy everyone.*

8. *The Urim and Thummim, mysterious objects that were in (or on) the breastplate of Israel's high priest and involved (we don't know how) in decision making (Exodus 28:30). Their use is mentioned in Ezra 2:63 and Nehemiah 7:65, but these verses shed no clear light on what Urim and Thummim looked like or how they were used.*

9. *Blaspheming against the Holy Spirit (Matthew 12:31; Luke 12:10), though no one is absolutely certain what this means. One reasonable guess is that it means attributing the work of God to the work of Satan and demons.*

10. *The eye (Matthew 6:22), and after many centuries, no one is still quite sure what he meant by the phrase.*

 ## LEVIATHAN, UNICORNS, AND SUCH

Be glad the Old Testament has been translated into English, because the original language, Hebrew, is notoriously difficult to learn and translate. Even after centuries of study, there are certain Hebrew words that puzzle scholars. This is particularly true of words referring to plants and animals. In some cases, translating is made even more of a mystery by the fact that the words may be referring to mythical animals, not real ones. See how much you know about these real—but possibly *unreal*—beasts of the Bible.

1. What beast, mentioned in Job 40:15, lives in the water and feeds on grass?
2. What sea beast is described in fearsome detail in Job 41?

3. What shaggy creatures of Greek mythology are mentioned by the prophet Isaiah?
4. What mythical horned creature, popular in art, may be referred to in Job 39:9 and Isaiah 34:7?
5. According to Psalm 104, what sea creature was formed to frolic in the sea?
6. What mythical beasts, mentioned many times in Psalms, are called "serpents" or "jackals" in most modern translations?

LEVIATHAN, UNICORNS, AND SUCH (ANSWERS)

1. The Behemoth—which may refer to a mythical water beast, or to a real beast such as a hippo or elephant

2. The leviathan, which, like the Behemoth, may be mythical or may be a real creature (possibly a crocodile or whale)

3. Satyrs, usually thought to be half-goat, half-man. Mentioned in Isaiah 13:21 and 34:14, they were probably (as modern versions have it) wild goats.

4. The unicorn. Translators struggle over a Hebrew word that refers to some type of horned beast. Many modern versions have "wild ox" instead of "unicorn."

5. The leviathan, again. This may be referring to a whale, but since translators aren't sure, many versions just use the word leviathan, which is a direct transliteration from the original Hebrew.

6. Dragons (as in the King James Version). Because there are no real dragons, modern versions do their best to connect the Hebrew words with an actual living creature.

"INSPIRED," YES, BUT HOW?

For hundreds of years people have agreed that the Bible was "inspired." But just what does that mean? The theory that God actually dictated the words doesn't hold water because it is obvious in the different books that the personalities of the authors show through clearly. They weren't just channeling God's words; and yet, in some mysterious way, the Bible's words really are "God's words." Somehow, rather beyond our comprehension, God "moved" the prophets, poets, apostles, and wise men to write, just as he "moved" kings and military leaders to act. Incidentally, the word *inspire* comes from the Latin *inspiratio,* meaning "to breathe into"—the "breath" coming from God, of course.

1. Which apostle stated that all Scripture is "inspired by God"?
2. According to 2 Peter, prophecy came because men were moved by what?
3. In the Gospels, which nuclear family was filled with the Holy Spirit?
4. What reluctant prophet was told by God, "Go, and I will be with thy mouth"?
5. Which prophet claimed that God "carries out the words of his servants and fulfills the predictions of his messengers"?
6. What pagan prophet assured his employer that he could only speak what God put into his mouth?
7. Which aide and successor of Moses was "full of the spirit of wisdom"?
8. What military man had the Spirit of the Lord come upon him before battling the pagan Ammonites?
9. Which king of Israel was told he would be "changed into a different person" when the Spirit came upon him?
10. What ritual marked the time when the Spirit came upon David?
11. Which prophet in David's court received a message from God, saying that David's dynasty would last forever?
12. What blind prophet was inspired by God to see through the disguise of a woman?
13. What fiery prophet, empowered by God, outran the horses of King Ahab?
14. Which prophet was moved by the power of God while listening to a harpist?
15. To whom did God give the plans for building the Temple in Jerusalem?
16. Where were the people gathered when the Spirit moved the prophet Jahaziel to speak?
17. Which king was considered evil for not recognizing that Jeremiah the prophet was inspired by God?
18. Which of Job's friends told him that the Spirit of God gives man understanding?
19. Which prophet foretold a leader who would bring justice to the nations with the power of the Spirit?
20. What young (and reluctant) prophet had his mouth touched by God, with the assurance he would speak on God's behalf?
21. What later prophet claimed the Lord's power enabled him to interpret the words of Jeremiah?

22. Which prophet stated he was filled with the Spirit and "with justice and might"?
23. In Genesis, who attributed his dream-interpreting ability to the Spirit of God?
24. What was the vocation of Bezalel, said to be filled with the Spirit of God?
25. What man had learned through the Holy Spirit that he would see the Christ before he died?
26. In chapter 1 of John's Gospel, who is the "man sent from God"?
27. What man, "full of the Holy Spirit," had a vision of Jesus standing at the right hand of God?
28. What man was led by the Spirit to preach the gospel to an Ethiopian eunuch?
29. What Christian, inspired by the Spirit, predicted a famine over the Roman Empire?
30. Which of Paul's letters begins with an announcement that the gospel had been promised long ago in the Holy Scriptures?
31. According to the Letter to the Hebrews, God in the past spoke through his prophets but has now spoken through whom?
32. In which New Testament book is the author continually given the command "Write"?

"INSPIRED," YES, BUT HOW? (ANSWERS)

1. *Paul, in 2 Timothy 3:16. Some modern versions have "God-breathed" (which is really more accurate) instead of "inspired."*

2. *The Holy Spirit (2 Peter 1:21). This passage emphasizes that God, not man, took the initiative in prophecy.*

3. *John the Baptist (Luke 1:15) and his parents, Elizabeth (1:41) and Zechariah (1:67)*

4. *Moses (Exodus 4:12)*

5. *Isaiah (44:26)*

6. *Balaam, the Moabite prophet that had been sent to curse Israel (Numbers 22:38; 23:26)*

7. *Joshua (Deuteronomy 34:9)*

8. *The judge Gideon (Judges 11:29)*

9. *Saul (1 Samuel 10:6)*

10. *His anointing by the prophet Samuel (1 Samuel 16:13)*

11. *Nathan (2 Samuel 7:4)*

12. *Ahijah (1 Kings 14), who was visited by the wife of King Jeroboam*

13. *Elijah (1 Kings 18:46)*

14. *Elisha (2 Kings 3:15)*

15. *David (1 Chronicles 28:19). The task of actually building the Temple fell to his son Solomon.*

16. *The Temple courts (2 Chronicles 20:14)*

17. *Zedekiah (2 Chronicles 36:12)*

18. *Elihu (Job 32:8)*

19. *Isaiah (42:1), in a passage that is known as one of the "Servant Songs," prophecies of a divine servant. Christians believe that Jesus fulfilled those prophecies.*

20. *Jeremiah (1:9)*

21. *Daniel (9:2)*

22. *Micah (3:8)*

23. *Joseph (Genesis 40:8; 41:16)*

24. *An artist involved in making the Tabernacle and its worship furnishings (Exodus 35:30-31). This is the rare case in Scripture of an "inspired artist."*

25. *Simeon, who did indeed see the infant Jesus (Luke 2:25)*

26. *John—not the author of the Gospel, but John the Baptist*

27. *Stephen, the first martyr (Acts 7:55)*

28. *Philip (Acts 8:29)*

29. *Agabus (Acts 11:28). Acts notes that the famine did indeed occur in the reign of Emperor Claudius.*

30. *Romans (1:2). By "scriptures," Paul was referring to what we now call the Old Testament.*

31. *His Son—that is, Christ*

32. *Revelation, where John is repeatedly told by Christ or an angel to write (1:11,19; 2:1,8,12,18; 3:1, 7, 14; 14:13; 19:9; 21:5). In no other book of the Bible are we so aware of the author being divinely compelled to write.*

 ## "CONTRADICTIONS," YOU SAY?

Does the Bible ever contradict itself? For centuries, readers have been mystified by what seem to be discrepancies in the biblical narratives. Most of these differences can be easily explained by a close reading of the text. Others may be due to errors that occurred in centuries of copying manuscripts. None reflect on the inspiration of the Scriptures. More important, none of these apparent contradictions in any way affects Christian belief and morality. I include these questions here, not to cast doubt on the Bible, but merely to test the reader's knowledge of some of these so-called contradictions.

1. In 1 Samuel 16:19-21, David comes to know Saul by being employed as his harpist. In 1 Samuel 17, how does David come to know Saul?
2. Matthew 27:6-8 says the priests bought the potter's field, but Acts 1:18-19 says someone else bought it. Who?
3. In Exodus 33:20, God tells Moses that no man can see God's face. According to Exodus 33:11, what man saw God face-to-face?
4. The Levites entered the service of the sanctuary at age 30—according to Numbers 4:3. At what age, according to Numbers 8:24, did they enter the service?
5. The mission of the 12 Israelite spies started at Paran—according to Numbers 13:3. In Numbers 20:1, where does the mission start?
6. According to Deuteronomy 10:6, Aaron died at Moserah. Where, according to Numbers 20:28, did he die?
7. Deuteronomy 15:4 says "There shall be no poor among you." What does Deuteronomy 15:11 say?
8. According to 1 Samuel 16:10-11, David had eight brothers. How many, according to 1 Chronicles 2:13-15, did he have?
9. According to Genesis 25:1, Abraham's second wife was Keturah. According to 1 Chronicles 1:32, who was Keturah?
10. In 1 Samuel 17, David is the slayer of Goliath. According to 2 Samuel 21:19, who killed the giant?
11. In 1 Samuel 31:3-4, Saul takes his own life after being wounded. In 2 Samuel 1, who claims he actually killed Saul?
12. According to 2 Samuel 14:27, Absalom had three sons. How many did he have according to 2 Samuel 18:8?
13. The Lord moved David to number the people of Israel according to 2 Samuel 24:1. In the story in 1 Chronicles 21, who moved David to do this?
14. According to 2 Kings 24:8, King Jehoiachin was 18 years old when he began to reign. How old was he in the account in 2 Chronicles 36?
15. Samuel was an Ephraimite, according to 1 Samuel 1. What tribe was he from in the account in 1 Chronicles 6?

16. According to 2 Chronicles 33:13-16, evil King Manasseh repented of his sins after being held captive in Babylon. What does the parallel account in 2 Kings 21 say about this repentance?

17. In Matthew's genealogy of the Messiah, Jesus is descended from David's son Solomon. What son of David is Jesus' ancestor in Luke's account?

18. In Luke's account of the temptation of Jesus, the last temptation is to jump from the pinnacle of the Temple. What is the last temptation in Matthew's version?

19. According to Matthew 8:5-13, a centurion asks that his servant be healed. In Luke 7:2-11, who does the asking?

20. In Matthew 8, the maniac lives in Gadara. In Luke 8 and Mark 5, where does he live?

21. Matthew 20:20 states that the mother of James and John requested that her sons be appointed to high office in the coming Kingdom. In Mark 10:35, who made the request?

22. In Matthew 26:34, Jesus predicts that Peter will betray him before the rooster crows once. In Mark 14:30, how many times is the rooster supposed to crow?

23. According to Matthew 27:3-10, Judas hanged himself. How did he kill himself according to Acts 1:18?

24. In John 19:19, we are told that the inscription on the cross read, "Jesus of Nazareth, the King of the Jews." According to Matthew 27:37, what was the inscription?

25. According to John's account of the post-Resurrection appearances, what two disciples ran to Jesus' tomb?

26. In Mark 2:26, Jesus says that Abiathar was priest during David's reign. According to 1 Samuel 21, who was priest at that time?

27. Matthew 5:3 has Jesus saying, "Blessed are the poor in spirit." What does he say in Luke 6:20?

28. James 1:13 says God does not tempt men. But Genesis 22:1 says God tempted a certain man. Who?

29. Solomon had 40,000 horses according to 1 Kings 4:26. How many did he have according to 2 Chronicles 9:25?

30. Matthew 27:9-10 attributes the prophecy about the potter's field to Jeremiah. Where is the prophecy found?

31. Mark 15:26 says the inscription on Jesus' cross read "The King of the Jews." What is it in Luke's account (23:38)?

32. Matthew's genealogy of Jesus says that Joseph's father was Jacob (1:16). According to Luke 3:23, who was it?

SOME TRULY PUZZLING THINGS

33. In which Epistle does Paul say, "Bear ye one another's burdens" and "Every man shall bear his own burden"?
34. What book of the Bible says, in the same chapter, "Answer not a fool according to his folly" and "Answer a fool according to his folly"?
35. According to 2 Samuel 6:23, David's wife Michal had no children. But according to 2 Samuel 21:8, she had children. How many?
36. Solomon stated in Proverbs 18:22, "Whoso findeth a wife findeth a good thing." Who, in the New Testament, stated, "It is good for a man not to touch a woman"?
37. Acts 9:7 says that the people traveling with Paul heard the heavenly voice Paul heard. But, according to Acts 22:9, someone said that the people did not hear the voice. Who said that?
38. Mark 1:12-13 says that Jesus immediately went into the wilderness after his baptism and was there for 40 days. Which Gospel claims that the day after his baptism he called Andrew and Peter to be his disciples?
39. According to 1 Corinthians 15:5, Jesus appeared to the 12 disciples after his resurrection. According to Matthew and Acts, how many apostles were there after his resurrection?

"CONTRADICTIONS," YOU SAY? (ANSWERS)

1. *Through the killing of Goliath*
2. *Judas Iscariot*
3. *Moses*
4. *Twenty-five*
5. *Kadesh Barnea*
6. *Mount Hor*
7. *"The poor will never cease to be in the land."*
8. *Seven*
9. *His concubine*
10. *Elhanan*
11. *Saul's Amalekite bodyguard*
12. *None*
13. *Satan*
14. *Eight*

15. *Levi*

16. *Nothing*

17. *Nathan*

18. *The temptation to rule the world*

19. *The servant*

20. *Gerasa*

21. *James and John*

22. *Twice*

23. *He fell headlong and burst apart.*

24. *"This is Jesus, the King of the Jews."*

25. *Peter and John*

26. *Abimelech*

27. *"Blessed are the poor."*

28. *Abraham*

29. *Four thousand*

30. *Zechariah 11:12-13. Neither Jeremiah nor Zechariah words the prophecy as it is quoted in Matthew.*

31. *"This is the King of the Jews." Obviously this is a case of very minor discrepancy.*

32. *Heli*

33. *Galatians (6:2 and 6:5). This is a case of poor translation, since in the Greek original, two different words are used, while the older English versions used the same word, burden, for both.*

34. *Proverbs (26:4 and 26:5)*

35. *Five. This apparent scribal error is corrected in some translations, where Merab, not Michal, is the mother of the five children.*

36. *Paul (1 Corinthians 7)*

37. *Paul*

38. *John (1:35)*

39. *Only 11. Matthew 27:3-5 says that Judas Iscariot hanged himself before Jesus' resurrection, and Acts 1:9-26 says that the new apostle, Matthias, had not yet been chosen at the time of the Resurrection.*

THE MYSTERY MYSTERY

Well, one thing is for sure—there is no mystery about where our word *mystery* comes from: It's from the Greek word *mysterion*, which occurs several times in the New Testament. The original word, however, didn't mean something puzzling or incomprehensible but something revealed, but only to a select few. A person initiated into one of the many bizarre cults of New Testament times received a *mysterion* on joining. The Christian authors took this meaning and gave it a new twist. For them, it referred to a divine truth—once hidden but now revealed to all people of faith. See what you know about the "mysteries" of the New Testament.

1. What book of the Bible speaks of the "mystery of the seven stars"?
2. What practice was Paul referring to when he spoke of one who "utters mysteries with his spirit"?
3. What one quality is much more important than being able to "fathom all mysteries"?
4. Which Epistle refers to the mystery "kept hidden for ages and generations"?
5. Who had the word *MYSTERY* written on her forehead?
6. What was Paul describing when he told the Corinthians, "Behold, I tell you a mystery"?
7. According to Ephesians 5, what human institution is a "mystery" symbolizing Christ and his church?
8. Which Epistle states that God made known "the mystery of his will"?
9. According to Colossians 2:2, who is the "mystery of God"?
10. What was the great mystery—which angered many Jews—Paul refers to in Romans 11:25?

THE MYSTERY MYSTERY (ANSWERS)

1. *Revelation (1:20)*

2. *Speaking in tongues (1 Corinthians 14:2)*

3. *Love (1 Corinthians 13:2)*

4. *Colossians (1:26)*

5. *The great harlot of Revelation (17:5), whatever she symbolizes*

6. *The final resurrection of all believers (1 Corinthians 15:51)*

7. Marriage (Ephesians 5:32)

8. Ephesians (1:9)

9. Christ. Paul's meaning is that Christ is God's revelation to humanity.

10. That Gentiles—non-Jews—were included in God's plan for salvation

WHAT WAS THAT VERSE AGAIN?

Some of the greatest mysteries of the Bible are the words of the Bible itself—particularly if you happen to be reading the King James Version. That well-loved Bible was first published in 1611, and the English language has changed dramatically (to put it mildly) in four hundred years. Add to that the fact that those translators back in the 1600s didn't have as deep a knowledge of Hebrew and Greek as we now possess, so in a few passages they were almost fumbling in the dark. As a result, that wonderful old KJV has become, over time, almost a puzzle to read, particularly in the passages below, which you can file under "Curious Quotations"—quaint, amusing, and maybe both. For each of the strange quotations listed, name the book of the Bible where it is found. (If you're really good, name the chapter and verse.)

1. At Parbar westward, four at the causeway, and two at Parbar.
2. Therefore will I discover thy skirts upon thy face.
3. The mountains skipped like rams, and the little hills like lambs.
4. All faces shall gather blackness.
5. The ships of Tarshish did sing of thee in thy market.
6. The herds of cattle are perplexed.
7. The voice of the turtle is heard in our land.
8. And they made two ouches of gold.
9. A bell and a pomegranate, a bell and a pomegranate, round about the hem of the robe to minister in.
10. I have put on my coat; how shall I put it on?
11. Dead flies cause the ointment of the apothecary to send forth a stinking savor.
12. Every man shall kiss his lips that giveth a right answer.
13. And kings shall be thy nursing fathers.
14. This thy stature is like to a palm tree, and thy breasts to clusters of grapes.

15. Destruction and death say, We have heard the fame thereof with our ears.
16. Associate yourselves, O ye people, and ye shall be broken in pieces.
17. And the rest of the tree of his forest shall be few, that a child may write them.
18. And on the eighth she shall take unto her two turtles.
19. Thou shalt not seethe a kid in his mother's milk.
20. Thy lips, O my spouse, drop as the honeycomb; honey and milk are under thy tongue; and the smell of thy garments is like the smell of Lebanon.
21. And it came to pass in the first month in the second year, on the first day of the month, that the tabernacle was reared up.
22. Behold, he formed grasshoppers in the beginning of the shooting.
23. So two or three cities wandered unto one city to drink water.
24. Let the floods clap their hands; let the hills be joyful together.
25. Every head was made bald, and every shoulder was peeled.
26. Her king is cut off as the foam upon the water.
27. And the sea coast shall be dwellings and cottages for shepherds, and folds for flocks.
28. And it waxed great, even to the host of heaven.
29. Then the king's countenance was changed, and his thoughts troubled him, so that the joints of his loins were loosed, and his knees smote one against the other.
30. He maketh them to skip like a calf; Lebanon and Sirion like a young unicorn.
31. And the wild asses did stand in the high places, they snuffed up the wind like dragons.
32. I have compared thee, O my love, to a company of horses in Pharaoh's chariots.
33. Thy bow was made quite naked.
34. The Lord will smite thee with the botch of Egypt, and with the emerods, and with the scab, and with the itch.
35. Cease ye from man, whose breath is in his nostrils.
36. Behold, I will corrupt your seed, and spread dung upon your faces, even the dung of your solemn feasts.
37. They are all adulterers, as an oven heated by the baker.
38. Feed thy people with thy rod.
39. And the man whose hair is fallen off his head, he is bald; yet is he clean.

40. Ye shall not eat one day, nor two days, nor five days, neither ten days, nor twenty days, but even a whole month, until it come out at your nostrils.
41. I am gone like the shadow when it declineth; I am tossed up and down as the locust.
42. And the unicorns shall come down with them, and the bullocks with the bull; and their land shall be soaked with blood, and their dust made fat with fatness.
43. Thy teeth are like a flock of sheep that are even shorn, which came up from the washing.
44. The words of a man's mouth are as deep waters.
45. Lift up your heads, O ye gates.
46. Thou shalt suck the breast of kings.
47. Will I eat the flesh of bulls, or drink the blood of goats?
48. When she saw Isaac, she lighted off her camel.
49. Thy neck is like the tower of David builded for an armory, whereon there hang a thousand bucklers.
50. Thou shalt not respect persons, neither take a gift.
51. So and more also do God unto the enemies of David, if I leave of all that pertain to him by the morning light any that pisseth against the wall.
52. Moab is my washpot; over Edom will I cast out my shoe.
53. The watchman said, The morning cometh, and also the night; if ye will inquire, inquire ye: return, come.
54. And he will take your menservants, and your maidservants, and your goodliest young men, and your asses, and put them to his work.
55. Their feet are swift to shed blood.
56. Now therefore go, and I will be with thy mouth.

WHAT WAS THAT VERSE AGAIN? (ANSWERS)

1. *1 Chronicles (26:18)*

2. *Jeremiah (13:26)*

3. *Psalms (114:4)*

4. *Daniel (8:10)*

5. *Ezekiel (27:25)*

6. *Joel (1:18)*

7. Song of Solomon (2:12)

8. Exodus (39:16)

9. Exodus (39:26)

10. Song of Solomon (5:3)

11. Ecclesiastes (10:1)

12. Proverbs (24:26)

13. Isaiah (49:23)

14. Song of Solomon (7:7)

15. Job (28:22)

16. Isaiah (8:9)

17. Isaiah (10:19)

18. Leviticus (15:29)

19. Deuteronomy (14:21)

20. Song of Solomon (4:11)

21. Exodus (40:17)

22. Amos (7:1)

23. Amos (4:8)

24. Joel (2:6)

25. Ezekiel (29:18)

26. Hosea (10:7)

27. Zephaniah (2:6)

28. Psalms (98:8)

29. Daniel (5:6)

30. Psalms (29:6)

31. Jeremiah (14:6)

32. Song of Solomon (1:9)

33. Habakkuk (3:9)

34. Deuteronomy (28:27)

35. Isaiah (2:22)

36. Malachi (2:3)

37. Hosea (7:4)

38. Micah (7:14)

39. Leviticus (13:40)

40. Numbers (11:20)

41. Psalms (109:23)

42. Isaiah (34:7)

43. Song of Solomon (4:2)

44. Proverbs (18:4)

45. Psalms (24:7)

46. Isaiah (60:16)

47. Psalms (50:13)

48. Genesis (25:64)

49. Song of Solomon (4:4)

50. Deuteronomy (16:19)

51. 1 Samuel (25:22)

52. Psalms (60:8)

53. Isaiah (21:12)

54. 1 Samuel (8:16)

55. Romans (3:15)

56. Exodus (4:12)

THE WORD TRANSLATING ITS WORDS

Since it was written long ago in three ancient languages (Hebrew, Aramaic, and Greek), the Bible would be a total mystery to us all, were it not for the necessary work of translators. Even they admit that the Bible has some words and phrases that are "stumpers." Happily, the original Bible writers themselves paused on occasion to explain the meaning of a name or phrase. For the meanings listed below, supply the proper name.

1. Sons of thunder
2. God with us
3. The place of the skull
4. King of peace
5. Teacher
6. Son of encouragement
7. Sorcerer
8. Little girl
9. Be opened

10. Sent
11. King of righteousness
12. Bitter
13. My God, my God, why have you forsaken me?
14. Confused
15. Red
16. Small
17. Shelters
18. Burning
19. Not my people
20. Not loved

THE WORD TRANSLATING ITS WORDS (ANSWERS)

1. Boanerges (Mark 3:17), a name Jesus bestowed on the two disciples John and James

2. Immanuel (Matthew 1:23)

3. Golgotha (Matthew 27:33), the place of Jesus' crucifixion

4. King of Salem (Hebrews 7:2)

5. Rabboni or Rabbi (John 1:38; 20:16)

6. Barnabas (Acts 4:36), the apostle

7. Elymas (Acts 13:8)

8. Talitha (Mark 5:41)

9. Ephphatha (Mark 7:34)

10. Siloam (John 9:7)

11. Melchizedek (Hebrews 7:2)

12. Marah (Exodus 15:23)

13. Eloi, Eloi, lama sabachthani? (Mark 15:34). Jesus spoke these words from the cross, and they are in the Aramaic form of Psalm 22:1.

14. Babel (Genesis 11:9), the famous site where human languages were confounded

15. Edom (Genesis 25:30)

16. Zoar (Genesis 19:22)

17. Succoth (Genesis 33:17)

18. Taberah (Numbers 11:3)

19. Lo-ammi (Hosea 1:9)

20. Lo-ruhamah (Hosea 1:6)

JESUS' BROTHERS OR "BROTHERS"?

Here is a point on which groups of Christians have really disagreed. The Bible makes it clear that Jesus of Nazareth had earthly brothers and sisters—but Catholic tradition teaches that these were not full siblings, children of Mary and Joseph, but rather Joseph's children by an earlier marriage. In other words, stepbrothers, and no blood relation to Jesus at all. Aside from this long-standing argument, most Bible readers don't really know that much about these siblings (or stepsiblings). So here's your chance to test your knowledge of these men and women who, at any rate, were people growing up under the same roof as the Savior of the world.

1. What two Epistles were supposedly written by brothers of Jesus?
2. According to Jesus, what people are truly his brothers and sisters?
3. In what town did everyone seem to know the names of Jesus' brothers?
4. In what town did Jesus stay along with his mother, brothers, and disciples?
5. What Jewish feast did Jesus' brothers encourage him to celebrate by going to Jerusalem?
6. Which of the Gospels states that Jesus' brothers "did not believe in him"?
7. Which brother of Jesus is the only one referred to as an "apostle"?
8. What book of the Bible mentions the apostles meeting in fellowship with Jesus' mother and brothers?

JESUS' BROTHERS OR "BROTHERS"? (ANSWERS)

1. James and Jude

2. Those who do the will of the heavenly Father (Matthew 12:48-50)

3. His hometown of Nazareth, of course (Matthew 13:55-56)

4. Capernaum (John 2:12)

5. The Feast of Tabernacles (John 7:2)

6. John (7:5). This was prior to Jesus' crucifixion and resurrection. Afterward, some did become believers.

7. James (Galatians 1:19)

8. Acts (1:14)

THANK HEAVEN FOR FOOTNOTES

First, the good news: For the most part, the Bible is not all that difficult to understand, particularly if you read one of the newer translations. The bad news: There are still lots of terms—matters of geography, measurements, turns of phrase—that would totally baffle today's reader. Happily, footnotes have been a feature of Bibles for centuries, and they certainly help make the Bible a less mysterious book. The questions here deal with some of these "footnote mystery-solvers."

1. When the Old Testament speaks of "the River," what river associated with modern Iraq is being referred to?
2. *Horn* is used figuratively throughout the Old Testament to refer to what quality?
3. "Passing through the fire" is referred to often in the Old Testament. What loathsome practice was meant?
4. What unit of measurement, meaning about two-fifths of an ounce, is also the name of Israel's currency today?
5. The "Sea of the Philistines," mentioned in Exodus 23:31, is probably what large body of water?
6. The land of Shinar, mentioned in Genesis and elsewhere, is an alternate name for what famous empire of the ancient world?
7. When 2 Kings says that Elisha "poured water on the hands of Elijah," what does it mean?
8. In what book of the Bible would you find such untranslatable terms as *sheminith, gittith, shiggaion, miktam, maskil,* and *alamoth*?
9. What word is used throughout the Bible to cover all sorts of disfiguring skin diseases?
10. Most Bibles use the name "Red Sea" to refer to what actual body of water?
11. *Caphtor* referred to what famous island off the coast of Greece?
12. The Old Testament refers often to the Sea of Kinnereth. What more famous name is it called in the New Testament?
13. What commonly used measurement of length equaled about 18 inches?
14. Acts 27:9 refers to "the Fast." Which Jewish holy day was meant?
15. What common measurement of weight equaled a little over a pound?
16. *Seed* commonly referred to a man's what?
17. In Exodus, "the river" referred to what very famous river of world history?

18. What is the meaning of the Hebrew word *selah*, found many times in Psalms and three times in Habakkuk?
19. A measurement equaling about 75 pounds had a "gifted" name. What was it?
20. The Feast of Dedication mentioned in John 10:22 is known today as the Jewish festival of what?
21. *Sea of the Arabah* and *Salt Sea* were Old Testament names for what famous (and salty) lake?
22. The Chaldeans, referred to many times in the Old Testament, were better known as what?
23. In some of the genealogies, such as 1 Chronicles 1, "father" could have what meaning other than literal "father"?
24. John's Gospel refers to the Sea of Tiberias. What more familiar name do we know it by?
25. What had a man done when he "slept with his fathers," a phrase used often in 1 and 2 Kings?
26. A "Sabbath day's walk," mentioned in Acts 1:12, was about how far?
27. A handsbreadth was roughly how wide?
28. The Great Sea (Joshua 1:4) and the Sea (Numbers 34:5) referred to what very large sea?
29. The Gospels and Acts refer often to "unclean" spirits. What is the meaning here?
30. A cor, or homer, was about how much by volume?

THANK HEAVEN FOR FOOTNOTES (ANSWERS)

1. *The Euphrates*

2. *Strength, power*

3. *Child sacrifice, something commonly practiced by pagan nations but prohibited by God's law*

4. *The shekel*

5. *The Mediterranean Sea. The Philistines' cities were on its coast.*

6. *Babylon*

7. *He was Elijah's personal servant (2 Kings 3:11).*

8. *Psalms. The terms are (we think) types of musical or poetic forms.*

9. *Leprosy. True leprosy was a real problem in ancient times, but it is clear in the Bible*

that the writers used "leprosy" to cover many other types of skin afflictions, most of them not nearly as serious as leprosy.

10. The Reed Sea—Yam Suph in Hebrew, which was the body of water crossed by the Israelites fleeing Egypt. It was definitely not the large sea lying between Africa and Arabia, now known as the Red Sea.

11. Crete (Deuteronomy 2:23 and elsewhere)

12. The Sea of Galilee

13. The cubit

14. Yom Kippur, the Day of Atonement

15. A mina

16. Descendants

17. The Nile, which in the Hebrew and Greek originals is never given a name

18. No one knows, and translators don't even try. It is probably a musical direction of some sort, perhaps meaning "pause here," but no one is sure.

19. Talent

20. Hanukkah

21. The Dead Sea

22. Babylonians

23. Ancestor, in the broad sense. Abraham, for example, was considered the "father" of all Jews.

24. The Sea of Galilee. For some odd reason, John used the name that the Romans gave to the lake (John 21:1).

25. Died. It also meant being buried with one's ancestors.

26. About three-quarters of a mile. The Jewish law limited the amount of travel on the Sabbath, so a "Sabbath day's walk" was shorter than a "day's walk."

27. Roughly three inches

28. The Mediterranean. The Hebrews never showed much imagination in naming this large and important body of water.

29. Evil spirits, that is, demons. Many modern versions choose to use "evil spirits" instead of "unclean spirits."

30. About six bushels

GODS, THE HOME VERSION

Ever heard the Hebrew word *teraphim*? Like many other words, it drives translators nuts, since, in most cases, we aren't quite sure what they (the word is plural) were. The best guess is that they were "household idols"—small, portable images of the gods that one worshipped—home-size, not temple-size. Whatever they were, they play an important part in some key stories of the Bible, making us wish we knew precisely what they were and what they signified to those people long ago. By the way, in most modern Bibles, the word is simply translated "idols."

1. What woman stole her father's teraphim before running off with her husband?
2. How did she hide them when her father came searching?
3. What man in the book of Judges used his wealth in silver to make teraphim and other idols?
4. Who saved her husband's life by hiding teraphim in his bed?
5. What saintly king prohibited the keeping of teraphim?
6. Which prophet said that the teraphim speak deceit?
7. Which prophet predicted that the people would live for a long time without any teraphim or any other religious emblems?
8. Which prophet sneered at the king of Babylon for consulting his teraphim for guidance?

GODS, THE HOME VERSION (ANSWERS)

1. *Rachel, wife of Jacob and daughter of Laban (Genesis 31:19). This is the first mention of teraphim in the Bible.*

2. *She sat on them, literally. See Genesis 31:35 for Rachel's creative cover-up story.*

3. *Micah (Judges 17), no relation to the later prophet with the same name*

4. *Michal, wife of David, who put the idol in bed, pretending it was David lying there sick (1 Samuel 19)*

5. *Josiah (2 Kings 23:24)*

6. *Zechariah (10:2). The teraphim don't literally speak, so he probably meant that people used them in some way to predict the future.*

7. *Hosea (3:4)*

8. *Ezekiel (21:21)*

CAN YOU KEEP A SECRET?

A secret refers to something hidden—or, at least, hidden from the general public view. In the Bible, God does many things in secret. And so (for both good and bad reasons) do human beings. See what you know about the various divine and human secrets in the Bible.

1. What scheming woman tried to wheedle a secret out of a long-haired muscleman?
2. According to Psalms, who knows the secrets of men's hearts?
3. In Exodus, what men repeatedly use their "secret arts"?
4. Who told people to do their praying and charitable works in secret?
5. What wealthy man was secretly a follower of Jesus?
6. What Bible book warns against worshipping false gods and idols in secret?
7. Who secretly sent two Israelite spies to check out Jericho?
8. What wicked king held a secret conference with wise men from the east?
9. Who was scolded by his father-in-law for fleeing secretly by night?
10. Who were given "the secrets of the Kingdom of Heaven" by Jesus?
11. According to Psalm 101, what will God do to a man who secretly slanders his neighbor?
12. Which judge was able to murder an enemy king by claiming he had a secret message for him?
13. What rebel son sent secret messengers through Israel to proclaim him king?
14. Which prophet did God ask, "Can anyone hide in secret places so that I cannot see him"?
15. Who encouraged Jesus to "go public" and not keep his miracles a secret?
16. With what secret sins did the prophet Nathan confront David?
17. To whom did Jesus say that he had always taught publicly, never in secret?
18. According to 1 Corinthians, who were "entrusted with the secret things of God"?
19. According to Proverbs, "a gift given in secret soothes _____."
20. To which prophet did God declare, "I have not spoken in secret, from somewhere in a land of darkness"?
21. What book of the Bible declares that food eaten in secret is tasty?

22. What book of the Bible declares that God sees our secret sins "in the light of his presence"?
23. According to Proverbs, a _____ man keeps a secret.
24. Who claimed that "it is shameful to mention what the disobedient do in secret"?
25. What book of the Bible condemns those who learn the "deep secrets of Satan"?

CAN YOU KEEP A SECRET? (ANSWERS)

1. Delilah, of course, who finally got Samson to reveal the secret of his strength (Judges 16)

2. God, of course (Psalm 44:21)

3. The magicians in Pharaoh's court. Egypt had a long history as a center of magic and the occult.

4. Jesus (Matthew 6:3-18), who was making the point that we ought to seek God's approval, not man's

5. Joseph of Arimathea (John 19:38)

6. Deuteronomy (13:6; 27:15)

7. Joshua (2:1)

8. Herod (Matthew 2:7)

9. Jacob, son-in-law of Laban (Genesis 31:27)

10. The disciples (Matthew 13:11)

11. Silence him (Psalm 101:5)

12. Ehud, who slyly assassinated the obese Eglon, king of Moab (Judges 3:19)

13. Absalom, the wayward son of King David (2 Samuel 15:10)

14. Jeremiah (23:24)

15. His brothers (John 7:4)

16. Committing adultery with Bathsheba and murdering her husband (2 Samuel 12:9)

17. The high priest (John 18:20)

18. Apostles (1 Corinthians 4:1)

19. Anger (Proverbs 21:14)

20. Isaiah (45:19)

21. Proverbs (9:17)

22. *Psalms (90:8)*
23. *Trustworthy (Proverbs 11:13)*
24. *Paul (Ephesians 5:12)*
25. *Revelation (2:24), which is probably referring to some form of Christian heresy*

PART 2

MULTITUDE OF MIRACLES

THE GOD OF BATTLES

In the Bible, Israel was a tiny nation surrounded by greedy, oppressive, war-loving empires. It seemed almost inevitable that in any military encounter, Israel would be the loser. But history has plenty of examples of small forces defeating larger ones, and so does the Bible. At times tiny David can whip the hulking Goliath, and at times the small army of Israel can whip the big battalions of the mighty empires—particularly if the Lord is on Israel's side. Call it mystery, or miracle, or whatever you like.

1. What army was defeated when an angel of the Lord struck down 185,000 soldiers?
2. What nation's army was destroyed in the Red Sea?
3. What nation was Israel fighting when Moses' arms, held aloft, caused Israel to win?
4. What weather phenomenon did the Lord use to defeat the Amorites when Joshua and his men were fighting them?
5. Which prophet's word caused the Syrian soldiers to be struck blind?
6. When Samuel was offering a sacrifice, what did the Lord do to rattle the Philistines?
7. What occurred when Jonathan and his armor bearer attacked the Philistines?
8. What made the Syrians flee, thinking the Israelites had joined forces with Egyptians and Hittites?
9. Who were the Judeans fighting when God helped them slaughter a half-million soldiers?
10. Which king led the people in singing and praising God, leading God to destroy the armies of the Ammonites, Moabites, and Edomites?

THE GOD OF BATTLES (ANSWERS)

1. *Assyria's (2 Kings 19:35)*

2. *Egypt (Exodus 14:13-31)*

3. *Amalek (Exodus 17:11)*

4. *Large hailstones (Joshua 10:6-13)*

5. *Elisha's (2 Kings 6:18-23)*

6. *Thundered from heaven (1 Samuel 7:10)*

7. *An earthquake (1 Samuel 14:11-15)*

8. *The Lord made a sound like a thundering army (2 Kings 7:6-7).*

9. *Israel (2 Chronicles 13:15-16)*

10. *Jehoshaphat (2 Chronicles 20:22)*

 ## JESUS, THE ULTIMATE MIRACLE MAN

Lots of people think of Jesus Christ as a great teacher. Well, he definitely was that, but to the people who knew him in the flesh he was much more than that. He was also the miracle man, particularly known for his compassionate miracles of healing. His miracles, even more than his wise teachings, convinced many people that he was indeed the Son of God. And of course, not long after his crucifixion, there was the greatest miracle of all.

1. In what town did Jesus work his first miracle?
2. What woman got up and started doing household chores after Jesus healed her of a fever?
3. What unproductive tree did Jesus wither by cursing it?
4. How was the woman who was hemorrhaging healed by Jesus?
5. Who appeared with Jesus at his miraculous transfiguration?
6. Which apostle did Jesus enable to walk (briefly) on water?
7. Which disciples did Jesus call to follow him after blessing them with an enormous catch of fish?
8. Whom did Jesus send to catch a fish that had a coin in its mouth?
9. When Jesus healed the blind man of Bethsaida, what did the man say people looked like?
10. What widow had her dead son brought to life by Jesus?
11. Where was Jesus when he healed the son of an official from Capernaum?
12. What was the affliction of the man Jesus healed by sending him to the pool of Siloam?
13. Why did the synagogue ruler complain when Jesus healed a woman who had been stooped for 18 years?
14. Where was Jesus when he miraculously escaped from a crowd that was going to push him off a cliff?

15. What was the other affliction of the deaf man Jesus healed in the Decapolis?
16. How many loaves of bread were used to feed the 5,000?
17. How was Joseph told about Jesus' miraculous conception?
18. Who announced Jesus' conception to Mary?
19. What was the affliction of the man Jesus healed after his famous Sermon on the Mount?
20. What little girl did Jesus raise from the dead after telling people she was only asleep?
21. What did Jesus say to calm the storm on the lake?
22. When Jesus healed a man of dumbness, what did the Pharisees accuse him of?
23. When Jesus healed a paralyzed man, what did the man pick up and carry home?
24. When Jesus healed 10 lepers, how many came back to thank him?
25. How many loaves did Jesus use to feed the 4,000?
26. What woman had her daughter healed, even after Jesus told her that he had been sent to the Jews, not to foreigners?
27. Which Gospel records the miraculous catch of fish after Jesus' resurrection?
28. Which apostle cut off a man's ear at Jesus' arrest, and then watched Jesus heal the ear?
29. In what town did Jesus heal a demon-possessed man in the synagogue?
30. What man of Bethany did Jesus bring back to life?
31. Which Gospel records the ability of the resurrected Jesus to walk through locked doors?
32. What was the affliction of the man Jesus healed on the Sabbath at the home of a Pharisee?
33. What Roman of Capernaum asked that Jesus heal his servant?
34. When Jesus was healing people, which prophet did he claim to be fulfilling?
35. Where did Jesus send the demons he drove out of the Gadarene demoniacs?
36. According to Matthew's Gospel, what Sabbath healing caused the Pharisees to plot to kill Jesus?
37. What did Jesus tell the two blind men not to do after he healed them?
38. What future disciple did Jesus see, through miraculous means, sitting under a fig tree?

39. When Jesus healed a man who was both blind and dumb, what demon did the Pharisees accuse him of consorting with?
40. When the disciples saw Jesus walking on the water, what did they think he was?
41. What was the affliction of the young boy who was throwing himself into the fire?
42. How did Jesus heal the two blind men who asked for his help?
43. Where in Jerusalem was Jesus doing his healing work when he caused the chief priests and the scribes to become indignant?
44. What miracle in Jesus' life is mentioned most in the New Testament?
45. Where did Jesus heal a man who had been sick for 38 years?

JESUS, THE ULTIMATE MIRACLE MAN (ANSWERS)

1. Cana (John 2:1-11), an obscure little town that would have been long ago forgotten if Jesus had not been present at a wedding there, when he turned water into wine

2. Peter's mother-in-law (Matthew 8:14-15)

3. A fig tree (Matthew 21:17-20)

4. She touched the hem of his garment (Matthew 9:20-22).

5. Elijah and Moses (Matthew 17:1-9)

6. Peter (Matthew 14:28-31)

7. Peter, James, and John (Luke 5:4-11)

8. Peter (Matthew 17:24-27)

9. Like trees walking (Mark 8:22-26)

10. The widow of Nain (Luke 7:11-15)

11. Cana (John 4:46-54)

12. Blindness (John 9:1-7)

13. He healed her on the Sabbath (Luke 13:11-14).

14. His hometown, Nazareth (Luke 4:29-30)

15. Almost mute (Mark 7:31-35)

16. Five (Matthew 14:15-21)

17. In a dream (Matthew 1:18-21)

18. The angel Gabriel (Luke 1:26-38)

19. Leprosy (Matthew 8:1-4)

20. Jairus's daughter (Matthew 9:23-25)

21. *"Peace, be still!" (Matthew 8:23-27)*
22. *Having demonic power (Matthew 9:34)*
23. *His bed (Matthew 9:1-8)*
24. *One (Luke 17:11-19)*
25. *Seven (Matthew 15:32-39)*
26. *The Canaanite woman (Matthew 15:22-28)*
27. *John (21:3-11)*
28. *Peter (Luke 22:49-51)*
29. *Capernaum (Luke 4:31-37)*
30. *Lazarus (John 11)*
31. *John (20:19-21)*
32. *Dropsy (Luke 14:1-4)*
33. *The centurion (Matthew 8:5-13)*
34. *Isaiah (Matthew 8:17)*
35. *Into a herd of pigs (Matthew 8:28-34)*
36. *The healing of the man with the withered hand (Matthew 12:10-14)*
37. *Not to tell anyone else (Matthew 9:27-31)*
38. *Nathanael (John 1:48)*
39. *Beelzebub (Matthew 12:24)*
40. *A ghost (Mark 6:45-50)*
41. *He was demon possessed (Matthew 17:14-18).*
42. *He touched their eyes (Matthew 20:30-34).*
43. *In the Temple (Matthew 21:14-15)*
44. *His resurrection*
45. *The pool at Bethesda (John 5:1-9)*

TRAVELING GOD'S WAY

Some of the greatest miracles in the Bible have to do with getting from Point A to Point B. You might call them "miracles of travel," in which the Lord manifested his power to make his chosen people's journey a little easier, or faster—or just downright astounding.

1. What two people walked on water in the midst of a storm?

2. Elijah and Elisha walked across the Jordan River on dry ground after Elijah struck the waters with what?
3. Elijah outran a king's chariot, running all the way from Mount Carmel to Jezreel, almost 10 miles. Who was the king?
4. How was Elijah taken up into heaven?
5. Israel crossed the Red Sea on dry ground and also crossed a river on dry ground. Which river?
6. What carried Philip from Gaza to Azotus?
7. Which prophet was able to travel for 40 days on the strength from a cake and water?
8. Who took Jesus to a pinnacle of the Temple in Jerusalem?
9. Ezekiel was lifted up by a spirit, which held him between earth and heaven. What was the spirit holding on to?
10. Who was taken up into heaven in the sight of his followers?
11. What man knew someone who had been caught up to the third heaven?
12. Which Old Testament prophet proclaimed that those "who wait upon the Lord shall renew their strength and mount up with wings like eagles"?

TRAVELING GOD'S WAY (ANSWERS)

1. *Jesus and Peter (Matthew 14:22-32). Jesus proved to be better at it than poor Peter was.*

2. *His cloak (2 Kings 2:8)*

3. *Ahab (1 Kings 18:41-46)*

4. *In a whirlwind (2 Kings 2:11)*

5. *The Jordan (Joshua 3)*

6. *The Spirit of the Lord (Acts 8:39-40)*

7. *Elijah (1 Kings 19:5-8)*

8. *The devil (Matthew 4:5-7)*

9. *A lock of Ezekiel's hair (Ezekiel 8:1-3)*

10. *Jesus (Acts 1:9)*

11. *Paul (2 Corinthians 12:1-7)*

12. *Isaiah (40:31). He was speaking figuratively, but as these previous questions have shown, sometimes the Lord's servants literally did mount up like eagles.*

THE MANY MIRACLES OF MOSES

Movie director Cecil B. DeMille gave us one of the great all-time movies, *The Ten Commandments*, and no small part of his choice to film the Moses saga was that it gave Hollywood an excuse to lay on the special effects. (That was 1956, and the effects were "state of the art" at the time.) If you've read the Old Testament, you know that Moses is one of its greatest figures, and a multitude of miracles were connected with this amazing man. See how much you remember about miracles in the life of Moses—either from the Bible, from the classic movie, or both.

1. What did Moses' staff turn into?
2. What bird served as miracle food for the Israelites?
3. What did Moses do to bring forth water from the rock at Kadesh?
4. What animal came forth out of the Nile in droves?
5. What miraculous thing happened to Moses' hand?
6. What was the unique feature of the hailstorm that God sent upon the Egyptians?
7. What did Moses mount on a pole as a way for healing the ailing Israelites?
8. What everyday substance was changed into a plague of lice?
9. What caused the boils on the Egyptians?
10. What did the Nile's waters turn into?
11. Who appeared on the Mount of Transfiguration with Moses and Jesus?
12. What did Moses cast into the bitter water at Marah to make it sweet?
13. What happened to Aaron's staff when placed in the Tent of Meeting?
14. What was done to stop the plague that killed 14,700 of the Israelites?
15. What voracious insect was a plague on the Egyptian flora?
16. What happened to rebellious Korah and his men?
17. What happened to 250 men who offered incense?
18. For how long did the thick darkness hang over the Egyptians?
19. What substance, called bread from heaven, fed the Israelites in the wilderness?
20. What hid the departing Israelites?
21. Who was made leprous because of her rebellious acts and then healed at her brother's request?

22. What did the Israelites put on their doorposts so the angel of death would pass over?
23. What did the Lord use to part the Red Sea?
24. What means did the Lord use to halt the Egyptian chariots?
25. What happened to the manna the Israelites tried to hoard?
26. Who was slain by the angel of death?
27. What was Moses supposed to do to the rock at Horeb to bring water from it?
28. What consumed the offering on the altar?
29. What did Moses do at Taberah when the fire of the Lord destroyed many Israelites?
30. What brought the locust plague to a halt?
31. When the plague of hail came, where was the one place it did not fall?
32. Whose rod was turned into a serpent that swallowed the Egyptian sorcerers' serpents?
33. What bit the Israelites, causing Moses to fix a brass figure on a pole?

THE MANY MIRACLES OF MOSES (ANSWERS)

1. A serpent (Exodus 4:2-4)

2. Quail (Exodus 16:11-13)

3. He struck it twice with his staff (Numbers 20:1-11).

4. Frogs (Exodus 8:5-7)

5. It became leprous, then became normal again (Exodus 4:7).

6. It was accompanied by fire that ran along the ground (Exodus 9:22-26).

7. A brass serpent (Numbers 21:5-9)

8. Dust (Exodus 8:16-17)

9. Ashes that were turned into dust (Exodus 9:8-12)

10. Blood (Exodus 7:19-25)

11. Elijah (Luke 9:28-36)

12. A tree (Exodus 15:23-25)

13. It sprouted and blossomed and bore almonds (Numbers 17).

14. An offering of incense was made (Numbers 16:46-50).

15. Locusts (Exodus 10:12-15)

16. They were swallowed up by the earth (Numbers 16:28-33).

17. They were consumed by fire from the Lord (Numbers 16:16-35).

18. Three days (Exodus 10:21-23)

19. Manna (Exodus 16:14-15)

20. A cloud (Exodus 14:19-20)

21. Miriam (Numbers 12)

22. Lamb's blood (Exodus 12:21-30)

23. A strong east wind (Exodus 14:21)

24. He made their wheels come off (Exodus 14:23-25).

25. It was filled with maggots (Exodus 16:20).

26. The firstborn among the Egyptians (Exodus 12:29-30)

27. Strike it (Exodus 17:1-6)

28. Fire from the Lord (Leviticus 9:22-24)

29. He prayed, and the fire died down (Numbers 11:1-2).

30. The Lord blew them away with a strong west wind (Exodus 10:16-20).

31. In Goshen, where the Israelites dwelled (Exodus 9:26)

32. Aaron's (Exodus 7:10-12)

33. Fiery serpents (Numbers 21:5-9)

DEATH DONE BIZARRELY

According to Genesis, it wasn't God's original intention for man to die. Death was Adam's punishment for disobedience. So, in a way, all human death is "unnatural," not something God built into the original order of the world. Even so, the human race grew accustomed to the hard truth that all of us must die, most of us from old age, disease, or warfare. But the questions below deal with some very unusual deaths in the Bible, some of them attributed to God himself (always for extreme human wickedness), and some involving some very peculiar lethal weapons.

1. What two cities were rained on by fire and brimstone?
2. What devoured Aaron's sons, Nadab and Abihu, when they offered "strange fire" to the Lord?
3. What Canaanite captain was killed when Jael, a Hebrew woman, drove a tent peg through his skull?

4. Who was killed for touching the Ark of the Covenant?
5. The Lord sent a pestilence on Israel that killed 70,000 people. What act of King David brought this on?
6. God sent fire from heaven to kill the soldiers who came to capture which prophet?
7. What husband and wife dropped dead after it was revealed they had lied about the price of the land they had sold?
8. Who was hanged on the very gallows he had prepared for Mordecai?
9. What people were killed by great hailstones from heaven?
10. Who, along with his household, was swallowed up by the earth for rebelling against Moses?
11. What man was slain by God for refusing to produce children with his widowed sister-in-law?
12. Who was the first individual who was killed by God for being wicked?
13. What did God do when the Israelites began to complain about the death of Korah and his followers?
14. In the Exodus story, what was the last plague sent upon the Egyptians?
15. Which son of Saul was murdered by two servants who stabbed him in the belly and carried his severed head to David?

DEATH DONE BIZARRELY (ANSWERS)

1. Sodom and Gomorrah (Genesis 19:24-25), of course

2. Fire from God (Leviticus 10:1-2). Translators still puzzle over what exactly is meant by "strange fire," though clearly God considered it wicked, whatever it was.

3. Sisera (Judges 4:18-21)

4. Uzzah (2 Samuel 6:6-7)

5. He conducted a census of the people of Israel (2 Samuel 24:1-5).

6. Elijah (2 Kings 1:9-12)

7. Ananias and Sapphira (Acts 5:1-10)

8. Haman (Esther 7:10)

9. Amorites (Joshua 10:8-14)

10. Korah (Numbers 16)

11. Onan (Genesis 38:9-10)

12. *Er (Genesis 38:7)*

13. *He sent a plague that killed 14,700 Israelites (Numbers 16:41-50).*

14. *The death of the firstborn (Exodus 12:29)*

15. *Ishbosheth, slain by Recab and Baanah (2 Samuel 4:5-8)*

THOSE TWO AMAZING "EL" PROPHETS

Two of the great miracle men of the Bible are the prophet Elijah and his friend and successor, Elisha. Not only were the two of them practically fearless (though Elijah did flee as a result of Jezebel's threats [1 Kings 19:3]) in standing up for the right (which is pretty miraculous in itself), but the two were literally surrounded by miracles in their lives. Careful readers of the Bible have noticed that many of the Elijah-Elisha miracles were duplicated (centuries later) in the life of an even greater prophet, Jesus himself.

1. What birds fed Elijah in the wilderness?
2. Whom did Elijah miraculously supply with flour and oil?
3. What did the bones of Elisha do to a dead man?

4. What did Elisha do to make an ax head float to the surface of the water?
5. Who was healed of leprosy when he followed Elisha's instructions?
6. Who appeared with Jesus and Elijah on the Mount of Transfiguration?
7. What happened to the children who made fun of Elisha's bald head?
8. What river did Elijah part by striking it with his cloak?
9. What did Elisha do to make the poisoned stew edible?
10. What happened to the Syrian soldiers when Elisha prayed?
11. How long was rain withheld after Elijah's prayer?
12. Who conceived a son after Elisha predicted she would?
13. What did Elijah call on to destroy the soldiers sent to arrest him?
14. Who was Elijah up against when fire from the Lord burned up a sacrifice and the water around the altar?

15. How many men did Elisha feed with 20 loaves of barley and some ears of corn?
16. How did Elisha raise the Shunammite woman's son from the dead?
17. What did Elisha's servant see after Elisha prayed that his eyes would be opened?
18. For whom did Elisha supply water miraculously?
19. What took Elijah into heaven?
20. Who fed Elijah after he prayed to the Lord to take his life?
21. What did Elisha do for the Syrian soldiers after leading them to Samaria?
22. What did Elisha supply the poor widow with?
23. How did Elisha purify the bitter water?
24. Who did Elijah miraculously outrun on the way to Jezreel?

THOSE TWO AMAZING "EL" PROPHETS (ANSWERS)

1. *Ravens (1 Kings 17:2-7)*
2. *A widow and her son (1 Kings 17:13-16)*
3. *Brought him back to life (2 Kings 13:20-21)*
4. *He threw a stick into the water (2 Kings 6:4-7).*
5. *Naaman the Syrian (2 Kings 5:1-14)*
6. *Moses (Luke 9:28-36)*
7. *They were torn apart by two bears (2 Kings 2:23-25).*
8. *The Jordan (2 Kings 2:8)*
9. *He poured flour into it (2 Kings 4:38-41).*
10. *They were struck blind (2 Kings 6:18).*
11. *Three and a half years (1 Kings 17:1)*
12. *The Shunammite woman (2 Kings 4:14-17)*
13. *Fire from heaven (2 Kings 1:10-12)*
14. *The prophets of Baal (1 Kings 18:17-38)*
15. *A hundred (2 Kings 4:42-44)*
16. *He stretched his body out on the boy's (2 Kings 4:32-37).*
17. *An angelic army (2 Kings 6:15-17)*
18. *The armies of the kings of Judah, Israel, and Edom (2 Kings 3:14-20)*
19. *A whirlwind (2 Kings 2:11)*

20. *An angel (1 Kings 19:4-8)*

21. *Prayed for the healing of their blindness (2 Kings 6:19-20)*

22. *Large quantities of oil (2 Kings 4:1-7)*

23. *He threw a container of salt into it (2 Kings 2:19-22).*

24. *Ahab (1 Kings 18:46)*

THE GREAT ESCAPES

The Great Escape was a popular movie of the 1960s, and it's no wonder. Audiences love a good story about a cleverly planned escape. There's something satisfying about seeing people in a prison, concentration camp, or other tight spot—hopelessly trapped—but then, through cleverness, pluck, and courage, their situation turns out to be not so hopeless after all. Among the Bible's many fascinating stories there are several examples of great escapes—many so unexpected and mysterious that we can only attribute them to the hand of God.

1. Paul, newly converted to Christianity, so enraged the Jewish leaders in a certain city that they decided to murder him. His friends let him down in a basket through the city wall. What city was it?

2. The judge Ehud stabbed the fat Moabite king Eglon while they were alone together. What simple maneuver did Ehud use to evade the king's guards?

3. Nebuchadnezzar breached the walls of Jerusalem, but the king and many others escaped. How?

4. The king of Sodom escaped his attackers by hiding where?

5. In Mark's Gospel, a young man who was following Jesus on the night of his betrayal just barely escaped from being apprehended himself. What was the sole garment the young man was wearing, and how did he escape?

6. Where did Joseph take Mary and the infant Jesus in order to escape the wrath of King Herod?

7. After Moses, who was still living in the royal household of Egypt, killed an Egyptian, where did he take refuge?

8. When a violent storm caused the death of all of Job's children, how many people in the household escaped the tragedy?

9. Jesus was threatened with stoning by people gathering in Jerusalem for the Feast of Dedication. How did he escape?
10. Of the many times Saul tried to kill David, one of the closest calls was when he threw a spear at David. What did David do?
11. How did Michal, David's wife, fool the messengers who came to fetch the runaway David?
12. Running from Saul, David took refuge in Gath, where the king was worried about having a popular folk hero in town. How did David keep himself from being a victim of the king's anger?
13. When Absalom was trying to usurp the crown from his father, David, a woman helped David by hiding two of his messengers from Absalom's men. How did she hide them?

THE GREAT ESCAPES (ANSWERS)

1. *Damascus (Acts 9:19-25)*

2. *He locked the door to the king's chamber and escaped through an upstairs porch (Judges 3:25-26).*

3. *There was a secret gate next to the king's garden (2 Kings 25:1-5).*

4. *In slime pits (Genesis 14:9-11)*

5. *The garment was a linen cloth. When the men grabbed him by the cloth, he fled away naked (Mark 14:51-52).*

6. *To Egypt (Matthew 2:13)*

7. *In Midian (Exodus 2)*

8. *One (Job 1:14-19)*

9. *We don't know—the Gospel account gives no explanation (John 10:22-39).*

10. *He merely sidestepped the spear so it went into a wall (1 Samuel 19:10).*

11. *She placed an idol (presumably human sized) in David's bed and told the messengers he was sick (1 Samuel 19:11-18).*

12. *He pretended to be crazy (1 Samuel 21:10-15).*

13. *She hid them in a well, spread a covering over the well, and scattered grain over it (2 Samuel 17:17-21).*

THE BIG MIRACLE: RESURRECTION

In the Old Testament, the great miracle, that sign that God really acted in the world, is the deliverance of the Hebrew slaves in Egypt. In the New Testament, it is the resurrection of Jesus from the grave. Believing (or not) in that miracle is a "deal breaker"—that is, you can't really be considered a Christian unless you believe Jesus rose from the dead. Well, let's admit it is hard to believe a dead man could come back to life again—but also hard to believe that the first Christians would have preached that message if it hadn't really happened. Whether a person believes in the miracle or not, there's no denying that it is the most important belief in the New Testament.

1. What Christian holiday is an annual celebration of Jesus' resurrection?
2. According to Matthew's Gospel, who moved the stone that sealed Jesus' tomb?
3. What woman, who had once been demon possessed, was among the first to see Jesus' empty tomb?
4. Who said the words "Why do you seek the living among the dead"?
5. What did the Jewish priests tell the people had happened to Jesus' body?
6. After his resurrection, Jesus commanded the disciples to make disciples in all nations. This command is called what?
7. In Luke's Gospel, two disciples encounter the risen Jesus while walking toward what village?
8. What day of the week was the empty tomb discovered?
9. Who was the first of the 12 disciples to walk into Jesus' empty tomb?
10. When Mary Magdalene first saw the risen Jesus, who did she mistakenly think he was?
11. In which Gospel does the risen Jesus "breathe" the Holy Spirit on the disciples?
12. What skeptical disciple refused to believe that Jesus was risen until he had actually touched him?
13. Which disciple was commanded by the risen Jesus to "feed my sheep"?
14. Where were Jesus and the disciples when he cooked them a breakfast?

15. Which disciple proclaimed the resurrection of Jesus in a famous sermon at Pentecost?
16. In Acts 4, what group of people was "greatly disturbed" because the disciples were preaching about the resurrection of the dead?
17. Who claimed he had healed a crippled man through the power of the risen Jesus?
18. In what city was Paul when philosophers mocked him for preaching about the Resurrection?
19. What two Jewish groups got into a quarrel when Paul spoke of the Resurrection?
20. Which Epistle states that Jesus was "raised to life for our justification"?
21. Which Epistle contains a long chapter on both Jesus' resurrection and the future resurrection of believers?
22. Which Epistle states that Abraham, centuries before Christ, had believed in resurrection?
23. In Luke's Gospel, what amazing thing happened to the risen Jesus at Bethany?
24. Which Gospel records that Jesus was taken up into heaven and seated "at the right hand of God"?
25. In the book of Acts, the risen Jesus promises the disciples that they will be baptized with what?
26. When the risen Jesus ascended to heaven, what hid him from the disciples' sight?
27. What martyr had a vision of the risen Jesus standing at the right hand of God?
28. Who claimed to be an apostle because of his encounter with the risen Jesus?

THE BIG MIRACLE: RESURRECTION (ANSWERS)

1. *Easter, of course*

2. *An angel (Matthew 28:2)*

3. *Mary Magdalene (Matthew 28:1; Mark 16:1)*

4. *The angels at the tomb (Luke 24:5)*

5. *That his disciples had stolen it during the night (Matthew 28:13)*

6. *The great commission*

7. *Emmaus (Luke 24:13-35)*

8. Sunday—or, as the Bible has it, "the first day of the week" (John 20:1)

9. Peter (John 20:3-8)

10. A gardener (John 20:15). Remember that Jesus' tomb was in "a garden."

11. John (20:22)

12. Thomas (John 20:24-25), the source of the expression "doubting Thomas"

13. Peter (John 21:15-17)

14. At the Sea of Galilee (or, in some versions, Sea of Tiberias, an alternate name for the same body of water) (John 21:1-11)

15. Peter (Acts 2)

16. The Jewish leaders in Jerusalem (Acts 4:2)

17. Peter (Acts 4:10)

18. Athens, in Greece (Acts 17:18)

19. The Pharisees (who believed resurrection was possible) and the Sadducees (who didn't) (Acts 23:6-9)

20. Romans (4:25)

21. 1 Corinthians. Its chapter 15 is the famous "Resurrection chapter."

22. Hebrews (11:19)

23. He ascended into heaven (Luke 24:50-51).

24. Mark (16:19)

25. The Holy Spirit (Acts 1:5)

26. A cloud (Acts 1:9)

27. Stephen (Acts 7:55)

28. Paul (1 Corinthians 9:1)

WATER WONDERS

One of the great movie moments of all time is the parting of the Red Sea in the classic *The Ten Commandments*. Come to think of it, that miracle is one of the great moments in human history, too. It wasn't the only time in the Bible that God and his servants worked some truly awesome miracles with water.

1. Who turned water into wine?
2. Who walked on the Sea of Galilee?
3. What did Moses do to heal the bitter waters of Marah?

4. Who was healed of leprosy after dipping seven times in the Jordan?
5. Which judge wrung out a bowlful of water from a fleece in answer to prayer?
6. What river was turned into blood?
7. Who healed Jericho's water supply by throwing salt into it?
8. Who made an ax head float on the water?
9. Who died when the parted Red Sea became unparted?
10. When the Israelites in the wilderness complained about lack of water, where did the water come from?
11. How did God water the thirsty army of Israel?
12. Who calmed the sea by speaking to it?
13. Who parted the Jordan by striking it with his cloak ?
14. What were the Israelite priests carrying when they crossed the Jordan on dry ground?

WATER WONDERS (ANSWERS)

1. *Jesus (John 2:1-10)*

2. *Jesus and Peter (Matthew 14:25-31)*

3. *He cast a tree into the waters (Exodus 15:23-25)*

4. *Naaman the Syrian (2 Kings 5:14)*

5. *Gideon (Judges 6:38)*

6. *The Nile (Exodus 7:20)*

7. *Elisha (2 Kings 2:19-22)*

8. *Elisha (2 Kings 6:4-7)*

9. *The Egyptians (Exodus 14:21-29)*

10. *A rock (Exodus 17:1-6; 20:1-11)*

11. *He ordered them to dig trenches, and in the morning they were filled with water (2 Kings 3:14-22).*

12. *Jesus (Mark 4:39)*

13. *Elijah (2 Kings 2:8-14)*

14. *The Ark of the Covenant (Joshua 3:7-17)*

DYING IN DROVES

Human nature hasn't really changed over the centuries, as proven by the long sad history of wars and other calamities humans bring on themselves. We're painfully aware that in the past century, millions of people perished in wars, concentration camps, and other forms of human-engineered cruelty, and the abominations continue. The Bible records several occasions when people died en masse, and while most of these were the result of war, on a few occasions the deaths were brought about by God himself, punishing human wickedness in a dramatic fashion.

1. Which judge and his men killed 120,000 Midianites?
2. What nation saw 185,000 of its soldiers slaughtered by an angel of the Lord?
3. When the Israelites lost 30,000 soldiers in the time of Samuel, who were they fighting?
4. Which king headed up the slaying of 47,000 Syrians?
5. When the Jews were allowed to defend themselves against the Persians, how many Persians were killed?
6. Which king of Israel killed 20,000 men of Judah in one day because they had forsaken the Lord?
7. For what offense did the Lord kill 50,070 men of Beth Shemesh?
8. For what sin of David did the Lord kill 70,000 Israelites with a plague?
9. Which king of Judah led an army that killed 500,000 soldiers of Israel?
10. What Syrian king fled when 100,000 of his soldiers were killed by the people of Israel?

DYING IN DROVES (ANSWERS)

1   Gideon (Judges 8:10)

2. Assyria (2 Kings 19:35)

3. The Philistines (1 Samuel 4:10)

4. David (1 Chronicles 19:18)

5. 75,000 (Esther 9:15-16)

6. Pekah (2 Chronicles 28:6)

7. *For looking into the Ark of the Covenant (1 Samuel 6:19)*

8. *Taking a census (2 Samuel 24:15)*

9. *Abijah (2 Chronicles 13:17)*

10. *Ben-hadad (1 Kings 20:29)*

 ## SETTING THE WORLD ON FIRE

Fire in ancient times served the obvious purposes of cooking and heating. But it often was a sign of God's presence—something that everyone who ever saw the movie *The Ten Commandments* knows. That movie depicted one of the most famous God-to-man confrontations in the whole Bible, but there were others—some even more dramatic—involving supernatural fire.

1. What two sinful cities were destroyed by fire and brimstone from heaven?
2. When the Israelites were wandering in the wilderness, what did they follow by night?
3. According to Daniel, this astonishing person has a throne like a "fiery flame." Who is he?
4. What did the seraph touch the trembling Isaiah's tongue with?
5. According to Revelation, where is the place reserved for those whose names are not in the Book of Life?
6. What did the cherubim use to guard the entrance to Eden?
7. How did God first appear to Moses?
8. What strange phenomenon accompanied the plague of hail in Egypt?
9. What mountain did the Lord descend upon in fire?
10. What two sons of Aaron were devoured by fire for making an improper offering to the Lord?
11. How did God deal with the Israelites who were complaining about their misfortunes in the wilderness?
12. Which judge of Israel was visited by an angel, whose staff caused meat and bread to be consumed by fire?
13. How did Elijah respond to an army captain's summons to present himself to King Ahaziah?

14. What two men saw a chariot of fire drawn by horses of fire?
15. Where, in answer to Elijah's prayer, did fire from the Lord consume both the sacrifice and the altar?

SETTING THE WORLD ON FIRE (ANSWERS)

1. *Sodom and Gomorrah (Genesis 19:24)*

2. *A pillar of fire (Exodus 13:21)*

3. *The Ancient of Days (Daniel 7:9)*

4. *A live coal from the altar (Isaiah 6:6)*

5. *A lake of fire and brimstone (Revelation 20)*

6. *A flaming sword (Genesis 3:24)*

7. *In a burning bush that was not consumed (Exodus 3:2)*

8. *Fire that ran along the ground (Exodus 9:23)*

9. *Sinai (Exodus 19:18)*

10. *Nadab and Abihu (Leviticus 10:1-2)*

11. *His fire devoured them (Numbers 11:1-3).*

12. *Gideon (Judges 6:21)*

13. *He called down fire from heaven on the captain and his men (2 Kings 1:9-12).*

14. *Elijah and Elisha (2 Kings 2:11)*

15. *Mount Carmel (1 Kings 18:16-40)*

DEAD, BUT NOT FOR GOOD

One reason humans fear death is that it appears to be the final word. This certainly isn't so, as proven by the great miracle of the Bible, the resurrection of Jesus. However, Jesus' return from the dead was neither the first nor the last time in the Bible that a person came back to life. Test your knowledge of these "life after life" events.

1. What man of Bethany was raised from his tomb by Jesus?
2. Eutychus, who died after falling out of a window during a sermon, was raised from the dead by whom?
3. Which prophet revived the son of the Zarephath widow?

4. Who raised a woman named Dorcas from the dead?
5. What prominent leader of Israel was summoned up from the dead by a witch?
6. A man came to life again when his body came into contact with the buried bones of which prophet?
7. What was the name of the town where Jesus raised a widow's son from the dead?
8. Who did Elisha raise from the dead?
9. According to Matthew, what marvelous event occurred in conjunction with Jesus' death on the cross?
10. Whose daughter did Jesus bring back to life?

DEAD, BUT NOT FOR GOOD (ANSWERS)

1. *Lazarus (John 11:1-44)*

2. *Paul (Acts 20:9-10)*

3. *Elijah (1 Kings 17:17-22)*

4. *Peter (Acts 9:36-41)*

5. *Samuel (1 Samuel 28:7-20)*

6. *Elisha (2 Kings 13:20-21)*

7. *Nain (Luke 7:11-15)*

8. *The son of the Shunammite woman (2 Kings 4:32-35)*

9. *Many godly people came out of their graves (Matthew 27:52-53).*

10. *Jairus's (Luke 8:41-42, 49-55)*

 ## BARREN WOMEN NO LONGER BARREN

You don't have to read very far in the Bible to figure out that childlessness in Bible times was considered a great curse, especially to women. Every woman wanted to have children, the more the better, so naturally all childless women prayed constantly for a child. In some cases those prayers were answered by God, who sometimes made it possible for woman of advanced age to give birth. And in one very notable case (you know who), the child did not even have a human father.

1. Whose mother was told by an angel that she would bear a son who would deliver Israel from the Philistines?
2. Who gave birth to a son when she was 90 years old?
3. What elderly couple produced a child, in accordance with the words of an angel?
4. Who prophesied to the Shunammite woman that, though her husband was too old, she would bear a child?
5. Why did God cause barrenness among the women of Abimelech's household?
6. What woman, long barren, gave birth to twins?

7. Who was taunted by her husband's other wife for being childless, though she later bore a son?
8. Whose astounded mother called herself the "handmaiden of the Lord" when told she would bear a child?
9. What beloved wife of Jacob gave birth after many years to Joseph and Benjamin?
10. What very old man remarried after his wife's death and continued to father children?

BARREN WOMEN NO LONGER BARREN (ANSWERS)

1. *Samson's (Judges 13:3-5). Interestingly, the Bible does not tell us her name.*

2. *Sarah (Genesis 21:1-5)*

3. *Elizabeth and Zechariah (Luke 1:7-9, 13, 18)*

4. *Elisha (2 Kings 4:13-17)*

5. *Abimelech had taken Sarah for himself (Genesis 20:17-18).*

6. *Rebekah (Genesis 25:21-26)*

7. *Hannah, mother of Samuel (1 Samuel 1:1-19)*

8. *Jesus' (Luke 1:26-38)*

9. *Rachel (Genesis 30:22-24; 35:18)*

10. *Abraham (Genesis 25:1-6)*

PART 3

DESCRIBING THE
INDESCRIBABLE GOD

UNSEARCHABLE AND UNTRACEABLE

One of the prophets asked, "Who has known the mind of the Lord?" The answer, of course, is "no one." Although in the Bible the Lord reveals himself to humanity, the fact remains that God and his purposes are still very, very mysterious. You might say that the Lord gives us all the information we *need* but definitely not all the information we *want*. Obviously the human mind is limited as to what we can (and should) understand. And the God of the Bible is not only bigger than the entire universe but much, much bigger than human understanding. This is why you find the words *unsearchable* and *untraceable* applied again and again to the Holy One.

1. According to Jesus, who alone knows the Father?
2. Which prophet raised the question, "Who has known the mind of the Lord"?
3. According to Paul, who is it that "searches the deep things of God"?
4. Which prophet did God ask, "Do I not fill heaven and earth"?
5. Complete this verse from Isaiah: "My thoughts are not your thoughts, neither are your _____ my _____."
6. Which king of Israel asked, "Will God indeed dwell on the earth"?
7. Complete this verse from Proverbs: "It is the glory of God to _____ a thing."
8. Who preached the "unsearchable riches of Christ" to the Gentiles?
9. Complete this verse from Ecclesiastes: "That which is far off, and exceeding _____, who can find it out?"
10. What book of the Bible states that "the secret things belong to the Lord our God"?
11. Who said, "Unto God would I commit my cause, he who does great and unsearchable things, marvelous things without number"?
12. Which apostle praised "the depth of the riches of the wisdom and knowledge of God"?
13. Complete this verse from Isaiah: "Truly, you are a God that _____ yourself, O God of Israel, the Savior."
14. According to Job, what does God use to conceal his heavenly throne?

UNSEARCHABLE AND UNTRACEABLE (ANSWERS)

1. The Son, of course (Matthew 11:27), meaning Jesus himself

2. Isaiah (40:12), who, ironically, probably understood the mind of the Lord better than most people

3. The Spirit (1 Corinthians 2:10)

4. Jeremiah (23:24)

5. Ways, ways (Isaiah 55:8)

6. Solomon (1 Kings 8:27), at the dedication of the Temple

7. Conceal (Proverbs 25:2)

8. Paul (Ephesians 3:8)

9. Deep (Ecclesiastes 7:24)

10. Deuteronomy (29:29)

11. Job's friend Eliphaz (Job 5:8)

12. Paul (Romans 11:33)

13. Hides (Isaiah 40:28)

14. A cloud (Job 26:9)

HAVE A HEART, LORD

God does indeed have a heart—not an organ that pumps blood, of course, but an invisible seat of emotions and will, and it is this heart that intrigued the writers of the Bible. While the Almighty is, in the fullest sense, unknowable and mysterious, we can learn a great deal from the Bible about how God's "heart" works. Suffice it to say that it is far bigger (spiritually speaking) than the human heart.

1. In Genesis, what caused God's heart to be "filled with pain"?
2. What place was God speaking of when he said, "My heart will always be there"?
3. Which king was God grieved that he had made king of Israel?
4. What book of the Bible says that the purposes of the Lord's heart stand through all generations?
5. What calamity sent on Israel grieved God's heart so much that he withdrew it?

6. In Jeremiah, God says his heart would not go out to the people even if what two heroes stood before him?
7. In what book of the Bible does God say in his heart, "Never again will I curse the ground because of man"?
8. Which king of Israel was "a man after God's own heart"?
9. Which prophet was assured by God that, though God spoke against the people's sins, his heart was still with them?

HAVE A HEART, LORD (ANSWERS)

1. *Man's wickedness, which led to God's decision to flood the world (Genesis 6:6)*

2. *The Temple (1 Kings 9:3)*

3. *Saul (1 Samuel 15:11)*

4. *Psalms (33:11)*

5. *A plague (2 Samuel 24:15-16)*

6. *Moses and Samuel (Jeremiah 15:1)*

7. *Genesis (8:21)*

8. *David (1 Samuel 13:14)*

9. *Jeremiah (31:20)*

HE'S GOT THE WHOLE WORLD IN HIS HANDS

Well, first off, God doesn't have a body. He is a spirit, and one of the Ten Commandments strictly prohibited making any kind of picture or statue that represented him. (See Exodus 20:4.) While other nations represented their gods in the forms of humans or animals (or sometimes a combination of the two), the Israelites did not, for the true God was invisible—and also too impressive to be represented by any kind of idol. Still, the Bible does refer many, many times to God's "body"—figuratively, that is. So certain events are attributed to the "hand of God," "eyes of God," and so forth. They aren't intended literally, of course, but they are human languages' way of stating that God acts and knows. See what you know about God's "body," beginning in this section with his "hands."

1. What person did Moses warn that the hand of the Lord would send a plague on livestock?
2. In the lifetime of the prophet Samuel, the Lord's hand was against which foreign nation?
3. What great prophet was touched by the Lord's hand while he listened to a harpist?
4. What poor man lamented that he had been struck by the hand of God?
5. What book of the Bible speaks of the Lord's hand holding a full cup of foaming wine?
6. According to Proverbs, whose heart is in the hand of the Lord?
7. What book of the Bible states that eating, drinking, and finding satisfaction in work are from the hand of God?
8. Which prophet stated that Jerusalem had drunk "a cup of wrath" from the hand of the Lord?
9. Who experienced some truly bizarre visions in Babylon when the hand of the Lord was upon him?
10. According to the New Testament, who now sits at the right hand of God?
11. What saintly martyr had a vision of someone standing at the right hand of God?
12. What shyster was struck blind by the hand of God?
13. What book of the Bible states that Christ is interceding for us at the right hand of God?
14. Who told Pharaoh that the plagues on Egypt were done by "the finger of God"?
15. What things were written in stone by the finger of God?
16. Who claimed that he drove out demons "by the finger of God"?
17. Complete this verse from Hebrews: "It is a _____ thing to fall into the hands of the living God."
18. According to Isaiah, which of God's hands "spread out the heavens"?

HE'S GOT THE WHOLE WORLD IN HIS HANDS (ANSWERS)

1. *The Egyptian pharaoh (Exodus 9:3)*
2. *The Philistines (1 Samuel 7:13)*
3. *Elisha (2 Kings 3:15)*
4. *Job (19:21)*

5. Psalms (75:8)

6. The king's (Proverbs 21:1)

7. Ecclesiastes (2:24)

8. Isaiah (51:17)

9. Ezekiel (1:3; 3:14)

10. Christ, of course (Mark 16:19; Acts 2:33)

11. Stephen, who saw Jesus there (Acts 7:56)

12. Elymas, the fake sorcerer (Acts 13:6-12)

13. Romans (8:34)

14. His court magicians (Exodus 8:19)

15. The commandments given to Moses (Exodus 31:18)

16. Jesus (Luke 11:20)

17. Fearful (or, in some translations, dreadful) (Hebrews 10:31)

18. The right (Isaiah 48:13)

☛ THE EYES OF THE LORD

If you look at the back of a U.S. one-dollar bill, you will see on the left side a pyramid with, at the top, an eye. That old symbol is, of course, intended to represent the eye of God, watching over all the doings of humanity. Though God does not possess physical eyes, the Bible makes it clear that he is aware of everything that happens, so "the eyes of the Lord" are mentioned numerous times.

1. What righteous man of Genesis "found favor in the eyes of the Lord"?
2. According to Judges, the Israelites did evil in the eyes of the Lord by serving what false gods?
3. According to Samuel, what request of Israel was evil in the eyes of the Lord?
4. What famously rich and wise man did evil in the eyes of the Lord by catering to his wives' religions?
5. What wicked king was told by Elijah that he had done evil in the eyes of the Lord?
6. What good king, guided by the priest Jehoiada, did right in the eyes of the Lord?

7. What form of sacrifice is condemned as evil in the eyes of the Lord in 2 Kings 17?
8. According to Psalm 33, the Lord's eyes are on what sort of people?
9. What kind of man is a disgrace in the eyes of God, according to Psalm 52?
10. According to Proverbs 15, where are the eyes of God?
11. Which prophet had a vision of seven lights that symbolized the eyes of God?
12. Which prophet lamented that the people believed that those who did evil were good in the eyes of the Lord?
13. Who stated that Christians should take pains to do what is right in the eyes of the Lord?
14. What heavenly creatures, seen in a vision by Ezekiel, were covered all over with eyes?
15. What famous building project did God "come down" from heaven to look at?
16. In which book of the Bible does God say, "I will hide my eyes from you"?
17. Which prophet said that God's eyes were too pure to look upon wickedness?
18. What does God look upon to remind himself never to flood the earth again?
19. What foreign army did God "look down upon" before throwing its men into confusion?
20. What was the first thing God "saw" that he declared "good"?

THE EYES OF THE LORD (ANSWERS)

1. Noah (Genesis 6:8)

2. The Baals and Asherahs, the false gods of Canaan (Judges 2:11; 3:7)

3. Their request for a king to rule over them (1 Samuel 12:17)

4. Solomon (1 Kings 11:16)

5. Ahab (1 Kings 21:20)

6. Joash, king of Judah (2 Kings 12:2). Don't confuse this Joash with a later Joash, king of Israel, who was quite wicked (2 Kings 13:10-13).

7. Sacrifice of children (17:17), commonly practiced by the pagan nations but forbidden in Israel

8. Those who fear him (33:18)

9. *A mighty man (52:1), that is, one who uses his power to oppress others*
10. *Everywhere, of course (15:3)*
11. *Zechariah (4:2, 10)*
12. *Malachi (2:17)*
13. *Paul (2 Corinthians 8:21)*
14. *The cherubim (Ezekiel 10:12). The eyes symbolized God's ability to see everywhere and everything.*
15. *The tower of Babel (Genesis 11:5)*
16. *Isaiah (1:15), referring to God ignoring the prayers of the wicked*
17. *Habakkuk (1:13)*
18. *The rainbow (Genesis 9:16)*
19. *The Egyptian troops that pursued the Israelites (Exodus 14:24)*
20. *Light, appropriately enough (Genesis 1:4)*

 ## WALKING, RIDING, FLYING WITH GOD

Obviously, because God is everywhere, he has no need of feet, legs, chariots, or wings. Yet the Bible, using human terms to describe the Unfathomable One, speaks of the Lord walking, riding, and even flying. These human terms have led to some of the more intriguing and poetic passages in the entire Bible.

1. In what lovely spot was God walking "in the cool of the day"?
2. Which king wrote that he took refuge in the shadow of God's wings?
3. According to Psalm 68, how many chariots does God have?
4. In which book of the Bible does God promise "I will walk among you and be your God"?
5. Which of Job's friends spoke of God "walking about in the vaulted heavens"?
6. In Genesis, what righteous man "walked with God" so that God "took him"?
7. In Psalm 18, God soars on the wings of what?
8. Which prophet foretold that the Lord would come on chariots like a whirlwind?
9. In which book of the Bible does Moses assure the Israelites that God himself walks about their camp to protect it?

10. Which prophet stated that God trampled the sea with his horses?
11. According to Psalm 104, God uses what weather phenomenon as his chariot?

WALKING, RIDING, FLYING WITH GOD (ANSWERS)

1. *The Garden of Eden (Genesis 3:8), where the guilty Adam and Eve were hiding from him*

2. *David, reputedly the author of Psalm 57. The image seems to be that of a mother bird covering her chicks with her wings.*

3. *Tens of thousands (68:17)*

4. *Leviticus (26:12)*

5. *Eliphaz (Job 22:14)*

6. *Enoch (Genesis 5:24). According to Hebrews 11:5, Enoch did not die but was taken into heaven.*

7. *The wind (18:10)*

8. *Isaiah (66:15)*

9. *Deuteronomy (23:14)*

10. *Habakkuk (3:15)*

11. *The clouds (104:3)*

THE VERY FACE OF GOD

Does God look like the white-bearded gentleman in Michelangelo's famous painting? Well, actually God doesn't "look" like anything, according to the Bible. But even so, the Book does refer often to his "face" and "mouth," figuratively, of course. In a way, a person's face is his most important feature, and that is true of God as well, even though his "face" is invisible.

1. With what man did God speak "face to face, as a man speaks with his friend"?
2. Who marveled that he had seen God face-to-face and lived to tell it?

3. Which king "sought the face of the Lord" to explain why a famine had taken place?
4. According to Psalm 34, the face of the Lord is against what type of people?
5. According to Deuteronomy, man does not live by bread alone but by what?
6. Which prophet frequently backed up his words with "the mouth of the Lord has spoken"?
7. Which prophet warned against false prophets who speak "visions from their own minds, not from the mouth of the Lord"?
8. According to Exodus 33, what part of God did Moses see instead of his face?
9. Why was Moses not allowed to see God's actual face?
10. In which book of the Bible does it say that the heavens were made by "the breath of his mouth"?

THE VERY FACE OF GOD (ANSWERS)

1. Moses (Exodus 33:11)

2. Jacob (Genesis 32:30)

3. David (2 Samuel 21:1)

4. Those who do evil (34:16)

5. Every word that comes from the mouth of God (Deuteronomy 8:3)

6. Isaiah (1:20; 40:5; 58:14)

7. Jeremiah (23:16)

8. His "back" (33:23)

9. No one could see God's face and live (Exodus 33:20). The Bible confuses many people because it says that Moses was not allowed to see God's face, but it also says (33:11) that Moses and God spoke face-to-face. Chalk it up as another mystery of the Bible.

10. Psalms (33:6)

☞ FEAR, AWE, DREAD, REVERENCE

In our contemporary culture, we like people who are "warm and fuzzy"—approachable, easygoing, and mellow. Yet, at the same time, we respect an authority figure who knows how and when to be tough—the drill sergeant, the teacher or coach or boss who demands a lot and makes us do better than we thought we could. Well, the God of the Bible is definitely more of a "tough love" type than a "warm and fuzzy" type. The Bible has a lot to say about God's love and compassion—but also a lot about the *fear* of the Lord, humans' awareness that they are dealing with the Ultimate Authority Figure. The God of love and tenderness is also the mighty, mysterious One. To use an overused word, God is *awesome*.

1. What was Abraham about to do when an angel said to him, "Now I know that you fear God"?
2. What two books of the Bible state that "the fear of the Lord is the beginning of wisdom"?
3. Who asked the question, "Does Job fear God for nothing"?
4. Which apostle told believers to "love the brotherhood, fear God, honor the king"?
5. According to Proverbs 10:27, the fear of the Lord adds _____ to life.
6. Which prophet, in a very tight spot, said, "I am an Hebrew; and I fear the Lord"?
7. What book of the Bible, near its end, advises, "Fear God, and keep his commandments: for this is the whole duty of man"?
8. Who was Joseph speaking to when he said, "Do this and you will live, for I fear God"?
9. Who was told to appoint elders over Israel, choosing men who feared God?
10. Which king stated that a ruler who fears the Lord is like the light of morning?
11. According to Psalms, what sort of person has "no fear of God before his eyes"?
12. In a parable of Jesus, what man admitted he feared neither God nor man?
13. Complete this verse from Proverbs: "Fear the Lord and _____ evil."
14. Which women disobeyed the Egyptian pharaoh because they feared God?

15. What book of the Bible tells the story of a man who "feared God and shunned evil"?
16. What book of the Bible records that the church grew in numbers, "living in the fear of the Lord"?
17. To whom did Moses say, "I know that you and your officials still do not fear the Lord God"?
18. In Luke's Gospel, who asked the question, "Don't you fear God"?
19. In what book of the Bible does an angel announce, "Fear God and give him glory, because the hour of his judgment has come"?
20. Complete this verse from Proverbs: "Better a little with the fear of the Lord than great _____ with turmoil."

FEAR, AWE, DREAD, REVERENCE (ANSWERS)

1. *Sacrifice his son Isaac, as God had commanded (Genesis 22:12). The angel stopped him.*

2. *Psalms (11:10) and Proverbs (9:10)*

3. *Satan (Job 1:9), who was eager to test Job's faithfulness*

4. *Peter (1 Peter 2:17)*

5. *Length*

6. *Jonah (1:9)*

7. *Ecclesiastes (12:13)*

8. *His 11 brothers, who did not yet recognize him (Genesis 42:18)*

9. *Moses (Exodus 18:21)*

10. *David (2 Samuel 23:3-4)*

11. *The wicked (Psalm 36:1)*

12. *The unjust judge (Luke 18:4)*

13. *Shun (3:7)*

14. *The Hebrew midwives, who had been ordered by Pharaoh to kill Hebrew baby boys (Exodus 1:17)*

15. *Job (1:1)*

16. *Acts (9:31)*

17. *The Egyptian pharaoh (Exodus 9:30)*

18. *One of the two thieves crucified with Jesus. He asked the question of the other thief, who had been hurling abuse on Jesus (Luke 23:40-41).*

19. *Revelation (14:7)*
20. *Wealth (15:16)*

👉 GOD OF LOVE AND WRATH

Some people claim there are two different Gods in the Bible—the kind, loving God taught in the New Testament, and the angry-at-sin, wrathful God of the Old Testament. Not so. The truth is, the same God is in both Testaments, and he is loving and forgiving, but also righteous and angry at human evil. The reason the Book mentions God's wrath so often is that humans need reminding that their sins are serious. One of the great mysteries of the Bible is not that God is often angry, but that he isn't *more* angry at humanity.

1. In which book of the Bible does God warn that "your wives shall be widows, and your children fatherless"?
2. In which book of the Bible do people drink "the wine of the wrath of God"?
3. Who warned his followers to avoid the "outer darkness," where there would be "weeping and gnashing of teeth"?
4. Why was the Lord angry with King Solomon?
5. Complete Psalm 103:8: "The Lord is merciful and gracious, _____ to anger."
6. Whom did God ask, "How long will this people provoke me"?
7. What object had Uzzah touched that made the Lord so angry with him?
8. In the Old Testament, the Lord is often angry because the Israelites are a _____-necked people.
9. According to 2 Kings, what one tribe of Israel remained after the Lord vented his anger on the nation?
10. According to Psalm 110, what people will God strike down on the day of his wrath?
11. In Jeremiah, the people are told to put on what type of cloth to turn away the Lord's anger?
12. What entire book is a lament about the Lord's anger being poured out on Jerusalem?
13. Which Epistle says that the wrath of God is revealed against all man's ungodliness?

14. In which book of the Bible do people beg to be delivered from the wrath of the Lamb?
15. In which book of the Bible does God say, "Take this wine cup of fury at my hand"?
16. Who warned a "brood of vipers" against God's wrath to come?
17. Which apostle told people not to be vengeful but to "leave room for God's wrath"?
18. According to John's Gospel, whoever rejects the _____ will face the wrath of God.

GOD OF LOVE AND WRATH (ANSWERS)

1. *Exodus (22:24)*

2. *Revelation (14:10)*

3. *Jesus (22:13), who had a lot to say about God's love also*

4. *Solomon had let his pagan wives lead him away from the Lord (1 Kings 11:9).*

5. *Slow*

6. *Moses (Numbers 14:11). The Israelites were notorious ingrates.*

7. *The Ark of the Covenant (2 Samuel 6:7)*

8. *Stiff (Jeremiah 17:23). To be "stiff-necked" means to be proud, not willing to bow down to God.*

9. *Judah, the one tribe not conquered by the Assyrians (2 Kings 17:18). Later, however, Judah was faithless enough that it was conquered by the Babylonians.*

10. *Kings (110:5)*

11. *Sackcloth, coarse cloth like burlap, and a symbol of sorrow and repentance (Jeremiah 4:8). The meaning is that the repentance, not the cloth itself, will change the Lord's mind.*

12. *Lamentations, as you might guess from its title*

13. *Romans (1:18)*

14. *Revelation (8:16-17). The Lamb is Christ, pouring out his anger on the wicked.*

15. *Jeremiah (25:15)*

16. *John the Baptist (Matthew 3:7), the "vipers" being the Pharisees and Sadducees*

17. *Paul (Romans 12:19)*

18. *Son, that is, Christ (John 3:36)*

GLORY BE!

The words *glory*, *glorious*, and *glorify* occur hundreds of times in the Bible, almost always in connection with God or Christ. In the Old Testament, the Hebrew word *kabod* carried the idea of weight, substance—that is, glory was something a "person of substance" would have, and God, of course, is the ultimate Person. Having said that, let's admit that the whole concept of glory is still kind of elusive and mystifying—just what we would expect of an invisible and unfathomable Lord. See just how much you know about the glory of God—and, in some cases, human glory as well.

1. According to Psalm 19, what declares the glory of God?
2. Why was a certain child named Ichabod?
3. Who was hidden in a rock and privileged to see the glory of God pass by?
4. Which king witnessed fire from heaven consuming a sacrifice while God's glory filled the Temple?
5. What book of the Bible describes a 180-day feast at which a foreign king displayed his own glory?
6. On what famous mountain did the glory of the Lord settle?
7. In which Old Testament book is God himself referred to as the "Glory of Israel"?
8. Who sang the famous song beginning "Glory to God in the highest"?
9. Which Old Testament book refers to God as the "King of Glory"?
10. What famous prayer ends with the words "and the glory forever"?
11. Which prophet proclaimed that the glory of the second Jerusalem Temple would be greater than that of the first Temple?
12. Who was David mourning when he said, "Your glory, O Israel, lies slain on your heights"?
13. Whom were the Israelites about to stone until the glory of God intervened?
14. What man, about to be martyred, had a vision of the glory of God?
15. According to Psalm 8, whom does God crown with glory and honor?
16. Who said that we share in Christ's sufferings in order to share in his glory?
17. In which Gospel does Jesus say, "Father, the time has come. Glorify your Son, that your Son may glorify you"?
18. In Psalm 26, "the place where your glory dwells" refers to what?

19. What miracle was the first revealing of Jesus' glory?
20. What woman led the women of Israel in a song praising God's awesome glory?
21. According to Psalm 16, what people are the "glorious ones" in the land?
22. Which two disciples wished to sit at Jesus' side when he was glorified?
23. What city is lighted by the glory of God?
24. Who claimed that people should eat and drink to the glory of God?
25. According to 1 Peter, who will give the "crown of glory" to believers?
26. What city is praised in Psalms with the words "Glorious things are said of you, O city of God"?
27. According to Paul, who keeps unbelievers from seeing the glory of Christ?
28. Which Epistle says that "the Son is the radiance of God's glory"?
29. Which prophet foretold that "the earth will be filled with the knowledge of the glory of the Lord"?
30. What book of the Bible promises that "the Lord will rebuild Zion and appear in his glory"?
31. Who began a song of praise with the words "My soul glorifies the Lord"?
32. Which disciple did Jesus predict would glorify God by his death?
33. What people were "sore afraid" when the glory of God shone around them?
34. Which prophet proclaimed that human glory is as temporary as the flowers of the field?
35. According to Proverbs, what is the glory of young men?
36. Jeremiah lamented that his people had exchanged the glory of God for what?
37. Who claimed that our momentary troubles are far outweighed by eternal glory?
38. What man did God challenge to "adorn yourself with glory and splendor"?
39. According to Psalms, what people exchanged the glory of God "for an image of a bull, which eats grass"?
40. Which Epistle says that God "will meet all your needs according to his glorious riches in Christ Jesus"?
41. According to Romans 1, what happened when man refused to glorify God?

42. Which Gospel refers to "the glory of the One and Only"?
43. In Exodus, what mighty act brings great glory to God?
44. According to Hebrews, who was glorified because he suffered death?
45. What form did God's glory take when he met with Moses in the Tent of Meeting?
46. According to 1 Corinthians 15, what is "sown in dishonor" but "raised in glory"?
47. Which prophet saw the glory of the Lord in the form of a rainbow?
48. In which book of the Bible would you find the words "All glorious is the princess within"?
49. What book of the Bible states that "a large population is a king's glory"?
50. Which prophet had a vision of angels calling out, "The whole earth is full of his glory"?

GLORY BE! (ANSWERS)

1. The heavens (19:1)

2. The name, which means "no glory," was given to the grandson of the priest Eli, in remembrance of the Ark of the Covenant being captured by Israel's enemies (1 Samuel 4:21-22).

3. Moses (Exodus 33:18-22)

4. Solomon (1 Chronicles 7:1)

5. Esther (1:4), describing the Persian king Ahasuerus

6. Sinai (Exodus 24:16)

7. Numbers (15:29)

8. The angels at the birth of Jesus (Luke 2:14)

9. Psalms (24:7-10)

10. The Lord's Prayer, of course (Matthew 6:13)

11. Haggai (2:9)

12. Saul and Jonathan, who had been killed fighting the Philistines (2 Samuel 1:19)

13. Moses and Aaron (Numbers 14:10)

14. Stephen (Acts 7:55)

15. Man (8:5)

16. Paul (Romans 8:17-18)

17. *John (17:1)*
18. *The Temple (26:8)*
19. *The turning of water into wine at Cana (John 2:11)*
20. *Miriam, Moses' sister, after the Egyptians were drowned in the Red Sea (Exodus 15)*
21. *The saints (16:3)*
22. *The brothers James and John (Mark 10:37)*
23. *The New Jerusalem—heaven, that is (Revelation 21:23)*
24. *Paul (1 Corinthians 10:31)*
25. *The chief Shepherd—that is, Christ (1 Peter 5:4)*
26. *Jerusalem (87:3)*
27. *The "god of this age," which means Satan (2 Corinthians 4:4)*
28. *Hebrews (1:3)*
29. *Habakkuk (2:14)*
30. *Psalms (102:16)*
31. *Mary, mother of Jesus (Luke 1:46). The King James Version has the familiar wording "My soul doth magnify the Lord."*
32. *Peter (John 21:19), who, like most of the others, died as a martyr for the faith*
33. *The shepherds of Bethlehem (Luke 2:9). "Sore afraid" is the King James Version's wording. Many modern versions use the word "terrified."*
34. *Isaiah (40:6)*
35. *Their strength (20:29)*
36. *Worthless idols (Jeremiah 2:11)*
37. *Paul (2 Corinthians 4:17)*
38. *Job (40:10)*
39. *The Israelites, who, having just been freed by God from Egypt, proceeded to worship a gold calf idol (Psalm 106:20)*
40. *Philippians (4:19)*
41. *They began worshipping idols (1:21-23).*
42. *John (1:14). The "One and Only" was Christ.*
43. *Drowning the Egyptian army in the Red Sea (Exodus 14)*
44. *Christ (2:9)*
45. *A cloud (Exodus 40:34)*
46. *The bodies of believers (15:43)*
47. *Ezekiel (1:28)*
48. *Psalms (45:13)*

49. *Proverbs (14:28)*

50. *Isaiah (6:3), in his famous vision in the Temple*

THE ULTIMATE POWER SOURCE

A God without power would be no God at all, right? Well, the God of the Bible is the last word in power. In fact, one of his frequent names in the Hebrew Old Testament is *El-Shaddai,* which most Bibles translate as "Almighty." From beginning to end, we see El-Shaddai manifesting his power in many different ways, so much so that you can't help but link the concept of power with the concept of mystery.

1. Who said that "with God all things are possible"?
2. Which prophet, full of the Lord's power, outran the king's horses and chariot?
3. Which apostle claimed that faith rested on God's power, not human wisdom?
4. What book of the Bible states that the "voice of the Lord breaks the cedars"?
5. Who asked Job the question, "Do you have an arm like God's"?
6. Which prophet foretold that the Lord will "lay bare his holy arm in the sight of the nations"?
7. What woman led the women of Israel in singing, "Your right hand, O Lord, shattered the enemy"?
8. What little-read prophet said that clouds are "the dust of God's feet"?
9. Which New Testament book says that all human beings have an instinctive knowledge of God's power?
10. What group of people was told by Jesus that they did not know the power of God?
11. Complete this verse from Psalm 68: "Proclaim the power of God, whose _____ is over Israel."
12. Which Old Testament book states that God overturns mountains in his anger?
13. In Genesis, what miracle is referred to by the words "Is any thing too hard for the Lord"?

14. What bold soldier said to his armor bearer, "Nothing can hinder the Lord from saving"?
15. Which prophet did God ask, "Is anything too hard for me"?
16. According to Jesus, what was proof that he had the power of God?
17. What three men were certain God's power could save them from death in the fiery furnace?
18. Which prophet said that "the Lord is the Rock eternal"?
19. Which Epistle describes the "whole armor of God" that believers wear?
20. What oppressive king was told that his own stubbornness was for a showing of God's power?
21. What body of water did God lead his people through "as through a desert"?
22. According to Isaiah, God measured the _____ in the hollow of his hand.
23. Who told the Virgin Mary that "nothing shall be impossible with God"?
24. Which prophet took comfort in knowing that his many persecutors would "stumble" because of the power of God?
25. In which book of the Bible does God say, "I kill, and I make alive; I wound, and I heal"?

THE ULTIMATE POWER SOURCE (ANSWERS)

1. Jesus (Matthew 19:26)

2. Elijah (1 Kings 18:46)

3. Paul (1 Corinthians 2:5)

4. Psalms (29:5). Psalm 29 is probably the ultimate "power of God song."

5. God (Job 40:9)

6. Isaiah (52:10)

7. Miriam, sister of Moses and Aaron (Exodus 15:6)

8. Nahum (1:3)

9. Romans (1:20)

10. The Sadducees (Matthew 22:29), who did not believe in an afterlife

11. Majesty (68:34)

12. Job (9:5)

13. Sarah, wife of Abraham, conceiving a child in her old age (Genesis 18:14)

14. *Jonathan, son of Saul (1 Samuel 14:6)*

15. *Jeremiah (32:27)*

16. *That he drove out demons (Luke 11:20)*

17. *Shadrach, Meshach, and Abednego, Daniel's three friends in Babylon (Daniel 3:17)*

18. *Isaiah (26:4)*

19. *Ephesians (6:10-18)*

20. *The pharaoh during the time of Moses (Exodus 9:16)*

21. *The Red Sea (Psalm 106:9)*

22. *Waters (Isaiah 40:12)*

23. *The angel Gabriel (Luke 1:37)*

24. *Jeremiah (20:11)*

25. *Deuteronomy (32:39)*

 ## LIGHTNING, UNGREASED BUT MYSTERIOUS

Thanks to Ben Franklin and a horde of other scientists, lightning isn't quite so mysterious to us as it was to the ancient world. Even so, it is just as beautiful, terrifying, and unpredictable as it was to the folks of Bible times, and it's no surprise that lightning—or something that reminded them of lightning—was often associated with images of the awesome God himself.

1. In Exodus, lightning accompanied which of the plagues of Egypt?
2. What person "saw Satan fall like lightning from heaven"?
3. Which prophet had a strange vision of four creatures that "sped back and forth like lightning"?
4. Whose throne is surrounded by lightning and thunder?
5. Whom did God ask, "Do you send the lightning bolts on their way"?
6. On what famous mountain was there thunder, lightning, and a thick cloud?
7. Which prophet had a vision of a heavenly being with a face like lightning and eyes like torches?
8. Which king spoke of the lightning that blazed forth from God's presence?
9. In the Gospels, who had an appearance like lightning and clothes white as snow?

10. What book of the Bible says that the Lord fills his hands with lightning?
11. According to Matthew 24, what event will seem like lightning?
12. In Revelation, what immoral city experienced an earthquake accompanied by lightning and thunder?
13. What nation is Psalm 78 referring to when it says God gave their livestock to bolts of lightning?
14. Where was Jesus when his clothes became bright as a flash of lightning?
15. What book of the Bible says the Lord's voice strikes with flashes of lightning?
16. Which prophet spoke of chariots flashing through the city streets like lightning?
17. The first mention of lightning in the Bible is connected with what beautiful place?
18. Which prophet told Ephraim that God's "judgments flashed like lightning upon you"?

LIGHTNING, UNGREASED BUT MYSTERIOUS (ANSWERS)

1. Hail (Exodus 9:23-24)
2. Jesus (Luke 10:18)
3. Ezekiel (1:13)
4. God's, of course (Revelation 4:5)
5. Job (24:35)
6. Sinai, where God gave the law to Moses (Exodus 19:16)
7. Daniel (10:6)
8. David (2 Samuel 22:13)
9. The angel at Jesus' empty tomb (Matthew 28:3)
10. Job (36:32)
11. Jesus' second coming (24:27)
12. Babylon (16:18)
13. Egypt (78:48). It is referring to the plague of hail and lightning in Exodus 9.
14. On the Mount of Transfiguration, with Moses and Elijah (Luke 9:29)
15. Psalms (29:7)
16. Nahum (2:4). The verse is regarded by some as a prophecy of city traffic.

17. *Eden. Genesis 3:24 speaks of a "flaming sword flashing back and forth" barring the way back to Eden. Some have interpreted the "sword" as lightning.*

18. *Hosea (6:5)*

JUDGE NOT, UNLESS YOU'RE GOD

In our contemporary society, one of the worst things you can say about someone is that he is "judgmental." Well, in fact, the Bible presents us with a God who is *very* judgmental—but that is a wonderful thing, since we certainly can't depend on human judges and judgment to bring justice to the world. God alone, knowing all and able to see past the surfaces of things, can judge rightly and fairly.

1. What book of the Bible depicts God as a judge opening the Book of Life?
2. Complete this verse from Proverbs: "All the ways of a man are clean in his own eyes, but the Lord weighs the _____."
3. Who stated that "whatever you have spoken in darkness shall be heard in the light"?
4. Who claimed that "every one of us shall give account of himself to God"?
5. Complete this verse from Psalms: "Justice and judgment are the habitation of your _____."
6. What distraught woman said to her husband, "May the Lord judge between you and me"?
7. Which prophet foretold God judging the nations in a place called the Valley of Jehoshaphat?
8. Complete this verse from Proverbs: "To do justice and judgment is more acceptable to the Lord than _____."
9. According to Paul, we must all appear before the judgment _____ of Christ.
10. What rebels are kept in chains until the Day of Judgment?
11. Which prophet said that though the Lord is slow to anger, he will not acquit the wicked?
12. Which Epistle says, "Behold the goodness and severity of God"?
13. Complete this verse from Psalms: "To you, O Lord, belongs mercy, for you render to every man according to his _____."
14. According to Jesus, what shall accompany him when he returns to judge the earth?

15. What book of the Bible says that God will bring every work, even every secret thing, into judgment?
16. Who claimed he feared no human judgment, not even his own, for his only judge was God?
17. According to 1 John, believers may have _____ in the Day of Judgment.
18. What future king said to his king, "The Lord judge between you and me"?
19. What suffering man was asked the question, "Can a mortal man be more righteous than God"?
20. What city was Abraham discussing when he asked God, "Shall not the Judge of all the earth do right"?
21. What book of the Bible claims that God shows no partiality and takes no bribes?
22. Which New Testament book says, "Behold, the Judge stands before the door"?
23. Complete this verse from Hebrews: "It is appointed to man once to ____, but after this the judgment."
24. Which prophet predicted the coming of a man who "shall not judge by what his eyes see, nor decide by what his ears hear"?
25. According to Jesus, every idle word spoken in secret shall be proclaimed upon the _____.

JUDGE NOT, UNLESS YOU'RE GOD (ANSWERS)

1. *Revelation (20:11-15)*

2. *Motives (16:2)*

3. *Jesus (Luke 12:3)*

4. *Paul (Romans 14:12)*

5. *Throne (Psalm 89:14)*

6. *Sarah, wife of Abraham (Genesis 16:5), in the first use of the phrase "may the Lord judge between us"*

7. *Joel (3:2)*

8. *Sacrifice (Proverbs 21:3)*

9. *Seat (2 Corinthians 5:10)*

10. *The rebel angels (Jude 1:6)*

11. *Nahum (1:3)*

12. *Romans (11:22)*

13. *Work (Psalm 62:12)*

14. *Angels (Matthew 16:27)*

15. *Ecclesiastes (12:14)*

16. *Paul (1 Corinthians 4:3-5)*

17. *Boldness, because they needn't fear punishment (1 John 4:17-18)*

18. *David, speaking to Saul (2 Samuel 24:12)*

19. *Job (4:17)*

20. *Sodom, where God clearly believed the right thing was to do destroy it (Genesis 18:25)*

21. *Deuteronomy (10:17)*

22. *James (5:9)*

23. *Die (Hebrews 9:27)*

24. *Isaiah (11:1-4). This prophecy was believed to have been fulfilled in Jesus.*

25. *Housetops (Luke 12:3)*

PART 4

THE END (OF TIME)

THE BEAST, ANTICHRIST, 666, ETC.

Who—or what—is the "beast" mentioned in Revelation? People have been guessing for two thousand years. Pick some powerful historical figure—Nero, Hitler, Stalin, Napoleon, even good people like Martin Luther and Abraham Lincoln—and chances are that some group of people thought he was the Beast, the Antichrist, the evil figure symbolized by the number 666.

Of course, we aren't sure if the Beast is a single person or perhaps a nation or even an ideology. We only know that he/it is opposed to God and his saints and will cause great suffering before the end comes. We won't ask you here to speculate about who (what) you think the Beast is (or was), but merely about what you know about the Bible's mysterious words about the Beast, the Antichrist(s), and the 666 person.

1. Who predicted that there would be "false Christs" who would deceive people by performing miracles?
2. What book of the Bible states that many antichrists have already come into the world?
3. According to John, what teaching identifies an antichrist?
4. Where, according to Revelation 11, does the Beast come from?
5. But, according to Revelation 13, where does the Beast come from?
6. From what wicked creature does the Beast derive his power?
7. What three fearsome animals does the Beast resemble?
8. What happened to the Beast that made the world follow him?
9. What people do not worship the Beast?
10. The second Beast comes from where?
11. What awesome miracle did the second Beast perform?
12. On what parts of the body are people required to get the "mark of the beast"?
13. Why did people have to get the mark of the Beast?
14. What exactly is 666?
15. What fate awaits those who worship the Beast or receive his mark?
16. Those who resist the Beast are depicted holding what musical instruments?
17. What physical affliction was poured out on those who had worshipped the Beast?
18. The three evil spirits that came out of the Beast's mouth looked like what?
19. What aide of the Beast is destroyed with him in a lake of burning sulfur?

20. Those who had not worshipped the Beast were entitled to reign with Christ for how long?
21. Who is thrown into the eternal fire along with the Beast and the false prophet?
22. What brief epistle of Paul foretold a "man of sin," who would do horrible things before Christ's return?
23. Which Old Testament prophet foretold a 10-horned beast with iron teeth, which would persecute the saints before the end of time?
24. In Ezekiel, what evil prince seems to fit the description of the Beast or the Antichrist?

THE BEAST, ANTICHRIST, 666, ETC. (ANSWERS)

1. *Jesus (Matthew 24:24)*

2. *1 John (2:18)*

3. *Denying that Jesus is the Christ, God's Son (1 John 2:22). By the way, anti doesn't only mean "against" but can also mean "in place of."*

4. *The abyss—meaning the lower depths (Revelation 11:7)*

5. *The sea (13:1)*

6. *The dragon (Revelation 13:2). Mysterious as Revelation is, we can be pretty certain that the dragon means Satan, the devil.*

7. *A leopard, bear, and lion (Revelation 13:2). Obviously this isn't literal but means to symbolize fear and terror by using images of three wild animals that humans greatly fear.*

8. *He recovered from a fatal wound—or, more precisely, one of his seven heads recovered from a fatal wound (13:3).*

9. *Those whose names are in the Book of Life—referring, obviously, to Christians (13:8)*

10. *Out of the earth (13:11)*

11. *Making fire come down from heaven (13:13)*

12. *The forehead or the right hand (13:16)*

13. *In order to either buy or sell (13:17)*

14. *The "number of the beast"—whatever that may mean (13:18). Christians have spilled a lot of ink trying to connect 666 with some specific person's name. But 666 may be merely symbolic—six being the "imperfect" number as opposed to the "perfect" number seven.*

15. *Eternal torment (14:11)*

16. *Harps, of course (15:2)*

17. *Painful sores (16:2)*

18. *Frogs (16:13)*

19. *The false prophet (19:20)*

20. *A thousand years—that is, a millennium (20:4)*

21. *The devil (20:10)*

22. *2 Thessalonians (2:3-4). Some translations have "man of lawlessness." Obviously Paul is referring to someone like the Beast of Revelation.*

23. *Daniel (7:23-27). Both Daniel and Revelation depict the Beast as having 10 horns, and both books explain that the 10 horns represent 10 kings.*

24. *Gog, the prince of Magog (Ezekiel 38–39). Revelation uses the names Gog and Magog to refer to two powers hostile to the saints (20:8).*

THE END TIMES: SOME KEY WORDS

Christians in the first century were certain that Christ would return to earth soon. Although it didn't happen, successive generations have lived in the knowledge that the end of the world might arrive at any time. Over the years Christians have developed an entire vocabulary to talk about the end times. There is no harm in studying the end times, so long as we understand a basic teaching of the Bible: The end is very much shrouded in secrecy, and God alone knows all the details.

1. Theologians and Bible scholars refer to the study of the end times as what?
2. What word, taken from Greek, often refers to the second coming of Jesus?
3. Where did the phrase "Second Coming" originate?
4. In the Old Testament, what common phrase referred to the coming day of God's judgment on humanity?
5. What famous creed states that Jesus will "come to judge the quick and the dead"?
6. What musical instrument is used to announce the end of time?

7. What word is often used to refer to the persecution of people of faith at the end of time?
8. People being caught up in the air when Jesus returns is known as what?

9. The idea of a Millennium, or thousand-year reign of believers on earth, is based on what book of the Bible?

10. What is the difference between a "premillennial" Christian and "postmillennial" Christian?

11. What is an "amillennialist"?

12. What name from the book of Revelation has come to refer to the final great battle between good and evil?

13. What two names, found in both Ezekiel and Revelation, refer to two wicked forces that war against God's people at the end of time?

14. What system of thought teaches that God's dealings with humanity are divided into seven "ages," with the last one being the age of Christ's return to earth?

15. Writings that are concerned with the events of the end times (such as the book of Revelation) are known as what type of literature?

16. What is "conditional immortality"?

17. The Book of Life containing the names of all the saved persons is mentioned in which New Testament book?

18. Where did the expression "doomsday" come from?

19. What is the source of the phrase "judgment seat"?

THE END TIMES: SOME KEY WORDS (ANSWERS)

1. *Eschatology, from the Greek word* eschaton, *meaning "end" or "last"*

2. *Parousia, meaning "presence" or "coming"*

3. *In Jesus' many predictions of returning to earth. His being born as a baby in Bethlehem was, of course, his first coming.*

4. *"Day of the Lord," which was later used by the first Christians. An entire set of questions is devoted to "Day of the Lord" (see pages 91–93).*

5. *The Apostles' Creed. The old word* quick *meant "living."*

6. *A trumpet, mentioned in Matthew 24:31, 1 Corinthians 15:52, 1 Thessalonians 4:16, and several times in Revelation. The phrase "the last trump" has become part of the end-times vocabulary. By the way, the Bible does not say that the angel Gabriel will blow the trumpet.*

7. *The Tribulation. The actual phrase "the great tribulation" is found in Revelation 7:14.*

8. *The Rapture, which is from the Latin word* rapio, *meaning "caught up." The image of believers being raised into the air occurs in many places, such as 1 Thessalonians 4:17.*

9. *Revelation, which in chapter 20 speaks of Satan being "bound" for a thousand years while the saints reign on earth, though afterward Satan will be released, then finally defeated.*

10. *The "pre" people believe Christ will return before the Millennium, whereas "post" people believe he will return afterward. Lots of ink has been spilled in the pre/post debate.*

11. *Someone who takes the thousand-year period (of Revelation 20) symbolically, not as a literal thousand years*

12. *Armageddon, the location of the "battle on the great day of God Almighty" (Revelation 16:16). It refers to the area of Mount Megiddo, an area where several famous battles were fought in ancient times.*

13. *Gog and Magog. In Ezekiel 38, Gog is apparently a prince in the country of Magog (wherever that was). But in Revelation 20:8 the names refer to two wicked nations (or forces).*

14. *Dispensationalism, which teaches that the seven ages are "dispensations," in which God deals with humanity in different ways. The system has been widely spread through the popular Scofield Reference Bible.*

15. *Apocalyptic, from the Greek word* apocalypsis, *"revealing" or "unveiling." In fact, Apocalypse is an alternate name for the book of Revelation.*

16. *The idea that immortality is a gift given to the righteous and that at the end of time the wicked will simply be annihilated*

17. *Revelation (20:15; 21:27)*

18. *The old meaning of* doom *was "judgment," which was a good thing for the righteous but a bad thing for the wicked.* Doomsday *meant "Judgment Day," something positive for believers but extremely unpleasant for everyone else. Since it was assumed that there were more bad than good people in the world,* doom *came to mean "ruin."*

19. *In ancient times—and today, for that matter—a judge pronounced his verdict while seated on an official "judgment seat." The New Testament emphasizes that everyone must appear before Christ's judgment seat (2 Corinthians 5:10).*

 ## GOOD HEAVEN!

Harps, golden streets, pearly gates. Yes, all those images are from the Bible, and a lot more besides. Of course, the Bible writers faced quite a task when depicting heaven: They were trying to describe the indescribable. So, in spite of all the Bible says about heaven (and it says a lot), heaven remains quite mysterious to us, which is as it should be. After all, it is literally "out of this world."

1. What man in Genesis "walked with God" so that God "took him"?
2. What is Sheol?
3. What great prophet was taken into heaven in a fiery chariot?
4. What suffering man stated that even though his body died, yet he would still see God?
5. What book of the Bible states that God will not allow his "Holy One" to see corruption?
6. What famous passage ends with "I will dwell in the house of the Lord forever"?
7. What is the only Old Testament book to explicitly speak of heaven and hell?
8. In the Beatitudes, what people will have the Kingdom of Heaven?
9. And what people did Jesus promise would have a great reward in heaven?
10. Complete this saying of Jesus: "Lay up for yourselves _____ in heaven."
11. What three men from Genesis did Jesus say will be present at the banquet of heaven?
12. According to Matthew 18, what do we have to become like in order to enter heaven?
13. What person did Jesus tell that those who are "born again" will have everlasting life?
14. What is "Abraham's bosom"?
15. Which Jewish group at the time of Jesus did not believe in an afterlife?
16. According to Matthew 22, what human institution does not exist in heaven?
17. What is the "eternal bread" that gives eternal life?
18. According to Jesus, what do we have to carry daily to follow after him?
19. What famous parable did Jesus tell when someone asked him, "What shall I do to inherit eternal life"?
20. To whom did Jesus say, "I am the resurrection and the life"?
21. What two long-dead men were seen with Jesus at the Transfiguration?
22. Finish this quote: "In my Father's house are many _____."
23. To what political figure did Jesus say, "My kingdom is not of this world"?
24. To what person did Jesus say, "Today you will be with me in paradise"?
25. The risen Jesus being taken up into heaven is known as what?

26. In Catholic teaching, what person (besides Jesus) was taken body and soul into heaven?
27. Who is at the "right hand" of God in heaven?
28. What book of the Bible depicts the saints in heaven holding harps?
29. Which Epistle states that "eye has not seen, nor ear heard" the things God has prepared for his people?
30. What famous oxymoron does Paul use to describe the bodies of believers in heaven?
31. Who had an "out of body" experience in which he went to "the third heaven"?
32. What book of the Bible refers to the "paradise of God"?
33. In which Epistle does Paul speak of believers sitting together in "the heavenly places in Christ Jesus"?
34. In the Catholic and Orthodox churches, a person believed to be in heaven is known as what?
35. According to Paul, every knee shall bow in heaven and on earth to do homage to whom?
36. According to the Letter to the Hebrews, who is the eternal High Priest in heaven?
37. Which Epistle states that Christians are "sojourners and pilgrims," passing through earth to their real home in heaven?
38. Which Epistle says that Christians receive "a kingdom that cannot be shaken"?
39. In Revelation, who has the "keys of hades and death"?
40. Who has a "marriage supper" in Revelation 19?
41. How many pearly gates does heaven have?
42. What color are the robes of the saints in heaven?
43. What object found in the Garden of Eden is also found in heaven?
44. Why isn't there a temple in heaven?
45. Why is there no sun in heaven?
46. What names are written on the gates of heaven?
47. What crystal-clear river flows in heaven?
48. In Revelation, heaven is also known as the New _____.
49. Which Epistle speaks of a "cloud of witnesses" watching us from heaven?

GOOD HEAVEN! (ANSWERS)

1. Enoch (Genesis 5:23-24). This is one of the most mysterious passages, hinting (but not making explicit) that Enoch did not die but was simply taken to heaven by God. It is the Bible's first hint that some people—good ones, anyway—will be "taken" by God.

2. In the Old Testament, the Hebrew word for the afterlife—neither heaven nor hell, just kind of a shadowy existence after death. English translations use "the grave" or some such term.

3. Elijah (2 Kings 2). Like Enoch, he was a righteous man "taken" by God.

4. Job (19:25), in a famous passage that suggests belief in heaven

5. Psalms (16:10-11). Christians apply this passage to Christ, of course, but also extend it to all Christians.

6. The "Shepherd Psalm," Psalm 23. "House of the Lord" probably meant the Temple but could also mean heaven.

7. Daniel (12:2-3), which states that the dead will someday be raised—either to eternal life or eternal shame

8. The poor in spirit (Matthew 5:3)

9. Those who were persecuted for righteousness' sake (Matthew 5:10)

10. Treasures (Matthew 6:19-21). He meant spiritual treasure, not earthly goods.

11. Abraham, Isaac, and Jacob (Matthew 8:10-11), three of the patriarchs of Israel

12. Little children (18:1-4)

13. Nicodemus (John 3:1-21)

14. Heaven, as seen in Luke 16:22-23. The patriarch Abraham was, Jews assumed, in heaven, so to be in "Abraham's bosom" (that is, at his side) meant to be in heaven.

15. The Sadducees, the ruling elite in Jerusalem. But most Jews did believe in an afterlife.

16. Marriage (22:30). People may marry "for life" but not "for eternity."

17. Not what, but whom. It was Jesus (John 6:51).

18. Our cross (Luke 9:23-24)

19. The parable of the Good Samaritan (Luke 10:25-37)

20. Martha, the sister of Lazarus, the man Jesus raised from the dead (John 11:25)

21. Moses and Elijah (Matthew 17:1-5). Presumably these two great saints left heaven to, temporarily, visit earth.

22. Mansions—or so the King James Version has it. Modern translations are more accurate with "rooms" or "dwellings."

23. Pilate, the Roman governor (John 18:36)

24. One of the two thieves crucified with him (Luke 23:39-43)

25. The Ascension

26. Mary, Jesus' mother. This is called the Assumption of Mary, and is not mentioned in the Bible.

27. Jesus. This is mentioned several times in the New Testament.

28. Revelation (15:2)

29. 1 Corinthians (2:9)

30. "Spiritual body" (1 Corinthians 15)

31. Paul, as he describes in 2 Corinthians 12:2-3. Actually, Paul is describing "a man" who had such an experience, but most scholars believe he was referring to himself.

32. Appropriately, the last one, Revelation (2:7)

33. Ephesians, where he uses "heavenly places" five times (1:3; 1:20; 2:6; 3:10; 6:12)

34. Saint, a word borrowed, of course, from the Bible

35. Christ, of course (Philippians 2:9-10)

36. Jesus (Hebrews 4:14; 8:1; 9:12)

37. 1 Peter (2:11)

38. Hebrews (12:28). The meaning is that heaven endures, while earthly powers do not.

39. Christ (1:17-18). The meaning is that Christ has power over death.

40. The Lamb—that is, Christ. He is "married" to his "bride," which means all Christians.

41. Twelve (Revelation 21:21). Actually, each gate is a pearl.

42. White, naturally—the color of purity (Revelation 7:9)

43. The tree of life (Genesis 3:22; Revelation 22:2)

44. God and the Lamb (Christ) are its temple (Revelation 21:22).

45. The glory of God provides light (Revelation 21:23; 22:5).

46. The names of the 12 tribes of Israel (Revelation 21:12)

47. The river of the water of life (Revelation 22:1-2)

48. Jerusalem (21:2)

49. Hebrews (12:1)

THE "H" WORD (HELL, THAT IS)

The idea of eternal punishment seems like a mystery. For some people, it is a mystery as to how a loving, compassionate God could allow people to suffer eternally. The Bible looks at hell from a different angle: The mystery is that God would choose to save anyone at all, given the way humans constantly thumb their noses at God and his ways. While the idea of hell is unfashionable right now, there's no doubt that the first Christians had very solid beliefs in both eternal bliss (heaven) and eternal agony (hell).

1. Who famously said that the way that leads to destruction is "broad"?
2. Which Old Testament prophet proclaimed that God takes no pleasure in the death of the wicked but desires that all people would turn from their evil ways?
3. According to Jesus, who will gather up all the wicked and toss them into a furnace of fire?
4. What sin, since it can never be forgiven, leads to eternal damnation?
5. In hell, what are human teeth doing?
6. If your hand causes you to sin, what should you do with it?
7. In a famous parable, what patriarch of Israel had a conversation with a rich man in hell?
8. Which Gospel says that some men are condemned because they loved darkness rather than light?
9. Which apostle stated that God cast sinning angels into hell?
10. What book of the Bible speaks of eternal torment in a "lake of fire"?
11. What is the "brimstone" that is part of hell?
12. What people did Jesus refer to as a "generation of vipers" that was in serious danger of hell?
13. Which Old Testament book is the only one to express a definite belief in hell and heaven?
14. Which Epistle cites Sodom and Gomorrah as examples of sin being destroyed by fire?
15. Which Old Testament book ends with a passage describing a fire that will never be quenched?
16. According to Jesus, what becomes of trees that do not bear good fruit?
17. Who warned that Jesus was coming to "burn up the chaff with unquenchable fire"?
18. In which Gospel does Jesus say that "whoever rejects the Son will not see life"?

19. Who was Jesus speaking of when he said "be afraid of the One who can destroy both body and soul in hell"?
20. What, according to Jesus, is easier than a rich man entering the Kingdom of God?
21. Who stated that the "wages of sin is death"?
22. According to James, what bodily organ is "set on fire by hell"?
23. According to Jude, what sort of people will end up in "blackest darkness" forever?
24. What book of the Bible speaks of the "great winepress of God's wrath"?
25. What is the "second death" spoken of in Revelation?
26. What is "annihilationism"?

THE "H" WORD (HELL, THAT IS) (ANSWERS)

1. Jesus (Matthew 7:13)

2. Ezekiel (33:11)

3. The angels (Matthew 13:41-43)

4. Blaspheming against the Holy Spirit (Mark 3:29), which is a mystery in itself. The most common interpretation is that it means attributing the work of Christ to Satan.

5. Gnashing, or grinding, an image used several times by Jesus in the Gospels. The idea is that a person in agony and regret would grind his teeth.

6. Cut it off—better to be maimed than to go to hell, according to Mark 9:43. The Bible isn't literally suggesting cutting one's hand off but making the point that whatever causes us to sin is a serious problem.

7. Abraham, who was in heaven with the poor beggar Lazarus (Luke 16:19-26)

8. John (3:18-19)

9. Peter (see 2 Peter 2:4)

10. Revelation (20:10-15)

11. Probably burning sulfur, mentioned in Revelation 21:8. Readers have noted that "fire and brimstone" are what destroyed the sinful cities of Sodom and Gomorrah (Genesis 19:24).

12. The Pharisees and teachers of the law (Matthew 23:33)

13. Daniel, which predicts a time when some will be raised for everlasting life, others for everlasting contempt (12:2)

14. Jude (verse 7)

15. Isaiah (66:24). Whether the prophet was actually referring to hell is not certain.

16. They are cut down and thrown into the fire (Matthew 7:19). The "trees" are human beings, of course.

17. John the Baptist (Luke 3:15-17)

18. John (3:36)

19. God (Matthew 10:28). Some people think it refers to Satan, but it is pretty clear in the context that this isn't so.

20. A camel passing through the eye of a needle (Mark 10:25)

21. Paul (Romans 6:23)

22. The tongue, which can do all kinds of evil things (James 3:6)

23. False teachers (verse 13)

24. Revelation (14:19). That passage is, by the way, the source of the phrase "grapes of wrath" in the "Battle Hymn of the Republic."

25. The eternal lake of fire (2:11; 20:6; 21:8). The "first death" refers to the normal physical death of each person.

26. The belief that the wicked are simply snuffed out, not punished eternally. It is difficult to square annihilationism with the Bible's rather blunt words about punishment being eternal.

 ## JESUS' SECOND COMING

The earliest believers in Jesus Christ held to the firm hope that he would return again, as he had promised. They didn't know when, and Jesus and his apostles had made it clear that no one could predict the time. That hasn't stopped clever (and occasionally deluded) people from making predictions, of course. Still, the time must remain a mystery. The message of the Bible is clear: Instead of speculating on the time of Christ's return, we should be ready at all times.

1. According to Jesus, who alone knows the time of the Second Coming?
2. To what dramatic (and wet) Old Testament event did Jesus compare the Second Coming?
3. Who will accompany Jesus at the Second Coming?
4. According to Luke's Gospel, who will Jesus be ashamed of when he returns?
5. Who stated that we expect the Lord to return from heaven because "our citizenship is in heaven"?

6. According to Paul, whose voice will be heard to announce the Lord's coming?
7. According to Peter, what type of crown shall believers receive when Christ appears?
8. Into what two groups of "animals" will Jesus divide the world when he returns?
9. Who stated that at Christ's return, we will all be changed "in the twinkling of an eye"?
10. In which book of the Bible does Christ twice promise "I will come on you as a thief"?
11. According to Jesus, what will happen to two men toiling in the field when he returns?
12. According to Paul, when Christ returns, what people will be raised up first?
13. Which Epistle promises that, when Christ comes again, "we shall be like him"?
14. The words "Amen. Come, Lord Jesus," appear near the end of what book of the Bible?
15. Which Gospel warns that the Second Coming will "close on you unexpectedly like a trap"?
16. Who tore his robes in rage when he heard Jesus say that he would return on the clouds of heaven?
17. According to Jesus, what type of deceivers would appear before he returned to earth?
18. What fate will befall believers before the Second Coming?
19. What city will be conquered by the Gentiles before the end comes?
20. Which Epistle states that the Lord's coming will be as sudden as a woman going into labor?
21. In one of Jesus' parables, what two plants represent the good and the wicked that will be separated at the Second Coming?

JESUS' SECOND COMING (ANSWERS)

1. *God the Father (Matthew 24:36)*
2. *The Great Flood of Noah's time (Matthew 24:37)*
3. *Angels (Matthew 16:27; 25:31; Luke 9:26)*
4. *Those who have been ashamed of Jesus and his words (Luke 9:26)*
5. *Paul (Philippians 3:20)*
6. *An archangel (1 Thessalonians 4:15)*

7. *A crown of glory (1 Peter 5:4)*

8. *"Sheep" and "goats," as explained in Matthew 25:31-46. The sheep represent the righteous, the goats the unrighteous.*

9. *Paul, in his famous "Resurrection Chapter," 1 Corinthians 15*

10. *Revelation (3:3; 16:15)*

11. *One would be taken, the other left (Matthew 24:40).*

12. *The "dead in Christ"—that is, Christians who have already died (1 Thessalonians 4:15-17)*

13. *1 John (3:2)*

14. *Appropriately enough, Revelation, the last book of the Bible*

15. *Luke (21:34-35)*

16. *The Jewish high priest (Matthew 26:64-65)*

17. *False prophets and false Christs (Matthew 24:24)*

18. *Severe persecution (Mark 13:9-13; Luke 21:12-19)*

19. *Jerusalem (Luke 21:24)*

20. *1 Thessalonians (5:3)*

21. *Wheat and tares (Matthew 13:24-43). Tares were a type of weed, which, at the "harvest," would be rooted up and burned.*

 ## THE MYSTERIOUS "DAY OF THE LORD"

The "Day of the Lord" is mentioned often in both Old and New Testaments. At times it seems to refer to any moment when God suddenly appears to punish sin and wickedness. But there are also passages that seem to refer to one final dramatic moment at the end of time, the day of final judgment on all humanity.

1. In a famous phrase used by Paul, the Day of the Lord will arrive like what?
2. Which prophets proclaimed that the Day of the Lord would come "like destruction from the Almighty"?
3. Which prophet predicted that silver and gold would be no help at all on the Day of the Lord's wrath?
4. Which apostle foretold that on the Day of the Lord the heavens would disappear with a roar?

5. According to Malachi, which prophet would return to earth as a forewarning of the Day of the Lord?

6. Who had to remind Christians that the Day of the Lord had not yet arrived?

7. According to Zephaniah, what would consume the whole earth on the Day of the Lord?

8. In Peter's famous Pentecost sermon, what did he say would happen to the sun on the Day of the Lord?

9. What book of the Bible laments that "in the day of the Lord's anger no one escaped or survived"?

10. Who prophesied that the Day of the Lord would be "a day of clouds, a time of doom for the nations"?

11. According to Joel, the Day of the Lord would arrive in what valley?

12. Which prophet warned, "Woe to you who long for the day of the Lord"?

13. Who asked the question, "The day of the Lord is great. Who can endure it"?

14. According to Zephaniah, what might provide a shelter on the Day of the Lord?

15. Who prophesied that the Day of the Lord would be a time when all nations would be paid back for all they had done?

16. Who foretold the looting of Jerusalem on the Day of the Lord?

17. According to Isaiah, who would be destroyed on the Day of the Lord?

18. Who prophesied that on the Day of the Lord, God would be like "a refiner's fire"?

THE MYSTERIOUS "DAY OF THE LORD" (ANSWERS)

1. *A thief in the night (1 Thessalonians 5:2)*

2. *Isaiah (13:6) and Joel (1:15) use almost precisely the same words.*

3. *Ezekiel (7:19)*

4. *Peter (2 Peter 3:10)*

5. *Elijah (Malachi 4:5)*

6. *Paul (2 Thessalonians 2:2)*

7. *Fire (Zephaniah 1:18)*

8. *It would be darkened (Acts 2:20).*

9. *Lamentations, appropriately enough (2:22)*

10. *Ezekiel (30:3)*

11. *The valley of decision (Joel 3:14)*

12. *Amos (5:18)*

13. *Joel (2:11)*

14. *Humility and righteousness (Zephaniah 2:3)*

15. *Obadiah (verse 15)*

16. *Zechariah (14:1-2)*

17. *Sinners (Isaiah 13:9), a theme echoed throughout the Bible*

18. *Malachi (3:2). If these words sound familiar, it might be because they are included in George Frederick Handel's* Messiah.

 ## EVERLASTINGLY ETERNAL

Eternity, if you pondered it long enough, might give you a headache. The human mind can imagine centuries, even millennia—but *eternity*? Like many things in the Bible, eternity is quite mysterious, mostly because our imaginations (and experience) are limited. In all likelihood, we won't really understand eternity until we get to heaven. In spite of all the mystery, however, the Bible does say a lot about eternity.

1. Who asked Jesus the famous question, "What shall I do to get eternal life"?
2. After the Great Flood, what sign was given of the everlasting covenant between God and earth?
3. What sin is, according to Jesus, eternal and unforgivable?
4. What two men carried the message of eternal life to the Gentiles after the Jews rejected it?
5. What country was given to Abraham's descendants as an "everlasting possession"?
6. Which Old Testament book speaks of the "everlasting arms" of God?
7. Which disciple affirmed that Jesus had "the words of eternal life"?
8. According to Psalm 119 (the longest chapter in the Bible), what is eternal?

9. Who prophesied about a virgin's son who would be called "Everlasting Father, Prince of Peace"?

10. Which king believed that God had established an everlasting covenant with his family?

11. According to Psalm 93, whose throne was established from all eternity?

12. According to Galatians, what person would be eternally condemned?

13. In Proverbs, what declares itself to be "appointed from eternity"?

14. Which prophet referred to God as "the Rock eternal"?

15. Which Old Testament book states that God "set eternity in the hearts of men"?

16. In Revelation, who proclaims the eternal gospel to the whole earth?

17. In the New Testament, what two sinful cities are cited as examples of punishment by everlasting fire?

18. What notable woman told Solomon that he had been made king because of God's eternal love for Israel?

19. According to Isaiah, what nation will be saved "with an everlasting salvation"?

20. What pagan king acknowledged that God's Kingdom is eternal?

21. Which Old Testament book speaks of eternal pleasures at the right hand of God?

22. To whom did God say, "I have loved you with an everlasting love"?

23. According to the New Testament, who was bound in everlasting chains until Judgment Day?

24. What pagan empire rashly boasted, "I will continue forever—the eternal queen"?

25. What is the only book that uses the phrase "eternal Spirit" of God?

26. According to Psalm 21, what person is granted "eternal blessings" by God?

27. Which Epistle states that believers have "an eternal house in heaven"?

28. What type of people receive God's everlasting love, according to Psalm 103?

29. What is the only Old Testament book to refer to God as "eternal King"?

30. Who prophesied that King Nebuchadnezzar of Babylon would bring "everlasting ruin" on Israel?

31. Which Epistle states that God's eternal power is evident to all humanity?
32. According to 1 John 3, what sort of person will not have eternal life?
33. Which apostle praised "the King eternal, immortal, invisible"?
34. In Genesis, what man "called upon the name of the Lord, the eternal God"?
35. According to John, what did God give so that men might have eternal life?
36. What nation, according to Psalms, has an everlasting covenant with God?
37. Who prophesied a time when God's people will be crowned with everlasting joy?
38. According to the Letter to the Hebrews, what sort of people gain eternal salvation?
39. Who prophesied that those who had died would awake to everlasting life or everlasting contempt?
40. According to Jesus, an eternal fire is prepared for whom?
41. Who urged believers to "fight the good fight" and "take hold of eternal life"?

EVERLASTINGLY ETERNAL (ANSWERS)

1. *The rich young ruler, who is not named (Matthew 19:16)*

2. *The rainbow (Genesis 9:16)*

3. *Blasphemy against the Holy Spirit (Mark 3:29)*

4. *Paul and Barnabas (Acts 13:46-48)*

5. *Canaan (Genesis 17:7-8)*

6. *Deuteronomy (33:27)*

7. *Peter (John 6:28)*

8. *The Word of God (Psalm 119:89, 142,160)*

9. *Isaiah (9:6), in a passage often read at Christmas (and sung as part of Handel's Messiah)*

10. *David (2 Samuel 23:5)*

11. *God's (93:2)*

12. *Anyone preaching a false gospel (Galatians 1:8-9)*

13. *Wisdom, which is the main theme of Proverbs (8:23)*

14. *Isaiah (26:4)*

15. *Ecclesiastes (3:11)*

16. *An angel (Revelation 14:6)*

17. *Sodom and Gomorrah (Jude 1:7)*

18. *The queen of Sheba (1 Kings 10:1-9)*

19. *Israel, of course (Isaiah 45:17)*

20. *Nebuchadnezzar, ruler of Babylon (Daniel 4:3, 34)*

21. *Psalms (16:11)*

22. *Israel (Jeremiah 31:3)*

23. *The rebel angels (Jude 1:6)*

24. *Babylon (Isaiah 47:7)*

25. *Hebrews (9:14)*

26. *The king (Psalm 21:6). We aren't sure which king this refers to, or whether it even referred to a particular individual.*

27. *2 Corinthians (5:1)*

28. *Those who fear him (103:17)*

29. *Jeremiah (10:10). However, the idea of God as eternal King is present through the whole Bible.*

30. *Jeremiah (25:9)*

31. *Romans (1:20)*

32. *Anyone who hates his brother*

33. *Paul (1 Timothy 1:17)*

34. *Abraham (Genesis 21:33). This is actually one of the few places in the Bible that refers to "eternal God."*

35. *His Son, Christ (3:15-17)*

36. *Israel (Psalm 105:10)*

37. *Isaiah (35:10)*

38. *Those who obey God (5:9)*

39. *Daniel (12:2)*

40. *The devil and his angels (Matthew 25:41)*

41. *Paul (1 Timothy 6:12)*

PART 5

WHAT'S IN A NAME?

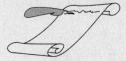

THAT'S MY NAME, YAH!

As you probably know, God's name in the Hebrew Old Testament is Yahweh, a name that, strictly speaking, can't even be translated but probably means something like "I am what I am." (See Exodus 3 for the famous story of God revealing his name to Moses.) Over time the Hebrew name came to be considered so sacred that many devout Jews would not say the name itself but would substitute the title *Adonai,* the Hebrew word for "lord." The practice continues in English Bibles, where in the Old Testament you'll see "LORD" (note the small caps) instead of Yahweh. Interestingly, the short form of Yahweh was simply Yah, and it made its way into lots of personal names, generally in the endings -iah or -jah—in other words, some of the most notable people (good and bad) in the Bible. So this section will test your knowledge of Bible characters, specifically those with "Yah names."

1. What wilderness prophet of Israel had a name meaning "Yah is God"?
2. Which prophet (with a much-read book full of prophecies of the Messiah) has a name meaning "Yah saves"?
3. What name meaning "Yah remembers" was the name of an Old Testament prophet and also the name of John the Baptist's father?
4. Which prophet, whose life ended in Egypt, had a name meaning "Yah lifts up"?
5. What military man, whose widow married King David, had a name meaning "Yah is light"?
6. Which king, whose name meant "may Yah give," instituted a major religious revival in the land of Judah?
7. This common name, meaning "servant of Yah," was borne by many men, notably the man who wrote the shortest book in the Old Testament. What was the name?
8. With a name meaning "Yah has hidden," this prophet wrote one of the last books of the Old Testament. Who was he?
9. This saintly king of Judah was a friend of the prophet Isaiah. The king's name meant "Yah is strength." Who was he?
10. Which son of King David, with a name meaning "my lord is Yah," made a failed attempt to become king himself?
11. Solomon's original name, given by the prophet Nathan, meant "beloved of Yah." What was the name?
12. One king of Judah went by two names, one meaning "Yah is strength" and the other meaning "Yah is strong." Who was he?

13. Both a king of Israel and a king of Judah had this name meaning "Yah has upheld." What was the name?
14. Judah's last king had the inappropriate name meaning "Yah is righteous." Who was the king?
15. What good prophet, persecuted by wicked King Ahab, had a name meaning "who is like Yah"?
16. What rotten king of Israel, with a short reign, had a name meaning "Yah opens"?
17. This wicked woman was, appropriately, the daughter of wicked King Ahab. Her name meant "Yah is exalted." Who was she?
18. This three-year king of Judah had a name meaning "my father is Yah." Who was he?
19. What man, whose name meant "Yah comforts," went from being a servant of the king of Persia to a major rebuilder of Jerusalem?
20. This name meaning "Yah is brother" was borne by several men, notably by the prophet involved in splitting Israel into two kingdoms. What is the name?

THAT'S MY NAME, YAH! (ANSWERS)

1. Elijah. (Remember that El was the Hebrew for "God." Also remember that in its original Hebrew form, Elijah's name would have been Eliyah.)

2. Isaiah

3. Zechariah. Incidentally, there are 35 men in the Bible with this name.

4. Jeremiah

5. Uriah

6. Josiah

7. Obadiah

8. Zephaniah

9. Hezekiah

10. Adonijah, whose coup was put down by his half brother Solomon

11. Jedidiah (2 Samuel 12:25)

12. Uzziah, also called Azariah, both names having the common idea of "strength"

13. Ahaziah

14. Zedekiah, who himself wasn't righteous at all

15. Micaiah (1 Kings 22)

16. *Pekahiah*

17. *Athaliah*

18. *Abijah*

19. *Nehemiah*

20. *Ahijah. See 1 Kings 11 for the prophet's story.*

 ## SOME TRULY HEAVENLY NAMES

How would you feel if you knew your name had been bestowed upon you by God himself? That did happen to a select few in the Bible, including the most famous person in the Bible (you know who) and also the man whose God-bestowed name was passed on to the most famous nation in the Bible, a nation that is still on the map.

1. Who was told to name his son Solomon?
2. Which prophet was told by God to name his son Maher-shalal-hash-baz?
3. Who told Joseph what Jesus' name would be?
4. Which prophet was told by God to name his son Lo-ammi?
5. Who told Hagar to name her son Ishmael?
6. What did God change Abram's name to?
7. Who was told by an angel that his son was to be named John?
8. Which prophet told the priest Pashur that his new name was to be Magor-missabib?
9. What did God call his human creation?
10. What new name did Jesus give to his disciple Simon?
11. What was Hosea told to name his daughter?
12. What was Sarai's name changed to?
13. What did God change Jacob's name to?
14. Who was told to name his firstborn son Jezreel?
15. Who told Mary that her son was to be named Jesus?

SOME TRULY HEAVENLY NAMES (ANSWERS)

1. *King David (1 Chronicles 22:9)*

2. *Isaiah (8:3)*

3. *An angel (Matthew 1:20-21)*

4. Hosea (1:9)

5. An angel (Genesis 16:11)

6. Abraham (Genesis 17:5)

7. Zechariah (Luke 1:13)

8. Jeremiah (20:3)

9. Adam (Genesis 5:2)

10. Peter (John 1:42)

11. Lo-ruhamah (Hosea 1:6)

12. Sarah (Genesis 17:15)

13. Israel (Genesis 32:28). Through his 12 sons and their descendants, Jacob's new name of Israel was passed on to the entire nation, a nation that still exists.

14. Hosea (1:4)

15. The angel Gabriel (Luke 1:30-31)

 ## WAITING FOR THE "EL"

El in Hebrew means "God," which is why so many Old Testament names contain an *el* either at the beginning or end of the word. (Names in Hebrew had to *mean* something, not just sound good. Daniel's name, for example, means "God is judge.") Each answer below contains an *el*. (A helpful hint in this section: Almost all the names are from the Old Testament.)

1. What outspoken prophet was a thorn in the side of wicked King Ahab and Queen Jezebel?
2. What town in Israel has a name meaning "God's house"?
3. Who was John the Baptist's aged mother?
4. Which prophet was noted as being bald?
5. What great leader of Israel anointed Saul and David as kings?
6. What was Jacob's new name after he wrestled all night with an angel?
7. According to one Old Testament prophet, there will come a day when young men will see visions and old men will dream dreams. Which prophet?
8. What was the original name of the young Israelite man named Belteshazzar?

9. Which prophet's name means "God is strong" or "God strengthens"?
10. Who told Mary that her son was to be named Jesus?
11. Which prophet did God tell to shave his head and beard?
12. Who was the mother of the Levitical priesthood?
13. Which prophet was reputed to be a hairy man (either because he himself was very hairy or because he wore a garment of hair)?
14. Which prophet, famous for his vision of the dry bones, was with the exiles in Babylon?
15. Which prophet predicted the outpouring of God's Spirit upon all people?
16. Which prophet outran a king's chariot and a team of horses?
17. Who was forbidden to mourn the death of his beloved wife?
18. Who told wayward King Saul that obeying God's voice was more important than sacrificing animals?
19. Who heard God's voice after running away from Queen Jezebel?
20. Who heard the voice of God as he watched four mysterious creatures flying under a crystal dome?
21. What famous rabbi was Paul's teacher?
22. What boy was called out of his sleep by the voice of God?
23. What upright young man was made ruler over the whole province of Babylon?
24. Who referred to Mary as the "mother of my Lord"?
25. Of which son of Abraham was it prophesied that he would be against everyone and everyone against him?
26. Which priest had two wayward sons who slept with the women who worked at the entrance of the Tabernacle?
27. What noble prophet's sons were notorious for taking bribes?
28. What soldier, David's oldest brother, picked at David for coming to the battle lines?
29. Which prophet's word caused the Syrian soldiers to be struck blind?
30. Which prophet triumphed when God consumed the offering on the altar and shamed the prophets of Baal?
31. Which priest scolded a distressed woman because he thought she had been drinking at the Tabernacle?
32. What two men saw a chariot of fire drawn by horses of fire?
33. The angel of the Lord appeared to the banished Hagar and told her what to name her child. What was the child's name?
34. What was the name of the angel who appeared to Mary and to Zechariah?

35. According to Revelation, what angel fights against Satan?
36. Who made an ax head float on the water?
37. What angel helped Daniel understand the future?
38. Which prophet parted the Jordan River by striking it with his cloak?
39. According to Jude's epistle, who disputed with Satan over the body of Moses?
40. Who told Saul that rebellion was as bad as witchcraft?
41. What name (which applied to Jesus) means "God with us"?
42. Which prophet was told to cut off his hair and scatter a third of it in the wind?
43. Which prophet experienced a furious wind that split the hills and shattered the rocks?
44. Which prophet had a vision of the four winds lashing the surface of the oceans?
45. Who had a vision of a river of fire?
46. Who lived by Kerith Brook, where he was fed by ravens?
47. What city was noted for its gold calf idols?
48. Which prophet ordered a king to shoot arrows out of a window?
49. Which prophet prophesied while accompanied by a minstrel?
50. Who was the prophet Samuel's father?
51. Who was the first of Israel's judges?

WAITING FOR THE "EL" (ANSWERS)

1. *Elijah (1 Kings). The name Elijah means "Yahweh is God."*

2. *Bethel—beth meaning "house," el meaning "God"*

3. *Elizabeth (Luke 1). Her name means "God is my oath."*

4. *Elisha (2 Kings 2). His name means "God is salvation."*

5. *Samuel, a name meaning "name of God"*

6. *Israel, of course (Genesis 32). The name means "wrestles with God."*

7. *Joel (2:28)*

8. *Daniel (1:6-7). His name was changed while he was in Babylon. Daniel means "God is judge."*

9. *Ezekiel*

10. *Gabriel, the angel (Luke 1:30-31). Gabriel means "strong man of God."*

11. *Ezekiel (5:1-4)*

12. *Elisheba, wife of Aaron (Exodus 6:23)*
13. *Elijah (2 Kings 1:8)*
14. *Ezekiel*
15. *Joel*
16. *Elijah (1 Kings 18:46)*
17. *Ezekiel (24:16-18)*
18. *Samuel (1 Samuel 15:22)*
19. *Elijah (1 Kings 19:13)*
20. *Ezekiel (1:24)*
21. *Gamaliel (Acts 22:3), whose name means "reward of God"*
22. *Samuel (1 Samuel 3:2-10)*
23. *Daniel (2:48)*
24. *Elizabeth (Luke 1:41-43)*
25. *Ishmael (Genesis 16:12), whose name means "God hears"*
26. *Eli (1 Samuel 2:22)*
27. *Samuel's (1 Samuel 8:1-3)*
28. *Eliab (1 Samuel 17:28)*
29. *Elisha's (2 Kings 6:18-23)*
30. *Elijah (1 Kings 18)*
31. *Eli, who scolded Hannah, future mother of Samuel (1 Samuel 1:9)*
32. *Elijah and Elisha (2 Kings 2:11)*
33. *Ishmael (Genesis 16:1-12)*
34. *Gabriel (Luke 1:5-38)*
35. *Michael (Revelation 12:7), whose name means "Who is like God?"*
36. *Elisha (2 Kings 2:19-22)*
37. *Gabriel (Daniel 8:15-26; 9:21-27)*
38. *Elijah (2 Kings 2:8-14)*
39. *Michael, the archangel (Jude 1:9)*
40. *Samuel (1 Samuel 15:23)*
41. *Immanuel (Matthew 1:23)*
42. *Ezekiel (5:2)*
43. *Elijah (1 Kings 19:11)*
44. *Daniel (7:2)*
45. *Daniel (7:10)*
46. *Elijah (1 Kings 17:1-4)*

47. *Bethel. Dan and Bethel were the two cities chosen by Israel's King Jeroboam as worship centers to substitute for the Temple of Jerusalem. Jeroboam set up calf idols in both towns (but since this is the "el" category, obviously Dan is not the correct answer).*

48. *Elisha (2 Kings 13:17)*

49. *Elisha (2 Kings 3:15-16)*

50. *Elkanah, a name meaning "God has possessed"*

51. *Othniel (Judges 3). (If you knew this one, consider yourself well versed in the Old Testament.)*

BROTHER "AH" AND FATHER "AB"

Many Old Testament names contain "Ab" or "Ah"—the reason being that the people of Old Testament times chose names carefully, every name having a meaning, and the meaning often had something to do with fathers and brothers. Test your knowledge of Old Testament characters, keeping in mind that each name here contains an "ab" or "ah," usually (but not always) at the beginning of the name.

1. What wicked king of Israel was Jezebel's husband?
2. What Hebrew patriarch had a name meaning "father of a multitude"?
3. What wife of David was once married to Nabal, whose name means "fool"?
4. What rambunctious, violent son of the judge Gideon proclaimed himself king and murdered 70 of his brothers?
5. What court counselor of David joined in the ill-fated conspiracy of David's son Absalom and later hanged himself?
6. Which prophet predicted that Jeroboam would rule over the 10 tribes that broke away from the rule of David's dynasty?
7. Which high priest managed to escape Saul's slaughter of 84 priests?
8. Who followed Rehoboam as king of Judah?
9. What young Shunammite maiden served as King David's "bed warmer" in his old age?
10. What soldier was a cousin of King Saul and commander in chief of his army?

11. What rebellious son of David had the (ironic) name meaning "father is peace"?
12. Which one of David's "mighty men" had a name meaning "brother of mother"?
13. Which of David's "mighty men" was a slingshot expert?
14. Which priest gave David Goliath's sword when David was fleeing from Saul?
15. What noted Jewish woman was Abihail the father of?
16. What son of Aaron the priest was struck down for "offering strange fire" to the Lord?
17. What cousin of David was the commander of the mighty men known as "the Thirty"?
18. What name did Jesus use for God?
19. Which priest, who served faithfully under David, was banished by David's son Solomon?
20. What man was given the Ark of the Covenant for safekeeping after it was returned from the Philistines?
21. What son of King Jeroboam died in childhood, as prophesied by the prophet Ahijah?
22. What two kings of Israel had wives named Ahinoam, whose name means "brother is pleasant"?
23. What false prophet was executed by King Nebuchadnezzar by being roasted in a fire?
24. Who was the commander in chief of David's armies?
25. Which son of David was noted for his luxurious mane of hair?
26. Who murdered a rival general while pretending to kiss him on the cheek in greeting?
27. Which older brother of David scoffed at the idea that David would kill Goliath?
28. Whose death caused David to order the people of Israel to tear their clothes?
29. Who received a letter from David, telling him to put Uriah in the heat of battle?
30. Who had his name changed (by God) from a name meaning "exalted father" to a name meaning "father of multitudes"?
31. Who had intercourse on a rooftop with all his father's concubines?
32. In which Epistles does Paul refer to Christians calling God "Abba, Father"?

BROTHER "AH" AND FATHER "AB" (ANSWERS)

1. Ahab, whose name combines both ah and ab, the name meaning something like "father's brother"

2. Abraham, whose name is appropriate for the founder of the Jewish nation

3. Abigail, whose name means "father of rejoicing"

4. Abimelech, whose name means "father is king"

5. Ahithophel, whose name means, appropriately, "brother of folly"

6. Ahijah, meaning "brother of Yah [God]"

7. Abiathar, meaning "father of abundance"

8. Abijah, meaning "father is Yah [God]"

9. Abishag, meaning (strangely enough) "the father errs"

10. Abner, the son of Ner, whose name means (surprise!) "Ner is father"

11. Absalom

12. Ahiam (2 Samuel 23:33)

13. Ahiezer (1 Chronicles 12:3), meaning "brother is help"

14. Ahimelech ("brother is king")

15. Esther, who became queen of Persia. Abihail means "father has power."

16. Abihu (Leviticus 10:1-3), which means "my father"

17. Abishai, whose name's meaning is uncertain

18. Abba, which is Aramaic for "dear Father" (Mark 14:36)

19. Abiathar ("father gives abundance"). Abiathar was banished because he supported Adonijah, Solomon's brother and rival for the throne of Israel.

20. Abinadab ("father is generous")

21. Abijah ("Yah [God] is Father")

22. Saul (1 Samuel 14:50) and David (1 Samuel 25:43). These are not the same woman, by the way.

23. Ahab ("brother's father") (Jeremiah 29:20-23). This is not the same man as King Ahab, of course.

24. Joab, meaning "Yah [God] is Father"

25. Absalom ("father is peace") (2 Samuel 14:26)

26. Joab, David's commander in chief, who murdered Amasa (2 Samuel 20:9)

27. Eliab ("El [God] is Father") (1 Samuel 17:28)

28. Abner's (2 Samuel 3:31). "Rending the garment" was an ancient symbol of grief and mourning.

29. Joab ("Yah [God] is Father") (2 Samuel 11:14-15). David had Uriah killed so he could marry Uriah's wife, Bathsheba.

30. Abraham, who was originally named Abram (Genesis 17:5)

31. Absalom ("father is peace") (2 Samuel 16:22)

32. Romans (8:15) and Galatians (4:6)

 ## NAMING WITH A PURPOSE

In Bible times, a child's name wasn't just chosen because it "sounded pretty." Biblical names had specific meanings, so the name was chosen more for its sense than its sound. Below are the meanings of the names of several biblical characters. Can you name the person in each case? (This isn't as hard as it looks. Except for 1, 2, 4, 6, and 9–14, all the names are found in the titles of books of the Bible. The other names are also familiar.)

1. man
2. prosperous
3. God is strong
4. God is Savior
5. help
6. great warrior
7. love's embrace
8. salvation of the Lord
9. God has helped
10. beloved
11. eagle
12. enlightened
13. the Lord sustains
14. the Lord is gracious
15. messenger
16. worshipper of the Lord
17. the Lord has consoled
18. star
19. something worth seeing
20. asked of God
21. exalted of God
22. dove

23. he that weeps
24. peace
25. honored of God
26. honorable
27. God is judge
28. the Lord is salvation
29. salvation
30. one with a burden
31. gift of the Lord
32. light-giving
33. rock
34. the Lord remembers
35. little
36. the Lord hides
37. the Lord has been gracious
38. praise of the Lord
39. festive
40. who is like the Lord
41. compassionate
42. affectionate
43. the Lord is God
44. polite
45. supplanter

NAMING WITH A PURPOSE (ANSWERS)

1. *Adam*
2. *Festus*
3. *Ezekiel*
4. *Elisha*
5. *Ezra*
6. *Gideon*
7. *Habakkuk*
8. *Isaiah*
9. *Lazarus*
10. *David*
11. *Aquila*

12. *Aaron*
13. *Ahaz*
14. *Ananias*
15. *Malachi*
16. *Obadiah*
17. *Nehemiah*
18. *Esther*
19. *Ruth*
20. *Samuel*
21. *Jeremiah*
22. *Jonah*
23. *Job*
24. *Solomon*
25. *Timothy*
26. *Titus*
27. *Daniel*
28. *Joshua*
29. *Hosea*
30. *Amos*
31. *Matthew*
32. *Luke*
33. *Peter*
34. *Zechariah*
35. *Paul*
36. *Zephaniah*
37. *John*
38. *Jude*
39. *Haggai*
40. *Micah*
41. *Nahum*
42. *Philemon*
43. *Joel*
44. *Mark*
45. *James (Jacob)*

PART 6

INVISIBLE BEINGS,
GOOD AND BAD

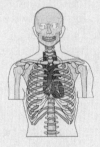

ANGELS, WINGED AND WINGLESS

At the end of the twentieth century, angels suddenly became trendy again, with a plethora of books on angels, angel trinkets, even entire stores devoted to angels. Readers of the Bible probably noticed that the cute and harmless angels of pop culture bore little resemblance to the angels of the Book. In fact, in the Bible there is nary one angel that could be described as "cute." Angels are God's messengers, sometimes operating secretly, but sometimes so intimidating in appearance that people are frightened out of their wits. See how much you know about these *real* angels of God.

1. Which apostle was released from prison by an angel who opened the prison's iron gate?
2. In what book of the Bible does the angel Raphael appear?
3. The angel of the Lord appeared to the banished Hagar and told her what to name her child. What was the child's name?
4. The prophet Balaam could not see the Lord's angel, but his talking donkey could. What was it about the angel that made the donkey turn away?
5. Joshua encountered an angel who was captain of the host of the Lord. What was the angel's purpose in appearing to Joshua?
6. The angel of the Lord instructed Philip to go to Gaza. What person did Philip encounter afterward?
7. What was the name of the angel who appeared to Mary and to Zechariah?
8. This man's mother was visited by the angel of the Lord, who told her she would have a son who would be dedicated as a Nazirite. Who was he?
9. Elijah was nurtured by an angel after his flight from Israel's evil queen. Who was the queen?
10. Jacob is the only person known to have wrestled with an angel. What kindly act did the angel perform after the wrestling match?
11. What Roman official was visited by an angel who told him God had heard his prayers?
12. Who was commissioned by an angel to save Israel from the Midianites?
13. What kind of angelic beings guarded the entrance to Eden?
14. Who had his lips touched by a live coal held by a seraph?
15. What foreign army had 185,000 men killed by the angel of the Lord?

16. What person did an angel prevent from the act of child sacrifice?
17. What two guides did the angel of the Lord provide for the Israelites in the wilderness?
18. What ungodly ruler in New Testament times was struck down by an angel?
19. Who was carried by angels to Abraham's bosom?
20. What angel helped Daniel understand the future?
21. Who was told by an angel that the angel's name was a secret?
22. According to Revelation, what angel fights against Satan?
23. What kind of angels did Isaiah see in the Temple praising God?
24. Who had a dream about an angel and goats?
25. What person saw the angel of the Lord in the form of a flame?
26. Which prophet was fed two meals by an angel?
27. According to Jude, who fought with Satan over the body of Moses?
28. Where was Jesus when an angel came and strengthened him?
29. Where was Paul when an angel assured him that he would be tried before Caesar?
30. How many angels will be at the gates of the New Jerusalem?
31. According to Jesus, what causes the angels to rejoice?
32. Who had a vision of four angels holding the four winds of the earth?
33. Which Gospel says that an angel rolled away the stone from Jesus' tomb?
34. At the end of time, what will an angel bind Satan with?
35. How many angels pour out the bowls of wrath on the earth?
36. Which prophet saw the Lord's angel riding on a red horse?
37. What is the name of the evil angel of the abyss in Revelation?
38. How many angels rescued Lot and his family from the doomed city of Sodom?

ANGELS, WINGED AND WINGLESS (ANSWERS)

1. *Peter (Acts 12:1-19)*

2. *He doesn't—unless your Bible happens to have the Apocrypha, where Raphael appears in the book of Tobit.*

3. *Ishmael (Genesis 16:1-12)*

4. *He was holding a drawn sword (Numbers 22:22-35).*

5. *To give him instructions on conquering Jericho (Joshua 5:13-15)*

6. *The Ethiopian eunuch (Acts 8:26-39)*

7. *Gabriel (Luke 1:5-38)*

8. *Samson (Judges 13:1-20)*

9. *Jezebel (1 Kings 19:1-8)*

10. *He blessed Jacob (Genesis 32:24-20).*

11. *Cornelius (Acts 10:1-8)*

12. *Gideon (Judges 6:11-23)*

13. *Cherubim (Genesis 3:24)*

14. *Isaiah (6:5-7)*

15. *The Assyrians (2 Kings 19:35)*

16. *Abraham (Genesis 22:11-18)*

17. *A pillar of fire and a pillar of cloud (Exodus 14:19-20)*

18. *Herod (Acts 12:23)*

19. *Lazarus (Luke 16:22)*

20. *Gabriel (Daniel 8:15-26; 9:21-27)*

21. *Samson's parents (Judges 13:17-18)*

22. *Michael (Revelation 12:7)*

23. *Seraphim (Isaiah 6:1-6)*

24. *Jacob (Genesis 31:11-12)*

25. *Moses (Exodus 3:1-22)*

26. *Elijah (1 Kings 19:5-8)*

27. *The archangel Michael (Jude 1:9)*

28. *Gethsemane (Luke 22:43)*

29. *On board ship during a storm (Acts 27:23-24)*

30. *Twelve (Revelation 21:12)*

31. *A repentant sinner (Luke 15:10)*

32. *John (Revelation 7:1)*

33. *Matthew (28:2)*

34. *A chain (Revelation 20:2)*

35. *Seven (Revelation 16:1-21)*

36. *Zechariah (1:8)*

37. *Abaddon or Apollyon (Revelation 9:11)*

38. *Two (Genesis 19:1-22)*

CHERUBS AND SERAPHS

Say *cherub* and people think of those adorable little infant angels often seen on Christmas cards. The cherubim depicted in the Bible are not like that at all—*cute* is the last word one would of think of applying to them. The Bible's cherubim and seraphim are often regarded as types of angels, but they are different enough and mysterious enough to warrant a section all to themselves.

1. The first cherubim mentioned in the Bible were stationed where?
2. What celestial weapon accompanied the first cherubim?
3. Gold cherubim images were found on the lid of what sacred object?
4. According to David's song in 2 Samuel 22, who "mounted the cherubim and flew"?
5. What famous building was embellished with numerous images of winged cherubim?
6. Which prophet had a vision of six-winged seraphim in the Jerusalem Temple?
7. And what did one of the seraphim touch to this prophet's mouth?
8. Which prophet mentions the cherubim so many times that his book has been called "the cherubim book"?
9. In Ezekiel 10, the cherubim are described as having four faces each. What creature's faces did they have?
10. In what foreign nation was Ezekiel when he had his vision of the cherubim?
11. In Ezekiel's vision, the cherubim's bodies were covered with what?
12. By what other name are the cherubim called in Ezekiel?
13. What is the only New Testament book to mention the cherubim?

CHERUBS AND SERAPHS (ANSWERS)

1. *At Eden, barring Adam and Eve's way back to the Garden (Genesis 3:24)*

2. *A flaming sword, flashing back and forth (Genesis 3:24)*

3. *The Ark of the Covenant (Exodus 25)*

4. *God (2 Samuel 22:11)*

5. *The Temple in Jerusalem, built by Solomon (1 Kings 6)*

6. *Isaiah (chapter 6)*

7. *A live coal from the altar. Thankfully, this was a vision, so Isaiah wasn't literally burned.*

8. *Ezekiel, who mentions them more often and describes them in more detail than anyone else*

9. *Human, ox, eagle, and lion (10:14). Over the centuries, people have read all kinds of meanings into the four faces.*

10. *Babylon. He was among the Jewish exiles deported there.*

11. *Eyes (10:12). We can safely assume that this symbolized the divine ability to see everything.*

12. *"Living creatures"*

13. *Hebrews (9:5), which refers to them as being part of the Ark of the Covenant*

THE DEVIL YOU SAY

You might be aware that the word *devil* is rooted in the Greek New Testament's word *diabolos* (which is also the root of our word *diabolical*). The *diabolos* was also called by his Old Testament name, Satan (a Hebrew word meaning "adversary"). Although the Bible says nothing at all about what the devil looks like (not a word about horns, red skin, or a pitchfork), it does have a great deal to say about this great adversary of humanity and God. The first 19 questions below deal with the devil/Satan himself. Questions 20 to 29 refer to his underlings, the demons.

1. In which Epistle does the apostle Paul refer to Satan as "the god of this world"?
2. What animal does 1 Peter compare Satan to?
3. Which Gospel uses the name Beelzebub for Satan?
4. What, according to the New Testament, is the final place for Satan?
5. In which Gospel does Jesus refer to Satan as "the prince of this world"?
6. What is Satan the father of, according to John's Gospel?
7. Which prophet spoke of the fallen Lucifer, usually taken to refer to Satan, as a fallen angel?

8. According to the parable of the sower, what happens when some-one hears the word of the Kingdom and does not understand it?
9. According to John's Gospel, Satan was from the very beginning both a liar and a _____.
10. In which Epistle does Paul call Satan the "spirit that worketh in the children of disobedience"?
11. According to Jude's epistle, who disputed with Satan over the body of Moses?
12. What book of the Bible speaks of a demonic fiend named Abaddon (in Hebrew) or Apollyon (in Greek)?
13. Which apostle spoke of the contrast between Christ and Belial (presumably another name for the devil)?
14. Which prophet spoke a lamentation for the king of Tyre in a passage that has traditionally been interpreted as referring to Satan instead of a human king?
15. In Luke's Gospel, Jesus refers to seeing the fall of Satan. What does he compare the fall to?
16. Whom did Satan provoke to do a census in Israel?
17. Which disciple did Satan enter?
18. Which disciple was told by Jesus that Satan wanted to sift him like wheat?
19. Which New Testament man did Satan provoke to lie to the Holy Spirit?
20. Who had seven sons that were overcome by an evil spirit they were trying to cast out of a man?
21. Which king of Israel was tormented by an evil spirit?
22. In the story of the demon-possessed boy healed by Jesus, what had the evil spirit been doing to the poor child?
23. What did the evil spirit do when Jesus cast him out of the man at Capernaum?
24. What possessed man ran around naked?
25. What was the affliction of the woman who had had an evil spirit for 18 years?
26. Which king had court prophets that had been the agents of a lying spirit?
27. What woman had Jesus driven seven demons out of?
28. In Revelation, for what reason do the demons perform miracles?
29. According to Jesus, when an evil spirit returns to a person, how many companions does it bring with it?
30. What does Satan masquerade as in the present world?

THE DEVIL YOU SAY (ANSWERS)

1. *2 Corinthians (4:4)*

2. *A roaring lion (1 Peter 5:8)*

3. *Matthew (12:24)*

4. *A lake of fire and brimstone (Revelation 20:10)*

5. *John (14:30; 16:11)*

6. *Lies (John 8:44)*

7. *Isaiah (14:12)*

8. *The wicked one (Satan) snatches from the heart what was sown (Matthew 13:19).*

9. *A murderer (John 8:44)*

10. *Ephesians (2:2)*

11. *The archangel Michael (Jude 1:9)*

12. *Revelation (9:11)*

13. *Paul (2 Corinthians 6:15)*

14. *Ezekiel (28:11-19)*

15. *Lightning (Luke 10:18)*

16. *David (1 Chronicles 21:1)*

17. *Judas Iscariot (Luke 22:3-4)*

18. *Peter (Luke 22:31)*

19. *Ananias (Acts 5:3)*

20. *Sceva (Acts 19:16)*

21. *Saul (1 Samuel 16:14-23)*

22. *Throwing him into the fire or water and making him foam at the mouth and grind his teeth (Mark 9:17-29)*

23. *Gave a loud scream (Mark 1:23-26)*

24. *The Gerasene demoniac (Luke 8:27)*

25. *She was bent and could not straighten up (Luke 13:11-16).*

26. *Ahab (1 Kings 22:2-22)*

27. *Mary Magdalene (Luke 8:2)*

28. *To bring the nations to war (Revelation 16:13-14)*

29. *Seven (Matthew 12:45)*

30. *An angel of light (2 Corinthians 11:14)*

WITCHCRAFT, SORCERY, AND SUCH

You might almost say that witchcraft is respectable today, with people openly identifying themselves as witches or "wiccans," unashamedly dabbling in the occult. Well, witchcraft certainly wasn't (isn't) respectable or even acceptable to the God of the Bible, and the Old Testament law codes were pretty severe toward witches. In the Bible's view, there is no good or "white" magic—all magic and sorcery are bad, man's selfish and misguided attempts to bend the world to his will instead of depending on the will of the Lord. The prophets spoke out against not only the occult dabblers in Israel itself but also the many neighbor nations that felt no shame about practicing sorcery. Incidentally, the broad category of "witches" also included people that today we would call "mediums," those who claim to communicate with the spirits of the dead.

1. What notorious queen of Israel practiced witchcraft?
2. What witch was consulted by a king who had outlawed all witches?
3. In what city did Paul find many believers who had formerly dabbled in witchcraft?
4. Which emperor had a bevy of magicians and psychics who could not interpret his strange dreams?
5. Which prophet claimed that Edom, Moab, Ammon, and Tyre all had sorcerers?
6. Who called on magicians to duplicate the miracles of Moses?
7. Who was the sorcerer Paul encountered on the isle of Paphos?
8. Which prophet called the city of Nineveh the mistress of witchcraft?
9. Who amazed the people of Samaria with his conjuring tricks?
10. What book of the Bible states, "Do not allow a sorceress to live"?
11. What book of the Bible claims that witchcraft is an "abomination unto the Lord"?
12. Who told Saul that rebellion was as bad as witchcraft?
13. Which Epistle mentions witchcraft as one of the works of the flesh?
14. Who called on magicians to interpret his dreams about cattle?
15. What names does the New Testament give to the magicians in Pharaoh's court in the time of Moses?

WITCHCRAFT, SORCERY, AND SUCH (ANSWERS)

1. Jezebel, the evil wife of wicked King Ahab (2 Kings 9:22)

2. The witch of Endor, who was visited by Saul (1 Samuel 28:7-25). While older transla-tions refer to her as a "witch," newer translations are probably right in calling her a "medium," one who "channeled" the spirits of the dead.

3. Ephesus (Acts 19:19)

4. Nebuchadnezzar, king of Babylon (Daniel 2:10)

5. Jeremiah (27:3-10)

6. Pharaoh (Exodus 7:11-12)

7. Elymas (Acts 13:6-8)

8. Nahum (3:4)

9. Simon the sorcerer (Acts 8:9)

10. Exodus (22:18)

11. Deuteronomy (18:9-12)

12. Samuel (1 Samuel 15:23)

13. Galatians (5:20)

14. Pharaoh (Genesis 41:8)

15. Jannes and Jambres (2 Timothy 3:8)

 GOBS O' GODS

According to the Bible, there is only one *true* God, but humanity has been very imaginative about worshipping all kinds of *false* gods and goddesses. This was condemned by saintly people of the Bible, not because they were bigoted and intolerant, but because worship of these gods often involved such practices as sexual orgies, mass sacrifice of children, and other degenerate practices. It's no surprise that some of these false gods were depicted as demonic in appearance—more like our concept of Satan than of a kind and loving God. No wonder many Jews and Christians began to wonder over time if the false gods were really demons in disguise, working to lead humanity away from worshipping and serving the true God. And no wonder the Bible comes out so strongly against bowing down to idols! See how much you know about the multitude of gods of the ancient world.

1. This fertility god of Canaan is mentioned more than any other foreign deity in the Bible. The prophet Elijah and, later, King Jehu of Israel, worked hard to stamp out his cult. What was his name?
2. This well-known Greek goddess had a magnificent temple in Ephesus, a city where Paul ran into trouble with some of her followers. Who was she?
3. The god of the Moabites also had child sacrifice as part of his worship. Solomon erected an altar for him, but Josiah tore it down. What was he called?
4. The people of Lystra were so dazzled by Paul and Barnabas that they called them by the names of two Greek gods. What were the names?
5. What fish-shaped god of the Philistines was disgraced when his statue was broken by the presence of the Ark of the Covenant?
6. This goddess of Canaan was associated with depraved worship practices. After Saul's death, his armor was placed in her temple by the Philistines. What was her name?
7. This Babylonian god is mentioned by Jeremiah as being filled with terror after the downfall of Babylon. What was his name?
8. The Ammonites' bloodthirsty god was widely known in Israel because of the horrible practice of children being sacrificed to him. What was the name of this god?
9. In Paul's speech to the men of Athens, he mentions the altar of a god. What is the altar's inscription?
10. After Gideon's death, what Canaanite god did the Israelites turn to?
11. Ezekiel saw a woman weeping for what god?
12. Who worshipped Succoth-benoth?
13. What gods did the Avites worship?
14. What was the god of Ekron, consulted by King Ahaziah?
15. What was Nehushtan?
16. What god did the Sepharites sacrifice their children to?
17. What nation was Milcom the god of?
18. While in the wilderness, what Moabite god did the Israelites begin to worship?
19. What god did Naaman the Syrian apologize to Elisha for worshipping?
20. What was the god of the men of Hamath?
21. What god did Amos say was symbolized by a star?
22. Who was King Sennacherib worshipping when his sons murdered him?

23. Whose ship had figures of the gods Castor and Pollux?
24. Who was the god of the men of Cuth?
25. What nation was Bel a god of?
26. Which prophet mentions Nebo as one of the gods of Babylon?

GOBS O' GODS (ANSWERS)

1. *Baal (Judges 2:11; 1 Kings 16:32; 18:19; 19:18; 2 Kings 10:18)*

2. *Artemis (the Greek name for the Roman goddess Diana, as in some translations) (Acts 19:23–20:1). Interestingly, the Artemis of Greek mythology is usually depicted as a slim and beautiful young virgin, but the archaeologists tell us that the Artemis worshipped in Ephesus was a kind of "earth mother" fertility goddess, with a woman's face and a body covered over with breasts.*

3. *Chemosh (Numbers 21:29; 1 Kings 11:7; 2 Kings 23:13)*

4. *Zeus and Hermes (also called Jupiter and Mercury in some Bible translations) (Acts 14:12)*

5. *Dagon (Judges 16:23; 1 Samuel 5:1-5; 1 Chronicles 10:10)*

6. *Astaroth, or Ashtoreth (Judges 2:13; 1 Samuel 7:3; 31:10; 1 Kings 11:33; 2 Kings 23:13)*

7. *Marduk (Jeremiah 50:2)*

8. *Moloch (Leviticus 18:21; 1 Kings 11:7; 2 Kings 23:10; Amos 5:26)*

9. *"To an Unknown God" (Acts 17:22-23)*

10. *Baal-berith (Judges 8:33)*

11. *Tammuz (Ezekiel 8:14)*

12. *The Babylonians (2 Kings 17:30)*

13. *Nibhaz and Tartak (2 Kings 17:31)*

14. *Baal-zebub (2 Kings 1:2)*

15. *The brass serpent Moses had made, which the Israelites later worshipped as if it were a god (2 Kings 18:4)*

16. *Adrammelech (2 Kings 17:31)*

17. *Ammon (1 Kings 11:5)*

18. *Baal-peor (Numbers 25:1-3)*

19. *Rimmon (2 Kings 5:17-18)*

20. *Ashima (2 Kings 17:30)*

21. *Rephen (Amos 5:26—see Stephen's words in Acts 7:43.)*

22. *Nisroch (2 Kings 19:36-37)*

23. *Paul's (Acts 28:11)*
24. *Nergal (2 Kings 17:30)*
25. *Babylonia (Jeremiah 51:44)*
26. *Isaiah (46:1)*

PART 7

BELIEVERS, AND WHAT THEY DO TOGETHER

ALTAR-ATIONS

In many churches today, an altar is the place where you kneel to take Holy Communion. But in the Bible, and throughout history, an altar was a place where a sacrifice took place, offering up an animal or other item to God. Thus, altars were special places, since God (or some god) was thought of as being present there, accepting whatever people had offered up to him. The altar in the great Temple of Jerusalem was thought of as being an especially sacred place. So although they were, physically speaking, nothing more than piles of stones, altars were also "holy places," associated with mystery and reverence.

1. Who almost sacrificed his much-loved son on an altar, but was stopped by an angel?
2. What military leader was killed while holding on to the horns of the altar?
3. What book of the Bible mentions a talking altar?
4. Who built the first altar?
5. Which king of Judah tore down Jeroboam's altar at Bethel and pounded the stones into dust?
6. Who built an altar and called it "The Lord Is My Banner"?
7. What kind of stone was, according to the Law, not supposed to be used in making an altar?
8. What was the altar in the Tabernacle made of?
9. Which of the 12 tribes nearly caused civil war when they built a magnificent altar on the banks of the Jordan?
10. Which judge built an altar and called it "The Lord Is Peace"?
11. Which king of Israel built a Baal altar to please his pagan wife?
12. Which judge's parents saw an angel going up to heaven in the flames on the altar?
13. Which judge and prophet built an altar to the Lord at Ramah?
14. Which king was told to build an altar in a threshing place?
15. What rebellious son of David sought refuge from Solomon by holding on to the horns of the altar?
16. Who took bones out of tombs and burned them on an altar to defile it?
17. Who had a vision of the Lord standing beside the altar?
18. Which king of Israel changed the religious institutions of the country by building an altar at Bethel?
19. What good king's birth was foretold hundreds of years before the fact by a prophet standing before the altar at Bethel?

20. What happened to Jeroboam's altar when he ordered his men to seize a prophet in front of it?
21. Which leader was told to tear down his father's altar to Baal?
22. What god's priests danced around the altar while they cut themselves with knives and daggers?
23. Which prophet triumphed when God consumed the offering on the altar and shamed the prophets of Baal?
24. Which priest of Judah placed a money box near the Temple's altar?
25. Who built an altar and named it for El, the God of Israel?
26. What evil king of Judah built an altar modeled on the altars of Syria?
27. Who rebuilt the Jerusalem altar when the exiles returned to Israel?
28. Who had his lips touched by a coal from the altar in the Temple?
29. Which prophet had a vision of an idol near the altar of God?
30. Which prophet foresaw the destruction of the altars of Bethel?
31. Who constructed the first altar covered with gold?
32. Which prophet spoke of the Jews weeping and wailing in front of the altar because God would not accept their offerings?
33. Which patriarch built an altar after he arrived in Canaan for the first time?
34. Which priest saw an angel standing beside the incense altar?
35. Where did Paul see an altar inscribed "To an Unknown God"?
36. Who had a vision of the souls of the martyrs underneath the altar?
37. Who told people to make peace with their brothers before they made a sacrifice on the altar?
38. In which book of the Bible does the Lord tell Moses to tear down all the pagan altars he finds?
39. Which priest led a movement in which the people tore down the Baal altars and killed Mattan, the priest of Baal?
40. What wicked king of Judah built altars for the worship of Baal and the stars?

ALTAR-ATIONS (ANSWERS)

1. *Abraham (Genesis 22:9)*

2. *Joab (1 Kings 2:28-34)*

3. *Revelation (16:7)*

4. *Noah (Genesis 8:20)*

5. *Josiah (2 Kings 23:15)*

6. *Moses (Exodus 17:15)*

7. *Cut stones (Exodus 20:25)*

8. *Acacia wood covered with bronze (Exodus 27:1)*

9. *Reuben, Gad, and part of Manasseh (Joshua 22:10)*

10. *Gideon (Judges 6:24)*

11. *Ahab (1 Kings 16:32)*

12. *Samson's (Judges 13:20)*

13. *Samuel (1 Samuel 7:17)*

14. *David (2 Samuel 24:18)*

15. *Adonijah (1 Kings 1:50)*

16. *Josiah (2 Kings 23:16)*

17. *Amos (9:1)*

18. *Jeroboam (1 Kings 12:32)*

19. *Josiah's (1 Kings 13:2)*

20. *It fell apart, and the ashes scattered (1 Kings 13:5).*

21. *Gideon (Judges 6:25)*

22. *Baal's (1 Kings 18:26-29)*

23. *Elijah (1 Kings 18)*

24. *Jehoiada (2 Kings 12:9)*

25. *Jacob (Genesis 33:20)*

26. *Ahaz (2 Kings 16:10)*

27. *The priest Jeshua (Ezra 3:2)*

28. *Isaiah (6:6)*

29. *Ezekiel (8:5)*

30. *Amos (3:14)*

31. *Solomon (1 Kings 6:20)*

32. *Malachi (2:13)*

33. *Abraham (Genesis 12:7)*

34. *Zechariah (Luke 1:11)*

35. *Athens (Acts 17:23)*

36. *John (Revelation 6:9)*

37. *Jesus (Matthew 5:24)*

38. *Exodus (34:13)*

39. *Jehoiada (2 Kings 11:18)*
40. *Manasseh (2 Kings 21:3-5)*

THE WATER RITUAL: BAPTISM

Sadly, Christians have literally fought each other (and even executed each other) over the "correct" way to baptize. (Full immersion? Sprinkling? Pouring?) They've also fought over whether it is proper to baptize infants. But one thing they all agree on: Baptism is an essential part of being a Christian, and that has been so since the very beginning. The water itself (whatever method is used) is not the important thing, of course; what matters is that the ritual symbolizes a deep and permanent inner change in the person.

1. Which Epistle mentions "one Lord, one faith, one baptism"?
2. Who referred to the Israelites' crossing of the Red Sea as a baptism?
3. What tradeswoman was baptized by Paul and Silas?
4. How many people were baptized on the Day of Pentecost?
5. Who baptized Paul?
6. What Roman official did Peter baptize?
7. What kind of baptism did John promise the Christ would administer?
8. What foreign dignitary did Philip baptize?
9. What man of Philippi took Paul and Silas home and was baptized by them?
10. In what city did Crispus, the synagogue ruler, believe Paul's message and submit to baptism?
11. Where did Paul baptize 12 men who had received the baptism of John?
12. Which Gospel opens with John the Baptist preaching in the desert?
13. In which Gospel does John try to dissuade Jesus from being baptized?
14. What did John the Baptist tell the tax collectors who came to him for baptism?
15. What magician came to be baptized by Philip?
16. Which Epistles compare baptism to burial?
17. Which Epistle says that the floodwaters at the time of Noah symbolize baptism?

THE WATER RITUAL: BAPTISM (ANSWERS)

1. *Ephesians (4:5)*

2. *Paul (1 Corinthians 10:1-2)*

3. *Lydia (Acts 16:14-15)*

4. *About 3,000 (Acts 2:41)*

5. *Ananias (Acts 9:17-18), not to be confused with the Ananias who lied about his financial gift to the church in Acts 5*

6. *Cornelius (Acts 10:23-48)*

7. *A baptism with the Holy Spirit and with fire (Luke 3:16)*

8. *The Ethiopian eunuch (Acts 8:38)*

9. *The jailor (Acts 16:26-33)*

10. *Corinth (Acts 18:8)*

11. *Ephesus (Acts 19:1-7)*

12. *Mark*

13. *Matthew (3:13-15)*

14. *Not to collect any more than was legal (Luke 3:12-13)*

15. *Simon the sorcerer (Acts 8:12-13)*

16. *Romans (6:4) and Colossians (2:12)*

17. *1 Peter (3:18-22)*

"I AM THE CHURCH, YOU ARE THE CHURCH"

It would have amazed the first Christians to hear of a church described as a "holy place," for in the Bible the church wasn't a place at all. It referred to the people who followed Christ. The old Sunday school song perfectly sums up the Bible's view of the church: "I am the church, you are the church, we are the church together." Instead of a holy *place,* the first Christians thought of themselves as a holy *fellowship,* dedicated to God. What was sacred was not any particular spot on the map, but the holy people whose minds were fixed on the Lord.

1. At what church were believers first called Christians?
2. What church began in the home of Lydia, the seller of purple cloth?

3. In what city was Paul accused of turning the world upside down?
4. What church had two bickering women named Euodia and Syntyche?
5. In what city did Paul raise up Eutychus, who had fallen to his death out of a window?
6. What church was the scene of a burning of wicked books?
7. What church was described by Revelation as "neither hot nor cold"?
8. Who founded the church at Colossae?
9. What church had a false prophetess named Jezebel as a member?
10. Who sent greetings from the church in Babylon?
11. What church suffered because of the "synagogue of Satan"?
12. What member of the Colossian church received a letter from Paul?
13. What church received Epistles from two different apostles?
14. At what church did Paul preach his first recorded sermon?
15. What church had a formerly demon-possessed girl as a member?
16. What was the first church to appoint deacons?
17. Who helped Paul establish the church in Corinth?
18. What church tolerated the heresy of the Nicolaitans?
19. What church had fallen prey to the legalistic Judaizers?
20. What is the most commended church in Revelation?
21. What church received from Paul an Epistle that has never been found?
22. What church took up a large love offering for the needy believers in Jerusalem?
23. On what Greek island did Titus supervise the churches?
24. What church saw the martyrdom of faithful Antipas?
25. What was the first church to send forth missionaries?
26. What church was Silas from?
27. What love-filled church sent members to accompany Paul all the way to Athens?
28. What church was noted for hating the Nicolaitan heresy?
29. To what church did Jesus say, "Behold, I stand at the door and knock"?
30. At what church did believers hold their property in common?
31. Who was sent by the Jerusalem church to oversee the church at Antioch?
32. To what church did Paul send Epaphroditus as a minister?
33. What church began at Pentecost?
34. What church had Crispus, a synagogue leader, as a member?

35. Where did Paul have a vision asking him to found churches in Europe?
36. At what church were Paul and Barnabas set apart by the Holy Spirit to do missionary work?
37. Who reported his vision of unclean animals to the church at Jerusalem?
38. At what church did Paul have a "loyal yokefellow"?
39. At what church did some people follow the teachings of Balaam?
40. What church was told by John to buy white clothing to hide its nakedness?
41. At what church did the Egyptian-born Apollos first serve?
42. What church did Timothy grow up in?
43. Which apostle was supposed to be the rock on which the church was built?
44. Who founded the church at Antioch of Pisidia?
45. From what Asian church was Paul driven out by unbelieving Jews?
46. What church was overseen by James?
47. In what church were Christians guilty of taking other Christians to court?
48. Who established the church at Ephesus?

"I AM THE CHURCH, YOU ARE THE CHURCH" (ANSWERS)

1. Antioch (Acts 11:26)

2. Philippi (Acts 16:15, 40)

3. Thessalonica (Acts 17:6)

4. Philippi (Philippians 4:1-3)

5. Troas (Acts 20:7-12)

6. Ephesus (Acts 19:19)

7. Laodicea (Revelation 3:15-16)

8. Epaphras (Colossians 1:7)

9. Thyatira (Revelation 2:18-29)

10. Peter (1 Peter 5:13), who may be using Babylon symbolically (as John does in Revelation)

11. Smyrna (Revelation 2:8-11)

12. Philemon

13. Ephesus (the Letter to the Ephesians from Paul and Revelation 2:1-7 from John)

14. *Antioch of Pisidia (Acts 13:16)*

15. *Philippi (Acts 16:18)*

16. *Jerusalem (Acts 6:1-7)*

17. *Priscilla and Aquila (Acts 18:2)*

18. *Pergamos (Revelation 2:12-17)*

19. *Galatia (Galatians 1:6-9)*

20. *Philadelphia (Revelation 3:7-13)*

21. *Laodicea (Colossians 4:16)*

22. *Antioch (Acts 11:30)*

23. *Crete (Titus 1:5)*

24. *Pergamos (Revelation 2:13)*

25. *Jerusalem (Acts 8:5, 14)*

26. *Antioch (Acts 15:34)*

27. *Berea (Acts 17:10-15)*

28. *Ephesus (Revelation 2:6)*

29. *Laodicea (Revelation 3:20)*

30. *Jerusalem (Acts 2:44-45)*

31. *Barnabas (Acts 11:22)*

32. *Philippi (Philippians 2:25)*

33. *Jerusalem (Acts 2:47)*

34. *Corinth (Acts 18:8)*

35. *Troas (Acts 16:9)*

36. *Antioch (Acts 13:2)*

37. *Peter (Acts 11:1-18)*

38. *Philippi (Philippians 4:3)*

39. *Pergamos (Revelation 2:14)*

40. *Laodicea (Revelation 3:18)*

41. *Ephesus (Acts 18:24-28)*

42. *Lystra (Acts 16:1)*

43. *Peter (Matthew 16:18)*

44. *Paul (Acts 13:14)*

45. *Iconium (Acts 14:5)*

46. *Jerusalem (Acts 15:13)*

47. *Corinth (1 Corinthians 6:1-4)*

48. *Paul (Acts 18:19; 19:1-10)*

PART 8

BIBLE WORDS AND PHRASES
EVERYWHERE

WORDS, WORDS: OUR BIBLE-SATURATED LANGUAGE

You might say that our language is "encoded" with the Bible. Without even realizing it, people are daily using words and phrases that are rooted in the Bible. While our culture may be in danger of becoming "biblically illiterate," there is little danger of the "hidden Bible" leaving our language and thought patterns anytime soon. Bible names and words crop up in the strangest places—houses, gardens, wine cellars, and in ordinary conversation. Test your awareness of how the Bible pervades everyday life and speech.

1. What wicked Old Testament queen's name now means "an evil and shameless woman"?
2. Which Old Testament prophet is the source of "whitewash," meaning to cover over crimes and corruption?
3. What Philistine giant's name is often applied to any oversized person or thing?
4. The phrase "forbidden fruit" is based on the story of what man and woman?
5. Which New Testament book's name has come to mean "the end of the world," especially if occurring with great violence and destruction?
6. The phrase "go the extra mile" is based on a saying by what person?
7. What group of people, often criticized by Jesus, had a name that now means "legalistic hypocrites, especially the religious kind"?
8. What pagan people, mentioned often in the Old Testament, had a name that has come to mean "crude, uncultured folk"?
9. What sinful city in the book of Genesis has given its name to sexual sins in general, one sexual sin in particular?
10. What long Old Testament book is the source of the phrase "at wit's end"?
11. What horrible hill, notable in Jesus' life, now means "place or experience of intense suffering"?
12. What do we call a comforter who is more prone to criticize than to provide real comfort?
13. What do we call a cab driver, particularly one who provides a wild, furious ride?
14. Which Old Testament city lends its name to a vegetable that is called an artichoke but isn't?

15. Which Old Testament conqueror's name now means "hunter," particularly an overbearing one?
16. What son of Abraham's name has come to mean "outcast"?
17. What purple-flowered vine, commonly found growing wild and in gardens, is named for an event in Jesus' life?
18. What long-lived Old Testament man's name is given to a wine bottle holding about six liters?
19. Which New Testament woman's name occurs in a word that now means "sickeningly sentimental"?
20. What do we call a person who goes out of his way to help someone?
21. What city visited by Paul lends it name to a wild, pleasure-loving person?
22. What do we call a scheming, beautiful, seductive woman, particularly one that leads a man to ruin?
23. What do we call the final battle at the end of time?
24. What pagan empire's name now means a place devoted to sensuous pleasure and materialism?
25. What biblical feast day now lends its name to Christians who emphasize spiritual gifts such as speaking in tongues and healing?
26. Which Old Testament town's name has come to mean a small church or chapel of a small denomination?
27. What biblical name is given to the summer cypress plant?
28. What do we call a person believed to bring bad luck?
29. What beloved friend of David's name has come to mean a New Englander?
30. What do we call grave robbers?
31. What plant is named after a kinsman of Jesus?
32. What do we call the practice of buying or selling a church office?
33. What plant is named for a painful plant in Jesus' life?
34. What Old Testament food's name now means "a sudden and unexpected source of gratification"?
35. What name is given to a hospital for people with contagious diseases, particularly leprosy?
36. Which disciple of Jesus has a tree named for him?
37. What do we call a long, eloquent lament?
38. Which New Testament garden's name now means "a place of intense mental or spiritual suffering"?
39. Which disciple's name can mean "a peephole"?
40. What king of Israel's name is used for an oversized drinking vessel?

41. What Old Testament time of liberation has come to mean simply "party time"?
42. What burial ground for paupers is named for the place purchased by Judas's betrayal money?
43. What yucca tree of the southwest U.S. is named for an Old Testament military leader?
44. What word means "showing great wisdom under trying circumstances" and is named for a wise king of Israel?
45. What Australian bird, noted for building mud nests, is named for Jesus' followers?
46. What cooking herb is also known as "Bible leaf"?
47. What "optical" phrase, found three times in the Bible, is a common phrase meaning "something dear and precious"?
48. What biblical type of ladder would you find on a ship or pier?
49. What seedy Asian grass is named for a very unfortunate Old Testament man?
50. What woman's garment is named for an Old Testament man with a famous garment?
51. The flowering yucca plant common in gardens also goes by what biblical name?
52. A leave of absence for education or training is called a what?
53. An adjective meaning "possessing incredible strength or size" is rooted in the name of an Old Testament hero. What is the word?
54. What flower is named for a son of King David?
55. The modern-day political movement to give Jews a homeland in Palestine goes by what name?
56. What yellow garden flower is named for a New Testament kinsman of Jesus?
57. A word meaning "bosom friend" comes from one of Paul's epistles. What is the word?
58. A lovely spot of unspoiled beauty is called a what?
59. What thorny tree of the tropics takes its name from the crown of thorns that was placed on Jesus' head?
60. What tall flowering garden plant is named for a biblical flower?
61. A tyrant is often called what (after a famous king in the Old Testament)?
62. What house plant with red berries is named for a biblical city?
63. What peculiar plant is named for a Canaanite city captured by Joshua?
64. What name was given to an annual contribution given by Roman Catholics to the pope?

65. A place that gives protection and safety from disaster is sometimes called what?
66. What is "Bible paper"?
67. On what food fish would you find "St. Peter's thumb mark"?
68. What place name, mentioned often in the Gospels, is given to the porch at the entrance to a church?
69. Which Old Testament prophet (and book) has come to be a common nickname for a Quaker?
70. What jumbo-sized wine bottle is named for a king of Israel?
71. Which disciple of Jesus has lent his name to tiny seabirds that flutter just above the surface of the ocean waters?
72. What two-word phrase from the Lord's Prayer has come to mean "heaven" or "the next world"?
73. "Risking one's neck" is from Romans 16:4, a verse in which Paul praises which Christian couple?
74. The phrase "thorns in our sides" is found in Numbers and in what very violent Old Testament book?
75. The expression "filthy lucre," used to refer to money in a disparaging way, is from which of Paul's letters?
76. The name Abigail, used as a generic name for a female servant, had its origin in the name of what king's wife?
77. What part of the human body is named for a man in the book of Genesis?
78. The phrase "I am with you in spirit" is from the writings of what Christian?
79. In a phrase from the Old Testament, peace and security are seen when a man sits under his own vine and _____ tree.
80. What group, famous for placing Bibles in hotel rooms, takes its name from a military leader in the book of Judges?
81. The Freemasons had a girls' auxiliary named for the daughters of what Old Testament man?

WORDS, WORDS: OUR BIBLE-SATURATED LANGUAGE (ANSWERS)

1. *Jezebel (1 and 2 Kings), the immoral pagan wife of Israel's King Ahab*

2. *Ezekiel (13:10-15; 22:28). Jesus may have been echoing Ezekiel when he used the term in the same way (Matthew 23:27).*

3. *Goliath, the giant slain by the shepherd boy (and later king) David*

4. *Adam and Eve, of course, who disobeyed God's command to stay away from the fruit of the tree of knowledge (Genesis 3)*

5. *Revelation, which in the original Greek is Apokalypsis (and is Apocalypse in Roman Catholic Bibles). The name is appropriate, since Revelation deals with wars, plagues, and the end of life as we know it.*

6. *Jesus, in his famous Sermon on the Mount: "If someone forces you to go one mile, go with him two miles" (Matthew 5:41).*

7. *The Pharisees, whom Jesus criticized not only for their hypocrisy but for their obsessive attention to unimportant details*

8. *Philistines. Not that they were particularly uncultured, but for some reason the English author Matthew Arnold (writing in the 1800s) used the name Philistine and gave it this new meaning.*

9. *Sodom, with sodomy being a word applied to homosexuality, based on the attempted male rape of the man Lot in Genesis*

10. *Psalms (see 107:27)*

11. *Calvary, the name of the hill on which Jesus was crucified. (The hill is also called Golgotha.)*

12. *A Job's comforter, named for Job's three so-called friends who, as Job himself said, were "miserable comforters"*

13. *A Jehu, named for the king who exterminated the idol-worshipping royal dynasty of King Ahab. In his plan to overthrow the royal family, Jehu (who had been anointed by God's prophet Elisha) had to do some fast maneuvering, and he was mentioned in the Bible as one who "driveth furiously" (2 Kings 9:20).*

14. *Jerusalem. The Jerusalem artichoke is actually a type of sunflower, but its edible roots are eaten and, mistakenly, called artichokes.*

15. *Nimrod, who was a "mighty hunter before the Lord" (Genesis 10)*

16. *Ishmael, Abraham's son by his maid Hagar. Genesis 16:12 describes him as "a wild man; his hand will be against every man, and every man's hand against him." (The narrator in the novel Moby Dick is a social outcast and named, appropriately, Ishmael.)*

17. *The passionflower, so called because the flowers' centers remind many people of a body on a cross. Jesus' crucifixion is often referred to as his passion—that is, intense suffering.*

18. *Methuselah, who according to Genesis 5, lived 969 years. As with the name Jeroboam, no one knows why the bottle has the name.*

19. *Mary Magdalene. The word is maudlin, an old shortened form of Magdalene. The word is based on the fact that many old paintings of Mary Magdalene show her as a weeping and repentant woman.*

20. *A Samaritan, or a Good Samaritan, so named for Jesus' parable of the Samaritan who helped the beaten traveler while the religious people passed by and gave no aid (Luke 10)*

21. *Corinth. A Corinthian (then and now) was one with high living and low morals. In fact, the word goes back even further than Paul's day, for Corinth had a long, pre-Paul reputation as sin city.*

22. *A Delilah, named for the Philistine mistress of Samson. She wormed out of him the secret of his strength, resulting in his capture and blinding by the Philistines (Judges 16).*

23. *Armageddon, from the book of Revelation's description of "the battle on the great day of God Almighty" (Revelation 16:14-16). Many people use the word to refer to a possible showdown of high-tech weaponry.*

24. *Babylon, noted in the Old Testament for its luxury and its idolatry. Also, in Revelation the name Babylon is used symbolically to refer to worldliness and corruption.*

25. *Pentecost, the Jewish feast day that, in Acts 2, is the day on which the Holy Spirit manifested himself by people speaking in tongues*

26. *Bethel. Much more common in England than the U.S., Bethel was often the name of a chapel of a Nonconformist church—that is, any denomination not part of the state-supported church of England.*

27. *Burning bush, named for the bush Moses saw that burned but was not consumed. The summer cypress has bright red foliage in the fall.*

28. *A Jonah, after the poor prophet who disobeyed the Lord's command to go to Nineveh. When he set sail for other parts, a storm struck the ship, and Jonah admitted that it was his fault (Jonah 1). He solved the problem by asking to be thrown overboard (and you know the rest of this fishy story, of course).*

29. *Jonathan. No one is sure why, although Old Testament names were very popular in the earliest days of New England.*

30. *Resurrectionists. Grave robbing is no longer practiced, but in times past, the so-called resurrection men would dig up graves, either to supply bodies to scientists or to rob the corpses of any jewels they were buried with. They were called "resurrectionists" because, as in the case of Jesus, there was an empty tomb.*

31. *St. John's bread, named for John the Baptist. More commonly called the carob plant, the St. John's bread yields sweet-tasting pods that, according to legend, were the food that John the Baptist lived on. Some scholars think that the "locusts" that the Gospels say John ate might have been carob pods.*

32. *Simony, named for Simon the magician who wanted to buy spiritual power from Peter (Acts 8). Simony was widely practiced years ago when the church was state-supported and high-ranking church leaders were well paid.*

33. *The Christ's-thorn plant, a name given to several prickly plants growing in the Middle East. The name, of course, comes from the crown of thorns put on the head of Jesus when he was being mocked by the Roman soldiers (Matthew 27:29).*

34. *Manna, the name of the food miraculously supplied to the Israelites after they fled from Egypt (Exodus 16)*

35. *Lazaretto, a name derived from Lazarus, the name of the leprous beggar in Jesus' parable of the rich man and the beggar (Luke 16)*

36. *The worst disciple, Judas. The Judas tree is cultivated for its showy red flowers. The name stems from the belief that Judas hung himself on a tree of this kind, and the flowers, once white, turned red. The redbud tree of the eastern U.S. is often called a Judas tree.*

37. *A jeremiad, named for the prophet Jeremiah, who lamented over the fate of fallen Jerusalem in the book of Lamentations*

38. *Gethsemane, the garden where Jesus agonized over his fate on the night he was betrayed (Matthew 26:36)*

39. *Judas. A peephole is sometimes called a Judas, a Judas hole, or a Judas window. The name obviously refers to Judas's treachery and deceit.*

40. *Joram (in some translations, Jehoram), though the cup's name is usually spelled jorum. As with other wine container terms, no one knows what the connection is.*

41. *Jubilee, the year of emancipation every 50 years. Slaves were liberated, and lands were restored to their former owners. Gradually the word came to mean a fiftieth anniversary, then, eventually, any time of celebration. (See Leviticus 25.)*

42. *It's called a potter's field (Matthew 27:7), at that time intended to be a place for burying foreigners, but later the term was extended to include burial for paupers and criminals and anyone else outside mainstream society.*

43. *The Joshua tree*

44. *Solomonic, for wise King Solomon*

45. *The apostle bird*

46. *Costmary, a name that itself means (in Greek) "fragrant root of Mary"*

47. *"Apple of the eye" (Deuteronomy 32:10; Psalm 17:8; Proverbs 7:2), which literally refers to the eye's pupil. In these three verses, the contexts indicates that the pupil is precious and protected.*

48. *A Jacob's ladder, which is the common name for a rope or chain ladder with wooden or metal rungs. The reference is to Jacob's dream of the ladder to heaven (Genesis 28).*

49. *Job's tears, a plant whose seeds are thought to resemble tears*

50. *A joseph, once used to refer to a long coat for women. The name comes from the "coat of many colors" that Jacob gave to his favorite son, Joseph (which aroused the jealousy of his 11 brothers, of course).*

51. *Adam's needle*

52. *A sabbatical, taking its name from Sabbath, of course, the biblical day of rest*

53. *Samsonian, rooted in the name Samson, the mighty judge of Israel*

54. *Solomon's seal*

55. *Zionism, named for the biblical Mount Zion, one of the hills of Jerusalem*

56. The very lovely Saint-John's-wort, named for John the Baptist

57. Yokefellow, which in fact is a translation of the Greek name Syzygus (Philippians 4:3). The Bible scholars still argue over whether Syzygus is an actual person's name or whether Paul was perhaps referring to a friend as his "yokefellow."

58. An Eden, of course, after the Garden of Eden in Genesis

59. The Jerusalem thorn

60. The rose of Sharon (Hibiscus family), which definitely is not the same plant referred to in Song of Solomon 2:1. Sharon, by the way, was the name of the Mediterranean coastal plain west of Israel.

61. A pharaoh, based on the oppressive Pharaoh in the book of Exodus

62. The Jerusalem cherry, which is not actually a cherry at all

63. The rose of Jericho, which rolls up when dry and expands when it is wet

64. Peter's pence, named for the tradition that the first pope was the apostle Peter.

65. An ark, after the boat that saved Noah and his family from the Flood

66. The very thin, very durable paper used in many Bibles, dictionaries, and other books that will (supposedly) be used frequently

67. The haddock. The "thumb mark" is the blotch behind the gill. No one is quite sure how Peter's name became attached to the fish, although Peter was (as the New Testament says) a fisherman.

68. Galilee. The name is commonly used in English churches, not quite so common in America.

69. Obadiah. No one knows exactly why.

70. Jeroboam. No one is sure why the bottle was named for the king.

71. Peter. The birds are called petrels, because Peter tried to walk on the sea as Jesus did (but, unlike the birds, he sank).

72. "Kingdom come," from Jesus' words "thy kingdom come" (Matthew 6:10)

73. His good friends Aquila and Priscilla, who "risked their necks" for Paul's sake. Some translations have "risked their lives," but the original Greek really means "risked their necks."

74. Judges (2:3); Numbers 32:55

75. Titus (1:7), which says that a church official should not be inclined to "filthy lucre"

76. David's. Abigail was one of his numerous wives. The connection of her name with "maid" is found in 1 Samuel 25:25.

77. The Adam's apple, of course. The bulge in the throat is, according to legend, the piece of the fruit that stuck forever in the throat of the sinning Adam.

78. Paul (1 Corinthians 5:3; Colossians 2:5)

79. Fig. The most often quoted verses about this pleasant existence are Micah 4:4 and Zechariah 3:10, but there are many other Old Testament references to "vine and fig

tree." (See 1 Kings 4:25; 2 Kings 18:31; Jeremiah 5:17; Joel 1:7.) Even in locales where figs aren't grown, Bible readers of the past often referred to "sitting under my own vine and fig tree."

80. *The Gideons*

81. *Job. The group was the Order of Job's Daughters (see Job 42:14-15).*

WORLD ATLAS, BIBLICAL NAMES

Wherever the Bible goes, there goes a wealth of names of people, places, and ideas, and lots of these end up on the world map. Given that our world is no longer as familiar with the Bible, people often forget that place names they see every day have their origin in the Old and New Testaments. You might say that the atlas of the world is "coded" with Bible names. Test your knowledge of some famous (and some not-so-famous) world sites named for people and places in the Scriptures.

1. Great Britain's royal court is officially known as the Court of St. _____. Which of Jesus' 12 disciples is the court named for?
2. Notre Dame cathedral in Paris is named for which New Testament woman?
3. A famous mountain in India is named for the disciple of Jesus who (according to legend) evangelized India. Which one? (Hint: doubt.)
4. The stunningly beautiful cathedral of Cologne, Germany, is dedicated to a famous trio of men in the New Testament. Who?
5. The site of the royal wedding of Prince Charles and Princess Diana was London's most famous cathedral. Which New Testament figure is the cathedral named for?
6. Dublin, one of the most Catholic cities in the world, does not possess a Roman Catholic cathedral. It does contain a procathedral, which is named, appropriately, for one of the Catholic Church's favorite saints. Who is she?
7. The grand church of the Vatican in Rome is named for the apostle who was (according to tradition) the first pope. Who was he?
8. France possesses two small islands off the eastern coast of Canada. One is Miquelon, and the other is named for one of Jesus' disciples. Which one?

9. Brazil's coast has some small rock islands named for an apostle who was shipwrecked. Which apostle?
10. Canada has both a major river (450 miles) and a major city named for an apostle and a New Testament author. Who?
11. Brazil's largest city (more than 7 million) is named for an active New Testament man. Who?
12. The nation of El Salvador in Central America is named for a title given to Jesus. What is it?
13. The old town of Santiago in Spain was probably one of the first "vacation hot spots" in Europe—mostly because it was supposed to be the resting place of one of Jesus' disciples. Which one?
14. The famous church Westminster Abbey in London is formally named for one of the most prominent apostles. Who was he?
15. The capital of the South American nation of Paraguay is named for a key event in the life of Jesus. What?
16. A famous church in London is the burial place of the famous John Smith, saved by Pocahontas. The church is named for a famous burial place in the New Testament. What place?
17. The most famous park in Dublin, Ireland, is a lovely green space named for a New Testament martyr. Who?
18. Heidelberg, Germany, has a stunning Gothic church named Heilig-Geist-Kirche. What person of the Bible is it named for?
19. Venice, Italy, has a cathedral and a plaza named for the city's patron saint, an author of a Gospel. Who was he?
20. Galway, Ireland, has a noted church named for one of the seven deacons in the book of Acts. The church became famous because Christopher Columbus supposedly prayed there before sailing for America. What is the name of the church?
21. The oldest church in London (built in 1123) was named for one of Jesus' lesser known apostles. Who?
22. One Caribbean island tops them all for its surplus of New Testament names—parishes (that is, counties) named for James, Peter, Joseph, John, Philip, Thomas, Andrew, and for Christ himself. What is the island?
23. The island of San Salvador in the Bahamas may be the first place Christopher Columbus landed. Who is the island named for?
24. Cuba, though officially Communist (and atheist), still has a city named Sancti Spiritus after a biblical figure. Who?
25. The great cathedral in Vienna, Austria, is probably one of the country's most photographed sights. What martyr is it named for?

26. The Caribbean island of Antigua has its capital and main harbor named for an apostle and Gospel author. Who?
27. Moscow's burial place of the czars is a cathedral named for whom?
28. In Budapest, Hungary, the city's grandest church is named for the "replacement" apostle who took the place of Judas Iscariot. Who?
29. The chief church in Geneva, Switzerland, is famous for being the church of Protestant leader John Calvin, who preached in it several times weekly. Which apostle is it named for?
30. The great university in Oxford, England, has a college named for which famous female follower of Jesus?
31. Russia's large city once known as Leningrad has returned to its former name, named for an apostle. Who?
32. A beautiful church in London's Covent Garden area is known as "the Actors' Church," but it is named for an apostle. Which one?
33. Both the city square and the cathedral in Munich, Germany, are named for the city's patron saint, a woman. Who was she?
34. Florence, Italy, is famous for its gorgeous baptism building (the Battistero) named for a Gospel writer. Who?
35. Of the many colleges at England's Cambridge University, the oldest has a curious name that includes an apostle's name. What is it?
36. The Vatican in Rome contains Nero's Circus. According to tradition, which apostle was executed there by order of Emperor Nero?
37. The cathedral of Frankfurt, Germany, is noted as the coronation site of the Holy Roman Emperors. Which of Jesus' lesser known apostles is it named for?
38. The most impressive church of France is probably the one off the coast of Normandy, almost an island, and named for an angel. What is it called?
39. Leipzig, Germany, has an old church famous for having composer Johann Sebastian Bach for its music director. Which doubting apostle was it named for?
40. Genoa, Italy, has a lovely church notable for being where Christopher Columbus was baptized. What martyr is it named for?
41. Autun, France, has a cathedral named for someone raised from the dead. Who?
42. What Caribbean island is named for Father, Son, and Holy Spirit?
43. The cathedral of Amalfi, Italy, is unique in being Arabic in design. Which apostle (a fisherman) of Jesus is it name for?
44. A small island republic of Africa is named for the apostle Thomas. What is the full name of the country?

45. The Canadian river connecting Lake Superior with Lake Huron is named for what New Testament woman?

46. What capital city of Central America is named for Joseph, the husband of Mary?

47. Teddy Roosevelt and his Rough Riders charged up a famous hill in Cuba, named for a New Testament man. Who?

48. What capital of a South American country is named for an apostle?

49. What Pacific island nation has a large city named Christchurch?

50. The South American nation Colombia has a Caribbean coastal city named for a New Testament woman. Who? (No, this one isn't named for Mary.)

51. What Pacific island chain bears the name of a wise Old Testament king?

52. Beléem, the name of a city in Brazil, is the Portuguese form of a famous New Testament town. Which one?

53. What large German city has an infamous red-light district named after the apostle Paul?

54. Panama has a city named for one of Israel's greatest heroes. Who?

55. Scotland is home to a town that is supposedly the birthplace of the game of golf. Which apostle is the town named for?

56. Ile Jesus (French for Jesus Island) lies near what metropolis in the Canadian province of Quebec?

57. A famous London landmark fortress has the Chapel of St. Peter ad Vincula—which means the Chapel of Peter in Chains (referring to Peter's imprisonment, Acts 12). What is the fortress called?

58. A portion of London's Westminster Abbey is notable for being the meeting place of the men who produced the King James Bible. What biblical name is given to the room?

59. What famous university of England has both a Christ's College and a Jesus College?

60. What Caribbean island with a French heritage is named for one of Jesus' disciples?

61. Which enormous Roman church, named for an apostle, is known as "the church of the pope"?

62. In what sprawling city would you find St. Andrew's Hill, St. Barnabas Street, St. James Square, St. Johns Gardens, St. Lukes Road, St. Mark Street, St. Marys Terrace, St. Paul's Churchyard, St. Stephens Gardens, St. Peters Terrace, and St. Thomas Way?

WORLD ATLAS, BIBLICAL NAMES (ANSWERS)

1. *James. Any ambassador to Great Britain is referred to (officially) as "Ambassador to the Court of St. James." The name stems from St. James Palace, a royal dwelling place until Buckingham Palace became the chief residence.*

2. *Mary, Jesus' mother, who is called (in French) Notre Dame (Our Lady). All the many Notre Dames across the globe are named for the Virgin Mary.*

3. *Thomas. The mountain is St. Thomas Mount. In fact, a very ancient Christian community exists in India, named the Mar Thoma (Sir Thomas) church.*

4. *The three wise men. The city's coat of arms contains the three crowns of the wise men (who, according to tradition, were also kings—remember "We Three Kings"?).*

5. *St. Paul. It is one of London's most famous landmarks, noted for its high dome. It survived several German bombings during World War II.*

6. *St. Mary (that is, Jesus' mother). A procathedral is a church that substitutes for a cathedral. Dublin does have two regular cathedrals—both of them Protestant.*

7. *Peter. St. Peter's Basilica is one of the most visited churches in the world. It is also one of the largest, having a capacity of 50,000 people.*

8. *Peter. The island is Saint Pierre—French for "St. Peter."*

9. *Paul. The islands are known as St. Paul's Rocks.*

10. *St. John, the name of a river flowing into the Bay of Fundy and also a large city in the province of New Brunswick*

11. *Paul. The city is São Paulo (St. Paul).*

12. *Savior. El Salvador is Spanish for "the Savior."*

13. *James. Santiago is Spanish for "St. James." In the Middle Ages, thousands of Christians traveled across Europe to visit the (alleged) cathedral of the buried saint. (Since James's martyrdom in Jerusalem is recorded in the book of Acts, only legend can account for how his body came to rest in a town in Spain.)*

14. *Peter. The church's official name is the Collegiate Church of St. Peter. It is noted as the burial place of many of England's most famous people, and is the usual site for coronations.*

15. *His ascension into heaven. Asunción is Spanish for "ascension."*

16. *The sepulcher (tomb) of Jesus. The name of the church is St. Sepulchre—that is, "Holy Tomb."*

17. *Stephen. The park is St. Stephen's Green.*

18. *The Holy Spirit, or Holy Ghost, which in German is Heilig-Geist*

19. *Mark—San Marco, in Italian*

20. *St. Nicholas. Nicholas is mentioned only once, in Acts 6:5 (and, no, he has no real connection with Santa Claus or Christmas).*

21. *Bartholomew. The church is named St. Bartholomew the Great.*

22. *Barbados*

23. *Jesus, the Savior. San Salvador is Spanish for "Holy Savior."*

24. *The Holy Spirit. Sancti Spiritus is Latin (no, not Spanish) for "Holy Spirit."*

25. *Stephen. It is St. Stephen's Cathedral, or, in the native tongue, Stephansdom.*

26. *St. John*

27. *Not really a who but a what—an archangel (that is, the highest order of angels). It is Archangel Cathedral, resting place of Czar Ivan the Terrible and some other Russian czars.*

28. *Matthias. The Matthias Church was the site of several coronations of Hungary's kings.*

29. *Peter. It is known as the Cathedral of St. Pierre.*

30. *Mary Magdalene. The college is known as Magdalen College (but it's pronounced "maudlin," strangely enough).*

31. *Peter. The city is St. Petersburg.*

32. *St. Paul*

33. *Mary. The square is Marienplatz (Mary's Square).*

34. *John. The building is the Battistero de San Giovanni (the baptistery of St. John). For years the building has been used for baptizing all infants born in Florence.*

35. *Peterhouse College, named for the apostle Peter, of course*

36. *Peter*

37. *Bartholomew*

38. *Mont-Saint-Michel—that is, St. Michael's Mount, named for the angel Michael*

39. *Thomas. In German, it is Thomaskirche (St. Thomas Church).*

40. *Stephen. In Italian, it is San Stefano.*

41. *Lazarus. It is known as the Cathedral of St. Lazare.*

42. *Trinidad—Spanish for "Trinity."*

43. *Andrew. It is on the coast, and, traditionally, Andrew is the patron saint of sailors.*

44. *São Tomé and Principe. The country was formerly a Portuguese colony, and São Tomé is Portuguese for "St. Thomas." (Principe is one island, São Tomé is another.)*

45. *Mary. The river is the Saint Marys.*

46. *San José (Spanish for "St. Joseph"), the capital of Costa Rica*

47. *John. The hill was San Juan Hill.*

48. *Santiago, Chile. Santiago is Spanish for "St. James."*

49. *New Zealand*

50. *Martha, sister of Mary and Lazarus. The city's name (which is Spanish) is Santa Marta.*

51. *The Solomon Islands*

52. *Bethlehem*

53. *Hamburg, with its notorious St. Pauli district*

54. *David*

55. *Andrew, who is considered the patron saint of Scotland. The town is St. Andrews (and, no, the Scots don't put an apostrophe in Andrews—for some strange reason).*

56. *Montreal*

57. *The Tower of London, famous for its many celebrity prisoners over the centuries*

58. *The Jerusalem Chamber. It is also notable because England's King Henry IV supposedly died in the room, fulfilling an old prophecy that he would "die in Jerusalem."*

59. *Cambridge*

60. *St. Barthelemy—French for "St. Bartholomew"*

61. *The Church of St. John Lateran ("Lateran" being the name of the Roman hill on which the church stands)*

62. *London, England, and these are not all the London streets named for people in the Bible.*

THE BIBLE IN WORSHIP

Let's admit that people who attend worship services, even on a weekly basis, aren't always paying close attention to what's going on. Christian worship, whether in a traditional stained-glass setting or a more free-wheeling modern style, is saturated with words, phrases, and actions rooted in the Bible. You might say this set of questions is about "decoding" Christian worship. You may be surprised to find just how Bible-rich the average worship service is.

1. Many pastors start their worship service with the words "This is the day that the Lord has made, let us rejoice and be glad in it." Where would you find that in the Bible?
2. "Holy, holy, holy" is a familiar phrase said (or sung) in many churches. Where does that phrase occur in the Bible?
3. What do you call a fixed set of Bible passages that are to be read in worship on particular days?

4. Some churches still practice "the holy kiss" in the worship service. Which New Testament books mention this practice?
5. "Peace be with you" is a part of many worship services. Where is that in the Bible?
6. Charismatic churches often "lift up hands to the Lord." What worshipful book of the Bible mentions this practice?
7. "Glory to God in the highest" is a common worship phrase. In the Gospels, who used these words?
8. "Father, Son, and Holy Spirit" are mentioned often in worship, but they are mentioned together in only one New Testament book. Which one?
9. Footwashing is still practiced in some churches. Which is the only Gospel to tell the story of Jesus washing the disciples' feet?
10. The Lord's Prayer is found in both Matthew's and Luke's Gospels. Which form is ordinarily used in Christian worship?
11. Which New Testament passage refers to infant baptism?
12. Which New Testament books mention speaking in tongues?
13. The Letter to the Ephesians refers to "making melody in your heart." Which denominations interpret this to mean that worship services should not have instrumental music?
14. Which apostle laid down the rule that women were not to be pastors?
15. The New Testament word *episkopos* is translated "bishop" in the King James Version, "superintendent" or "overseer" in some newer translations. Which New Testament books discuss the necessary qualifications for a bishop?
16. In what city was the first church building constructed?
17. In the early church, how often was the Lord's Supper celebrated?
18. Which New Testament letters are called the Pastoral Letters because they contain advice to deacons and pastors?
19. Which New Testament letter contains the most advice on conducting Christian worship?
20. What musical instruments are mentioned in connection with Christian worship?
21. Which Old Testament book was used as a "hymnal" by the early church?
22. What book of the Bible refers to a Christian marriage service?
23. In the Roman Catholic mass, what familiar praise word is said (or sung) after the reading from the New Testament?
24. When songs or prayers from the Bible are sung in worship, what are they called?

25. What type of contemporary churches are noted for singing Bible passages set to music?
26. In the liturgical churches (Roman Catholic, Episcopalian, and some other denominations), what words are said after a person finishes a Scripture reading?
27. And what does the congregation say immediately afterward?
28. If you are in a church with a large Bible resting on a stand shaped like an eagle, what denomination is the church?
29. What book of the Old Testament is reprinted in the Episcopalians' worship book, *The Book of Common Prayer*?
30. Which books of the Bible are read in Roman Catholic churches but not in Protestant churches?
31. The church season known as Epiphany celebrates which two key events in the life of Jesus?
32. The famous "love passage" in the Bible, so often read at church weddings, is from which New Testament book?
33. In baptism, people are baptized "in the name of the Father, the Son, and the Holy Spirit." Which New Testament book indicates that this is the proper form for baptism?
34. The passage beginning "I know that my Redeemer liveth" is read in many Christian funerals. Which Old Testament book is it from? (No, not Psalms.)
35. The word *Hallelujah* (or *Alleluia*) occurs frequently in worship. What is the only book of the Bible that actually contains the word?
36. Some denominations celebrate the Feast of Holy Innocents on December 28. What event in the Gospels is commemorated on this day?
37. What biblical event is commemorated every Sunday?
38. Many Christian burial services quote the words "I am the resurrection and the life." Who said this, and what book are they recorded in?
39. In the liturgical denominations, what three divisions of the Bible are always read from in each worship service?
40. In which book of the Bible would you find the Apostles' Creed?
41. How many church buildings are mentioned in the Bible?

THE BIBLE IN WORSHIP (ANSWERS)

1. Psalms (118:24)

2. Isaiah (6:3). The words were said by the angels Isaiah saw in the Temple.

3. Lectionaries. They are used in Catholic, Orthodox, Episcopal, and other churches.

4. Romans (16:16), 1 Corinthians (16:20), 2 Corinthians (13:12), 1 Thessalonians (5:26). It apparently was common practice in New Testament times.

5. 1 Peter 5:14

6. Psalms (134:12); 1 Timothy 2 also mentions "lifting up holy hands."

7. The angels who announced Jesus' birth (Luke 2:14)

8. Matthew (28:19), Jesus' "great commission," in which he tells the disciples to baptize in the name of the Father, Son, and Spirit

9. John (13)

10. Matthew's

11. None. So far as we know, infants were not baptized in the early church.

12. Acts (2:4; 19:6) and especially 1 Corinthians (12–14)

13. The Churches of Christ and some other noninstrumental churches

14. Paul, notably in 1 Timothy 2:12, which states that women are not to have authority over men

15. 1 Timothy and Titus

16. No one knows, since church buildings are not mentioned in the New Testament. In the early church, all churches were "house churches," meeting in private homes.

17. Apparently at every worship service (1 Corinthians 11)

18. 1 Timothy, 2 Timothy, Titus

19. Probably 1 Corinthians, which addresses such issues as the Lord's Supper, speaking in tongues, spiritual gifts, and order in worship

20. None are, which is why some denominations do not use instruments in worship

21. The book of Psalms

22. Not one. The New Testament gives the impression that Christians had been married either in a Jewish service or in a Roman civil ceremony.

23. Alleluia

24. Canticles. This word usually refers not to the Psalms but to other Bible passages that are poetic and are often sung or chanted.

25. The "praise churches," that is, charismatic churches

26. "The Word of the Lord"

27. "Thanks be to God."

28. Probably Episcopalian

29. The Psalms

30. The books of the Apocrypha, that is, the books between the Old and New Testa-

ments. Most Protestant churches do not believe that the Apocrypha is inspired—at least, not in the same way as the Old and New Testaments are.

31. *The visit of the wise men and also the baptism in the Jordan*

32. *1 Corinthians 13: "Love is patient, love is kind."*

33. *Matthew's Gospel, in which Jesus commands the apostles to "go and make disciples" and baptize them with this formula (Matthew 28:19)*

34. *Job (19:25)*

35. *Revelation (19:1, 3, 4, 6). But in the original Hebrew Old Testament, the Hebrew words Hallelu jah occur many times—and in our English translations, it almost always appears as "Praise the Lord" (which is what it means, of course).*

36. *King Herod's slaughter of the infant boys of Bethlehem when Jesus was born (Matthew 2:16)*

37. *The resurrection of Jesus, who was raised on the first day of the week*

38. *Jesus, of course, spoken before he raised Lazarus from the dead (John 11)*

39. *Old Testament, Gospel, Epistle. (Also, a Psalm is usually said—or sung—or chanted.)*

40. *It isn't in the Bible.*

41. *None. The first generation of Christians did not have (or seem to want) special buildings in which to worship. They met in homes, or wherever they could gather a group of believers together.*

 ## THE BIBLE-ENCODED AMERICAN MAP

What was said of the world atlas is true of the American map as well. The U.S. landscape is "coded" with the Bible, for there are hundreds—more accurately, *thousands*—of American places with biblical names. In this section you can test your acquaintance not only with the Bible but with the U.S. map.

1. The oldest city under the U.S. flag is named for what New Testament man?
2. What is the largest U.S. city with a biblical name?
3. What is the only U.S. capital named after a city in the Old Testament?
4. The oldest town in the U.S. with a biblical name is what?
5. The pagan city of Babylon lends its name to only one U.S. city. In which state would you find it?

6. In which state would you find a city named after ancient Israel's pagan neighbor, Moab?
7. What renowned Greek city, mentioned in the book of Acts, lends its name to cities in several states?
8. Which state has both Bethlehem and New Bethlehem?
9. Which state has a city named after Boaz, the husband of Ruth?
10. Which commonly mentioned biblical city would you *not* find on a U.S. map?
11. Which California city with a biblical name had Clint Eastwood as its mayor?
12. Which state has a city containing the name of Naaman, the Syrian officer cured of leprosy?
13. Which state has the city of New Egypt?
14. The Sangre de Cristo Mountains (Spanish for "blood of Christ") are in which western states?
15. What is the only state with a city named Dothan, the dwelling place of the prophet Elisha?
16. Minnesota's capital city is named after which Bible character?
17. The city of Beersheba lends its name to only one U.S. city. In which state?
18. The New Testament city Philippi has only one U.S. counterpart. In which state?
19. Arkansas has a lake named for what "mighty hunter" of the Old Testament?
20. Only one state has a city named after the first Christian martyr, St. Stephen. Which state?
21. Which southwestern state has a city named Trinity?
22. The city of Smyrna, mentioned in Revelation, gives its name to cities in three states. Which three?
23. Which two states have cities named Rome?
24. The New Testament village Emmaus lends its name to a town in which state?
25. In which state would you find Bethany, Bethel, and Bethlehem?
26. In which state is there a city named for John the Baptist?
27. Which two states have a Mars Hill, named for the place where Paul preached to the Athenians?
28. Two adjoining states have cities with similar names—Zion and Zionsville. What are the two states?
29. Which East Coast state has a city named after an angel?
30. Which state has both a town and a college named for the New Testament city Berea?

31. Only one state has a Nebo, named for the mountain from which Moses saw the Promised Land. Which state?
32. In which state would you find Mount Sinai?
33. Which Great Lakes state has the city of New Palestine?
34. The town of Ephrata (possibly from Ephratha, an alternate name for the town of Bethlehem) can be found in which state?
35. Which state has the city of Pisgah, named for an important mountain in the Old Testament?
36. Which Middle Eastern nation lends its name to several U.S. cities?
37. Which southern state has a city named Hiram, an important figure in the story of Solomon?
38. Two of the U.S. Virgin Islands are named after apostles. Which two?
39. In which state would you find the Apostle Islands National Lakeshore?
40. Which large southern California city is named for one of Jesus' disciples?
41. St. Simons Island is found on the coast of which southern state?
42. Utah has a national park named for a famous hill in Jerusalem. What is it?
43. The oldest U.S. city, St. Augustine, Florida, has a historic fort named for a New Testament character. Which one?
44. Which Illinois city with a biblical name was the birthplace of two major figures in the 1925 "evolution" trial—attorney William Jennings Bryan and defendant John Scopes?
45. This North Carolina national forest with a biblical name is the site of Mount Mitchell, the highest point east of the Mississippi River. What is it?
46. Which San Francisco suburban city is named for one of the four Gospel writers?
47. Which North Carolina town with a hyphenated name is named (partly) for a biblical city?
48. Which city in Illinois with a biblical name has aroused controversy in the ongoing church-state issue?
49. Which Delaware resort town is popular as the summer haven for DC residents?
50. San Simeon, named for the Simeon in Luke's Gospel who blesses the child Jesus, is in what state (which happens to have a lot of "San" names)?
51. The land of Gilead is mentioned often in the Old Testament. Where is Mount Gilead State Park?

52. Ephraim, named for one of the tribes of Israel, was founded by Moravian settlers in which Great Lakes state?
53. In which state is Bible Hill?
54. What New Hampshire town, named for an Old Testament site, was home of the poet Robert Frost?
55. Port Angeles, which means "port of angels," is on the coast of which Pacific state?
56. The St. Joseph River happens to be in the same state that has a St. Mary's River. Which state?
57. The reconstructed pioneer village of Little Norway is in a town named for the biblical Mount Horeb. What state is it in?
58. California has a famous geological "problem" named for one of the apostles. What is it?
59. What DC church named for one of Jesus' disciples is known as "the Church of the Presidents"?
60. The New Testament city of Sardis has a namesake in only one U.S. state. Which one?
61. St. Matthews, Kentucky, is a suburb of what large city?
62. The well-known Cathedral Church of St. Peter and St. Paul in DC is better known by what name?
63. Annapolis, Maryland, has one of the oldest, most prestigious (and smallest) U.S. colleges, named for an apostle. What is the name of the school?
64. Which southern city has St. Paul's Church, noted for being the church where Confederate president Jefferson Davis received the news that the Confederacy was about to fall?
65. California has a national park honoring a curious tree named for an Old Testament leader. What is the park's name?
66. Which Texas city has a name that means (in Latin) "body of Christ"?
67. Which DC suburb is named for a New Testament site where people were healed?
68. There are counties named Trinity in which two states?
69. Shiloh, Bethel, and Mount Olive lie within a few miles of each other in which Great Lakes state?
70. Thaddeus, one of the lesser known of Jesus' apostles, has a namesake town in which southern state?
71. Tabor, a mountain mentioned in connection with the judges Barak and Deborah, has a namesake in which Plains state?
72. St. Elizabeth, St. Thomas, and St. James lie within a few miles of each other in which state?

73. The towns Bethlehem and St. Bethlehem are both in which southern state?

74. New Philadelphia and Philadelphia are both in which northeastern state?

75. The town of Joppa in Illinois lies on the banks of which major river?

76. What is the only state with a county named Lebanon?

77. The county of Titus lies in what state (which happens to have 254 counties)?

78. Elihu, one of Job's friends in the book of Job, has a namesake in which southern state?

THE BIBLE-ENCODED AMERICAN MAP (ANSWERS)

1. *John the Baptist. The city (surprise!) is San Juan, Puerto Rico. As a commonwealth, Puerto Rico is part of the U.S., though not one of the 50 states. The city's full name, which is Spanish, is San Juan Bautista (St. John the Baptist). Originally, San Juan was the name used for the whole island of Puerto Rico.*

2. *Philadelphia, Pennsylvania. The city is mentioned in Revelation 3, but founder William Penn also chose the name because it meant "brotherly love."*

3. *Salem, Oregon. Salem is mentioned in connection with the priest-king Melchizedek (Genesis 14), and the Israelites later assumed that Salem was the same as Jerusalem. The name means "peace," and it has been a popular name on the U.S. map.*

4. *Salem, Massachusetts—named by its Puritan settlers*

5. *New York*

6. *Utah. This is a rare case of a pagan name from the Bible used as an American place name.*

7. *Athens. There are at least eight in the U.S.*

8. *Pennsylvania*

9. *Alabama*

10. *Strangely enough, Jerusalem, the most frequently mentioned city in the Bible. It's possible, however, that there are a few unincorporated spots in the U.S. named Jerusalem.*

11. *Carmel. (See 1 Kings 18 for a good story about Carmel.)*

12. *Delaware. The city is Naamans Gardens.*

13. *New Jersey*

14. *Colorado and New Mexico*

15. *Alabama*

16. *St. Paul*

17. *Tennessee. The town is Beersheba Springs.*

18. *West Virginia*

19. *Nimrod (Genesis 10:9)*

20. *South Carolina*

21. *Texas*

22. *Tennessee, Georgia, and Delaware*

23. *Georgia and New York*

24. *Pennsylvania*

25. *Connecticut*

26. *California. The city's name is San Juan Bautista.*

27. *North Carolina and Maine*

28. *Illinois and Indiana*

29. *Maryland. The city is St. Michaels, named for the archangel Michael.*

30. *Kentucky*

31. *North Carolina*

32. *New York*

33. *Indiana*

34. *Washington*

35. *Ohio*

36. *Lebanon. There are at least five in the U.S.*

37. *Georgia*

38. *St. Thomas and St. John*

39. *Wisconsin. There are 12 islands, naturally.*

40. *San Diego—Spanish for "St. James"*

41. *Georgia*

42. *Zion*

43. *Mark. Castillo de San Marcos is Spanish for "Fort of St. Mark."*

44. *Salem*

45. *Pisgah National Forest*

46. *San Mateo—Spanish for "St. Matthew"*

47. *Winston-Salem. (Salem is the biblical part, of course.)*

48. *Zion*

49. *Rehoboth Beach*

50. *California*

51. *Ohio*

52. *Wisconsin*

53. *Tennessee*

54. *Salem*

55. *Washington*

56. *Michigan*

57. *Wisconsin*

58. *The San Andreas Fault—San Andreas being Spanish for "St. Andrew"*

59. *St. John's Episcopal*

60. *Georgia*

61. *Louisville*

62. *The National Cathedral (or Washington Cathedral)*

63. *St. John's College (founded in1696)*

64. *Richmond, Virginia*

65. *Joshua Tree National Monument*

66. *Corpus Christi*

67. *Bethesda, Maryland*

68. *Texas and California*

69. *Ohio*

70. *Alabama*

71. *Iowa*

72. *Missouri*

73. *Tennessee*

74. *Pennsylvania*

75. *The Ohio*

76. *Pennsylvania*

77. *Texas*

78. *Kentucky*

"HIDDEN" BIBLE: SO MANY TITLES AND PLOTS

There have been thousands of books, poems, plays, and movies based on the Bible, and some have been quite successful. But aside from those, quite a lot of Bible phrases, images, and stories are "embedded" in many books and films, often in the form of titles, character names, and plots. As you work through the questions below, you may be surprised at how many writers have chosen, for various reasons, to use the Bible—"undercover," you might say—in their works.

1. What classic 1951 science fiction movie clearly based its plot on the life of Jesus? (Hint: big robot.)
2. Conservative commentator Sean Hannity's book *Deliver Us from Evil* takes its title from what familiar Bible passage?
3. What noted American author wrote the novel *East of Eden,* which takes its title from Genesis?
4. What contemporary comic strip by Stephen Pastis takes its name from a passage in Jesus' Sermon on the Mount?
5. Ernest Hemingway wrote a novel titled *The Sun Also Rises.* Which Old Testament book did he take his title from?
6. The Lillian Hellman play *The Little Foxes,* about a conniving southern family, takes its title from what book of the Bible?
7. The narrator in the novel *Moby Dick* has what biblical name?
8. American playwright Thornton Wilder wrote a popular comedy titled *The Skin of Our Teeth.* From which book of the Bible did he borrow the title?
9. Russian author Fyodor Dostoyevsky's novel *The Possessed* is a story of political terrorists, but he took his name from a character in the Gospels. Which character?
10. American poet Archibald MacLeish wrote an unusual stage play in 1958, *J. B.* Which Old Testament character is this based on? (Hint: the character's name sounds a lot like J. B.)
11. Louis Bromfield's 1924 novel *The Green Bay Tree* takes its name from the Psalms' description of a certain type of man. What type?
12. American playwright John Van Druten wrote the curiously titled play *The Voice of the Turtle.* From which Old Testament book does the play take its name?
13. Russian novelist Leo Tolstoy, famous for *War and Peace,* wrote a novel with a biblical title. What was it?

14. English poet Matthew Arnold, writing in the 1800s, borrowed the name of an Old Testament nation and used it to refer to people who are uncultured and crude. What nation?

15. The popular 1981 movie *Chariots of Fire* takes its title from an incident in the life of which prophet?

16. Thornton Wilder's play *The Angel That Troubled the Waters* takes its title from an incident in the Gospel of John. What incident?

17. Mississippi novelist William Faulkner's novel *Absalom, Absalom* is named for the wayward son of which king of Israel?

18. What heartwarming 1963 film with Sidney Poitier took its title from Jesus' statement about "Solomon in all his glory"?

19. In 1947, Ben Ames Williams wrote a Civil War novel titled *A House Divided*. What person in the Bible used the phrase "A house divided against itself cannot stand"?

20. The Pulitzer prize–winning play *There Shall Be No Night* takes its title from which New Testament book?

21. English poet Robert Browning titled several of his poem collections *Bells and Pomegranates*. Believe it or not, he took the title from the Old Testament. To what do "bells and pomegranates" refer?

22. American novelist Edith Wharton wrote a novel titled *The Valley of Decision*. From which Old Testament book of prophecy did she take the title?

23. Sidney Howard, noted for writing the script for *Gone with the Wind*, wrote a play with a biblical title: *The Silver Cord*. From which book of the Old Testament does this mysterious title come?

24. *The Four Horsemen of the Apocalypse*, by modern Spanish novelist Vicente Blasco Ibanez, takes its name from which New Testament book?

25. What movie of Swedish director Ingmar Bergman takes its title from 1 Corinthians 13:12?

26. American novelist Winston Churchill wrote *The Inside of the Cup*, which takes its title from Jesus' attacks on which group of people?

27. John Steinbeck's novel *To a God Unknown* takes its title from which New Testament book?

28. Samuel Sewall, an author in colonial America, wrote an anti-slavery tract in 1700 titled *The Selling of _____*. Which Old Testament character, sold into slavery, is named in the title?

29. American novelist Albion Tourgee wrote many novels about the Reconstruction era in the South. One of the novels, *Bricks without Straw*, takes its title from which Old Testament book?

30. The famous American short story *The Gift of the Magi* takes its title (but not its plot) from Matthew's story of the wise men and their gifts to the baby Jesus. Who wrote this famous story?

31. English comic author Jerome K. Jerome wrote *The Passing of the Third Floor Back,* about a New Testament character living in a modern boarding house. What character?

32. French novelist Marcel Proust published a novel titled (in English) *Cities of the Plain.* To which two immoral Old Testament cities does the title refer?

33. Irish poet W. B. Yeats wrote a mysterious poem about the modern world, containing the famous line "Things fall apart, the center cannot hold." What biblical title did he give to this poem?

34. American novelist Winston Churchill's 1915 novel *A Far Country* takes its title from which famous parable of Jesus?

35. American novelist Zora Neal Hurston's 1934 novel is named _____'s *Gourd Vine.* Which Old Testament prophet's name fills in the blank?

36. English philosopher Thomas Hobbes wrote a pessimistic book of political philosophy named (curiously) for a mythical beast in the book of Job. What was the beast?

37. French author Andre Gide's novel *Strait Is the Gate* takes its title from Jesus' words about a narrow gate. What does the narrow gate lead to?

38. Upton Sinclair wrote a modern novel titled *They Call Me Carpenter.* It contains such characters as Mr. Carpenter, Judge Ponty, and Mary Magna. What Bible character is it based on?

39. American novelist Winston Churchill wrote *The Dwelling Place of Light.* From which Old Testament book is this title?

40. Thornton Wilder's play *The Trumpet Shall Sound* takes its title from a description of Christians' resurrection. In which New Testament Epistle does this appear?

41. What Pulitzer prize–winning novel by William Faulkner bases its plot on the life of Jesus?

42. American novelist Henry James took the title *The Wings of the Dove* from what Old Testament book?

43. What artsy movie directed by Ingmar Bergman takes its title from the book of Revelation?

44. The 1934 movie *Our Daily Bread,* showing people working hard during the Great Depression, takes it title from what famous Bible passage?

45. T. E. Lawrence, the famous "Lawrence of Arabia," titled his

memoirs *Seven Pillars of Wisdom.* The title is taken from what book of the Old Testament?

46. *Lord of the Flies,* a much-read 1955 novel by Nobel Prize winner William Golding, takes its title from what pagan god mentioned in the Bible?

47. The much-loved science fiction novel *Stranger in a Strange Land* by Robert Heinlein takes its name from what Old Testament book?

48. The old Katharine Hepburn movie *A Bill of Divorcement* took its title from which Old Testament book of laws?

49. The 1978 movie *Days of Heaven* takes its name from which Old Testament book?

50. Ecclesiastes 7:4 is the source of the title of Edith Wharton's gloomy 1905 novel *The House of _____.*

"HIDDEN" BIBLE: SO MANY TITLES AND PLOTS (ANSWERS)

1. The Day the Earth Stood Still, *with its gentle "alien" named Klaatu posing as a normal human named Mr. Carpenter (get it?). Klaatu is actually killed but raised to life again.*

2. *The Lord's Prayer: "Lead us not into temptation, but deliver us from evil" (Matthew 6:13).*

3. *John Steinbeck, also famous for his* Grapes of Wrath. *"East of Eden" is where Cain dwelled after he murdered Abel.*

4. Pearls before Swine, *which features Pig, Rat, and other cleverly named characters. The phrase comes from Matthew 7:6, in which Jesus warns his followers not to "cast your pearls before swine."*

5. *Ecclesiastes. "The sun also rises, and the sun goes down" (1:5).*

6. *The Song of Solomon. "The little foxes that spoil the vines" (2:15).*

7. *Ishmael, son of Abraham. The novel begins with the words "Call me Ishmael."*

8. *Job. "I escaped by the skin of my teeth" (19:20).*

9. *The demoniac who was healed by Jesus. The demoniac was "possessed" by a "legion" of demons. Dostoyevsky believed the political agitators were similarly possessed.*

10. *Job*

11. *The wicked. "I have seen the wicked in great power, spreading himself like a green bay tree" (Psalm 37:35).*

12. *The Song of Solomon (2:12). The "turtle" is actually referring to a turtledove.*

13. *Resurrection*

14. *The Philistines. The term is still often used as Arnold used it.*

15. *Elisha (2 Kings 6:17), in which the prophet and his servant were guarded by heavenly chariots. The English poet William Blake used "chariot of fire" in one of his poems, which (if you listen carefully) you can hear sung by a choir in the movie.*

16. *Jesus' healing of the man at the pool of Bethesda in Jerusalem (John 5:1-15). Verse 4 says that an angel occasionally stirred up ("troubled") the pool's waters, and whoever entered the water first would be healed of his sickness.*

17. *David. The title comes from David's lament for the dead Absalom (2 Samuel 18:33).*

18. Lilies of the Field, *from Jesus' words "consider the lilies of the field."*

19. *Jesus, of course—referring to accusations that he could cast out demons because he himself was the prince of demons (Matthew 12:24). The phrase "a house divided" is often attributed to Abraham Lincoln because he used it in one of his most famous speeches.*

20. *Revelation (21:25). The words are a description of the New Jerusalem.*

21. *The decorations on the fringe of Israel's high priest's clothing (Exodus 28:33). No one knows what Browning meant by his title.*

22. *Joel. "The day of the Lord is near in the valley of decision" (3:14).*

23. *Ecclesiastes. "Remember your Creator before the silver cord is loosed, or the golden bowl is broken" (12:6).*

24. *Revelation, which is sometimes called the Apocalypse. The title refers to the symbolic horses in Revelation 6, symbolizing war, conquest, famine, and death.*

25. Through a Glass Darkly, *Paul's description of how we view heavenly things dimly in this life*

26. *The Pharisees. "Woe to you, scribes and Pharisees, hypocrites! For you cleanse the outside of the cup and dish, but inside they are full of extortion and self-indulgence. Blind Pharisee, first cleanse the inside of the cup and dish" (Matthew 23:25-26). (By the way, this Winston Churchill is not the same man as the British prime minister.)*

27. *Acts. When Paul preached to the Athenians, he refers to seeing a monument inscribed "To a God Unknown" (Acts 17:23).*

28. *Joseph, who was sold by his brothers to be a slave in Egypt*

29. *Exodus. It refers to the Hebrews being forced by the Egyptians to make bricks without straw (Exodus 5).*

30. *O. Henry*

31. *Christ*

32. *Sodom and Gomorrah. In fact, the original French title is* Sodome et Gomorrhe. *The novel, true to its title, deals with the theme of homosexuality.*

33. *The Second Coming*

34. *The Prodigal Son. Jesus says, "The younger son gathered all together, and journeyed to a far country, and wasted his possessions with riotous living" (Luke 15:13).*

35. *Jonah. The vine, described in Jonah 4, is the one that sheltered Jonah from the sun while he sulked over the salvation of pagan Nineveh.*

36. *Leviathan. God says to Job of the leviathan, "Any hope of overcoming him is vain" (Job 41:9). Hobbes' book does not refer to this mythical beast but to the almighty power of a government.*

37. *To life, while the wide gate leads to destruction: "Strait is the gate and narrow is the way, which leadeth unto life, and few there be that find it" (Matthew 7:14). "Strait" means "narrow," not "straight."*

38. *Jesus, of course, who is the "Carpenter" of the title*

39. *Job. In 38:19, God asks Job, "Where is the way to the dwelling place of light?"*

40. *1 Corinthians. 15:52 says, "The trumpet shall sound, and the dead shall be raised incorruptible, and we shall be changed."*

41. *A Fable, in which the main character, a soldier, is born in a cow shed. At the book's end, his body has mysteriously disappeared from its grave.*

42. *Psalms, where 55:6 reads, "Oh, that I had the wings of the dove."*

43. *The Seventh Seal. Chapters 5 through 8 of Revelation depict the various "seals" at the end of time, bringing disasters on humanity.*

44. *The Lord's Prayer: "Give us this day our daily bread."*

45. *Proverbs, where 9:1 refers to wisdom building its house with seven pillars*

46. *Beelzebub (see 2 Kings 1:2 and Matthew 12:24). The name Beelzebub literally translates as "lord of the flies." The popular novel has been made into a movie more than once.*

47. *Exodus 2:22, in which Moses, having fled the Egyptian court, gives his newborn son a name meaning "stranger."*

48. *Deuteronomy (24:1)*

49. *Deuteronomy, again (11:21), and also Psalms (89:29)*

50. *Mirth. In case you were curious, the verse reads, "The heart of the wise is in the house of mourning; but the heart of fools is in the house of mirth."*

CATCH THE SPIRIT

THAT'S THE SPIRIT

If you think the Holy Spirit is an "it," and if you spell it with a lower-case *s*, you must not be familiar with the Bible because the Spirit is definitely a "he" (that is, a person, not a thing), and he definitely deserves a capital *S*. In Christian tradition, the Spirit is one of the three "persons" of the Holy Trinity—and of the three, probably the least understood. That is appropriate, for the workings of the Spirit are often quite mysterious and unfathomable.

1. What bird symbolizes the Holy Spirit?
2. In creation, what was the Spirit doing "over the face of the waters"?
3. Which New Testament man was filled with the Spirit "even from his mother's womb"?
4. What man—as if you couldn't guess—was conceived through the power of the Spirit?
5. Where was Jesus when the Holy Spirit descended upon him?
6. Where did the Spirit lead Jesus after his baptism?
7. What false prophet, sent to curse Israel, instead blessed it under the influence of the Spirit?
8. What man in the Gospels had been told by the Spirit he would not die until he had seen the Messiah?
9. After his temptation, where did Jesus return "in the power of the Spirit" to preach?
10. In what town was Jesus rejected after announcing to the people that the Spirit of the Lord was upon him?
11. On what Jewish holy day did the apostles receive the Holy Spirit?
12. Which Gospel states that the apostles received the Spirit when the resurrected Jesus "breathed on them"?
13. What was the vocation of Bezalel, said in Exodus to have been filled with the Spirit of God?
14. Who were the 70 Spirit-filled men that Moses appointed to aid him?
15. What muscleman, not a particularly spiritual person, had the Spirit come upon him "mightily"?
16. What successor of Moses received the Spirit when Moses laid hands on him?
17. What tall, handsome king prophesied under the power of the Spirit?
18. What building's plans were "given by the Spirit"?

19. Who stated that blaspheming against the Spirit was the one unpardonable sin?
20. In Psalm 51, what man said to God "take not your Holy Spirit from me"?
21. In which Gospel does Jesus refer to the Spirit as the "Comforter"?
22. Which prophet foretold a descendant of Jesse upon whom the Spirit of the Lord would rest?
23. Who prophesied an outpouring of the Spirit on a multitude of people, in which "old men shall dream dreams, young men shall see visions"?
24. According to Matthew 10, at what time in a person's life would the Spirit tell him what to say?
25. What did Jesus say was proof that "the Kingdom of God has come upon you"?
26. In which Gospel does Jesus say that the Spirit will convict the world of sin?
27. Which prophet quoted God as saying, "My Spirit remains among you—do not fear"?
28. What amazing—and controversial—gift was bestowed upon Jesus' apostles on the Day of Pentecost?
29. Who predicted a time when people would be baptized by the Holy Spirit?
30. In which Gospel does Jesus foretell that his disciples will speak in "new tongues"?
31. Which prophet gave us this familiar quote: "'Not by might nor by power, but by my Spirit,' says the Lord"?
32. In Christian tradition, speaking in tongues at Pentecost was thought to "reverse" what famous story in Genesis?
33. What fisherman spoke out boldly to the Jewish authorities because he was "filled with the Spirit"?
34. Which apostle spoke of the "sword of the Spirit"?
35. According to 1 Corinthians, what is the "temple" in which the Holy Spirit dwells?
36. What group of Christians did Paul give the command "Quench not the Spirit"?
37. According to Paul, the _____ man does not receive the things of the Spirit.
38. Who are the "living epistles," written not by ink but by the Spirit?
39. According to Ephesians, Christians should be controlled by _____, not by alcohol.

40. What book of the Bible does the author say (several times) was revealed to him when he was "in the Spirit"?
41. In what city did Paul baptize believers, who then received the Spirit?
42. What husband-wife couple in Acts died mysteriously and suddenly because they "lied to the Spirit"?
43. In Acts, what seven men were "full of the Holy Spirit and wisdom"?
44. Who paid with his life by telling the Jewish leaders "You always resist the Holy Spirit"?
45. What other dramatic event occurred to Paul when he received the Holy Spirit?
46. In what Roman soldier's home did the Holy Spirit fall upon all those who heard the gospel?
47. In the very last chapter of the Bible, what does the Spirit invite people to do?

THAT'S THE SPIRIT (ANSWERS)

1. The dove, based on the Holy Spirit descending on Jesus in the form of a dove (Matthew 3:16; Mark 1:10)

2. Hovering, or (in the King James Version) brooding (Genesis 1:2)

3. John the Baptist (Luke 1:15)

4. Jesus, of course (Matthew 1:20)

5. At the Jordan River, being baptized by John (Matthew 3:13-17; Mark 1:9-11; Luke 3:21-22)

6. Into the wilderness, where he underwent his temptation (Matthew 4:1; Luke 4:1)

7. Balaam, the prophet of Moab (Numbers 24:2)

8. The aged Simeon (Luke 2:25-32)

9. Galilee, his home region (Luke 4:14)

10. Nazareth, his hometown (Luke 4:17-29)

11. Pentecost (Acts 2), with the result that Pentecost in time became a Christian holiday as well

12. John (20:22)

13. An artist, or craftsman, the man who constructed the worship vessels for Israel (Exodus 31:3-4), and the only case in the Bible of an artist having the Spirit

14. *The elders of Israel, who took some of the administrative burden from Moses (Numbers 11:17)*

15. *The judge Samson (Judges 14:6; 15:14)*

16. *Joshua (Numbers 27:18)*

17. *Saul (1 Samuel 19:23-24)*

18. *The Temple in Jerusalem (1 Chronicles 28:11-13)*

19. *Jesus (Mark 3:28-29), though people still debate what "blaspheming against the Spirit" really means. The most likely interpretation is that it means attributing Christ's work to Satan.*

20. *King David (Psalm 51:11)*

21. *John (14:16; 15:26). The Greek word is* paraklete, *which is translated as Comforter, Counselor, Helper, Advocate, and so on.*

22. *Isaiah (11:1-2). Jesse was the father of King David. Isaiah's prophecy meant that a descendant of David (Jesus was one) would be specially endowed with the Spirit, and Christians applied the prophecy to Jesus.*

23. *Joel, in a passage (2:28-32) believed to be fulfilled in the early church*

24. *At the hour of trial. Persecuted believers have taken great comfort in this.*

25. *He was able to cast out demons through the power of the Spirit (Matthew 12:28).*

26. *John (16:8)*

27. *The little-read and little-quoted Haggai (2:5)*

28. *Speaking in unknown tongues (Acts 2)*

29. *John the Baptist (Matthew 3:11)*

30. *Only in Mark (16:17)*

31. *Zechariah (4:6)*

32. *The story of the tower of Babel (Genesis 11), which began with men speaking one language but ended with God striking them with a diversity of languages, unable to understand each other*

33. *Peter (Acts 4:1-8)*

34. *Paul (Ephesians 6:10-18), in his famous passage on the spiritual "armor" of Christians*

35. *The body of the Christian (1 Corinthians 6:18-20)*

36. *The Thessalonians (1 Thessalonians 5:19-21)*

37. *Natural (1 Corinthians 2:14)*

38. *Christians (2 Corinthians 3:3)*

39. *Being filled with the Spirit (Ephesians 5:18)*

40. *Revelation (1:10; 4:2; 17:3; 21:10)*

41. *Ephesus (Acts 19)*

42. *Ananias and Sapphira, whose troubling tale is told in Acts 5:1-11*

43. *The seven deacons, appointed to aid the church of Jerusalem (Acts 6:3)*

44. *The martyr Stephen (Acts 6–7)*

45. *His sight was restored. He had been blinded on the road to Damascus, and he received his sight and the Spirit at the same time (Acts 9:17).*

46. *Cornelius (Acts 10), the first case of the Spirit being given to Gentiles (non-Jews)*

47. *"Take the water of life freely" (Revelation 22:17).*

 ## FRUIT AND CHARISMATA: WHAT THE SPIRIT GIVES

The previous section dealt with the Holy Spirit throughout the Bible. This section focuses on what the Spirit bestows upon believers, then and now. Some of these bestowals are called fruit, others are called gifts. (The Greek word translated "gifts" is *charismata*—a word you've probably heard before.) All of these are rather mysteriously and wonderfully given by the Spirit as he sees fit, and all of them—and all the people who receive them—somehow mysteriously work together to benefit what the New Testament calls the "body of Christ," that is, believers throughout the world. Some of the gifts are very "everyday," while others, such as healing and speaking in tongues, are more mysterious (and occasionally even controversial).

1. In which of Paul's epistles does he list the fruit of the Spirit?
2. In Paul's list of the fruit, which comes first?
3. Which of these is *not* in the list of the fruit of the Spirit: joy, wisdom, self-control, peace, kindness?
4. In which two Epistles does Paul list the gifts of the Spirit?
5. The spiritual gift called *dynameis* in the original Greek is usually translated as what?
6. Agabus, mentioned in Acts, was an example of a Christian possessing what spiritual gift?
7. What gift was useful at a time when many false prophets and evangelists were roaming around?
8. Barnabas, Paul's friend and fellow missionary, possessed what gift?
9. What two "word" gifts are mentioned (but not described) in 1 Corinthians 12:8?
10. What office, claimed by the 12 disciples of Jesus and by Paul, could also be given as a spiritual gift?

11. Fill in the blank in this verse from Paul: "We have different gifts, according to the _____ given us."
12. In the "gift chapters," who does Paul say is the head of the "body"?
13. By what other name is the gift of glossolalia known?
14. Christians who place a lot of emphasis on the gifts of the Spirit are called what?
15. The belief that spiritual gifts ended with the age of the apostles is called what?

FRUIT AND CHARISMATA: WHAT THE SPIRIT GIVES (ANSWERS)

1. Galatians (5:22-23), a much-quoted passage in the New Testament

2. Love, which is appropriate, given that Paul wrote a famous chapter (1 Corinthians 13) in praise of love

3. Wisdom. However, 1 Corinthians 12:8 speaks of "the word of wisdom" that is given "through the Spirit."

4. 1 Corinthians 12 ("gifts of the Spirit") and Romans 12:3-8 ("spiritual gifts"). The two lists are similar, and both emphasize the use of the gifts to benefit others.

5. Miracles, of which there were plenty among the first Christians (and, come to think of it, later Christians as well)

6. Prophecy (1 Corinthians 12:10). Christian prophets weren't necessarily foretellers (though Agabus was) but more often were "forth-tellers"—boldly proclaiming the Word of God.

7. Discernment of spirits, mentioned not only in the lists of gifts (1 Corinthians 12:10) but elsewhere in the New Testament (1 Thessalonians 5:2-21; 1 John 4:1).

8. Exhortation, also called encouragement (Romans 12:8)

9. The "word of wisdom" and "word of knowledge"

10. Apostleship (1 Corinthians 12:28). Paul's listing of this hints that it was not limited to those who had known Jesus in the flesh. Note that it is listed first among the gifts.

11. Grace (Romans 12:6)

12. Christ, of course

13. Speaking in tongues. Given the controversy surrounding this gift, there's a separate set of questions devoted to it.

14. Charismatics, or Pentecostals, or both. The term charismatic comes from Greek charismata, "gifts." "Pentecostal" is based on the account of the descent of the Holy Spirit at Pentecost (Acts 2). As a rule of thumb, Pentecostals make up entire denominations (the Assemblies of God being the largest), whereas charismatics are scattered throughout various denominations.

15. Cessationism, from the idea that the gifts "ceased" once Christianity was widely spread and the New Testament completed. It was taught by such influential theologians as Augustine and John Calvin and by many prominent evangelicals in the 1800s and 1900s. As you may surmise, charismatics and Pentecostals are not cessationists.

SPEAKING OF SPEAKING IN TONGUES

One of the great mysteries is that Christians have often persecuted other Christians, sometimes to the point of execution. Christians have even been persecuted for exercising the spiritual gifts that are praised in the New Testament. Among these—perhaps the most mysterious, and perhaps the most "fakeable" too—is glossolalia, also called speaking in tongues. Paul the apostle spoke in tongues himself and praised the gift—but also wanted some restrictions on it. Curiously, after the age of the apostles, the gift seemed to vanish—aided by the fact that the official church came to frown on it. It never completely died out, and it experienced an amazing rebirth in the twentieth century in what came to be called the charismatic movement. Speaking in tongues remains very controversial and very mysterious. In short, it is a fascinating subject.

1. Along with speaking in tongues, what related gift is listed among the gifts of the Spirit?
2. At the sending of the Holy Spirit at Pentecost, what visual sign appeared over the apostles' heads?
3. Which apostle preached to a group of Gentiles and witnessed them speaking in tongues?
4. In what city did people begin to speak in tongues when Paul laid his hands on them?
5. According to Paul, what gift is better than speaking in tongues?
6. In which Gospel did the risen Jesus foretell that his followers would speak in unknown tongues?
7. According to Paul, unless we have _____, tongues is nothing but noise.
8. In the early 1900s, Christians who had experienced speaking in tongues began to teach that it was "indisputable proof" of what?
9. The modern Pentecostal movement is often traced to the 1906 Azusa Street revival. In what U.S. city did that take place?

SPEAKING OF SPEAKING IN TONGUES (ANSWERS)

1. *The interpretation of tongues (1 Corinthians 12:10, 30)*

2. *Tongues of fire, appropriately enough (Acts 2:2-3)*

3. *Peter, preaching to the family of the Roman soldier Cornelius (Acts 10:46)*

4. *Ephesus (Acts 19:6)*

5. *Prophesying (1 Corinthians 14:5). However, he hoped both gifts would be exercised.*

6. *Mark (16:17)*

7. *Love (1 Corinthians 13:1)*

8. *The baptism of the Holy Spirit. Many Pentecostals still teach that any person who has had Spirit baptism will speak in tongues.*

9. *Los Angeles*

THE BODY, LITERAL AND SPIRITUAL

MATTERS OF THE HEART

Yes, technically the heart is that collection of cardiac tissue that pumps blood through the body. But the literal heart is far less interesting than the figurative heart, the seat of human emotions, both good and bad. The Bible has little to say about the physical heart, but lots to say about the spiritual-emotional heart, that mysterious entity inclined to do all sorts of good—and evil—things.

1. Who told his mistress "all his heart" and lost his hair (and eyesight and freedom) as a result?
2. What evil Old Testament king had his heart repeatedly hardened by God?
3. When a man looks at a woman with lust in his heart, what sin has he committed?
4. Whose wife "despised him in her heart" because he was dancing merrily in the streets and exposing a little too much flesh?
5. What handsome prince "stole the hearts of the men of Israel"?
6. Who told the Israelites to "circumcise the foreskins of their hearts"?
7. What pagan king's heart was "merry with wine"?
8. Which Old Testament book commands, "Thou shalt not hate thy brother in thy heart"?
9. According to Paul, what sort of people had been given up to the lusts of their own hearts?
10. To whom did God say, "The Lord looketh on the heart"?
11. What did God do when he perceived that man's heart was "only evil continually"?
12. Who claimed to be "meek and lowly in heart"?
13. According to Jesus, where is a person's heart?
14. Who takes away the Word sown in people's hearts?
15. Which king was "a man after God's own heart"?
16. Who was sent by God "to turn the hearts of the fathers to the children"?
17. According to Hosea, which two vices "take away the heart"?
18. What pagan king lost his mind and had his heart changed from a man's to a beast's?
19. Whose heart "fainted" when he heard that his long-lost son was still alive?
20. Who kept in her heart all the things people said about her newborn child?

21. Who entered Judas's heart to urge him to betray Jesus?
22. Which prophet said, "Rend your heart and not your garments"?
23. Who says in his heart, "There is no God"?
24. Who offered sacrifices on the possibility that his children had cursed God in their hearts?
25. What kind of heart is the Lord near to?
26. What book of the Bible says that even in laughter the heart may be sorrowful?
27. What rebel was killed by three darts, shot into his heart by Joab?
28. What book of the Bible says that the Lord's people have become as heartless as ostriches in the desert?
29. According to Malachi, which prophet will come back to turn the hearts of the children to their fathers?
30. Who said that the Old Testament Law allowed divorce because of people's hardness of heart?
31. Which prophet claimed that God would make a new covenant that would be written on the hearts of the people of Israel?
32. What will happen to the pure in heart, according to Jesus?

MATTERS OF THE HEART (ANSWERS)

1. Samson, who, unfortunately, told Delilah "all his heart" (Judges 16)

2. The pharaoh at the time of Moses (Exodus 7:3)

3. Adultery (Matthew 5:28)

4. David, whose wife Michal thought his dancing was undignified (2 Samuel 6:16)

5. David's son Absalom, who led a rebellion against his father (2 Samuel 15:6)

6. Moses (Deuteronomy 10:16), who was speaking figuratively, of course

7. The Persian king Ahasuerus (Esther 1:10)

8. Leviticus (19:17). This is a remarkable verse, since Leviticus is mostly concerned with offerings and sacrifices.

9. Homosexuals (Romans 1:24)

10. Samuel, who was in the process of choosing a king for Israel (1 Samuel 16:7)

11. Decided to destroy the earth with a flood (Genesis 6:5)

12. Jesus (Matthew 11:29)

13. Where his treasure is (Matthew 6:21)

14. Satan (Mark 4:15)

15. David (1 Samuel 13:14)

16. John the Baptist (Luke 1:17)

17. "Whoredom and wine" (Hosea 4:11)

18. Nebuchadnezzar of Babylon (Daniel 4:16)

19. Jacob, father of Joseph (Genesis 45:26)

20. Mary, Jesus' mother (Luke 2:51)

21. Satan (John 13:2)

22. Joel (2:13). He was referring to the practice of rending (tearing) the garments to express grief and claiming that it was more important to grieve inwardly than outwardly.

23. The fool (Proverbs 14:1)

24. Job (1:5)

25. A broken one (Psalm 34:18)

26. Proverbs (14:13)

27. Absalom, David's son (2 Samuel 18:14)

28. Lamentations (4:3)

29. The prophet Elijah (Malachi 4:6)

30. Jesus (Matthew 19:8)

31. Jeremiah (31:33)

32. They will see God (Matthew 5:8).

BREATHING LESSONS

There's nothing particularly mysterious about breathing—or is there? In both the Old and New Testaments, the words used for "breath" and "spirit" are the same. (It's *ruach* in Hebrew, *pneuma* in Greek, and either word can also mean "wind"—see pages 248-9 for more about that.) Unlike us modern, scientifically minded types, the people of Bible times saw breath—necessary for life, of course—as something divinely given. (Not a bad idea, when you think about it.) They were perceptive enough to realize that when a person stopped breathing, his "spirit" (literal and figurative) had gone. They also credited God's divine "breath" with a lot of power. See how much you know about breath/spirit in the Bible.

1. Which apostle taught that all Scripture is "God-breathed"?

2. What happened when the risen Jesus "breathed on" his disciples?
3. What Jewish fanatic was "breathing out threatenings and slaughter against the disciples of the Lord" but later became an apostle?
4. Which prophet had a vision of a valley of dry bones, brought to life when God breathed into them?
5. What lump of dust came to life when God breathed into it?
6. What military leader went into Canaan and "utterly destroyed all that breathed, as the Lord commanded"?
7. What chilly weather phenomenon did Job think came from the breath of God?
8. What praise-filled book ends with the words "Let every thing that hath breath praise the Lord"?
9. Which prophet warned against worshipping gold and silver idols that have no breath in them?
10. In Luke's Gospel, what did Jesus say before he breathed his last?
11. What is the only known case of halitosis in the Bible?
12. In the book of Revelation, what people were brought to life when God breathed into them?
13. Who, according to 2 Thessalonians, will Christ overthrow by the breath of his mouth?
14. In the King James Version, what phrase is used to mean "breathed his last breath"?
15. Which sensuous Old Testament book describes a lover whose breath has the fragrance of apples?
16. Which prophet described God blowing on the fires of hell to kindle the blaze?
17. According to Mark's Gospel, what did Jesus do just before he breathed his last?

BREATHING LESSONS (ANSWERS)

1. *Paul, writing to Timothy (2 Timothy 3:16). Some translations have "inspired" instead of "God-breathed," though in fact "God-breathed" is a perfect translation of the Greek wording.*

2. *They received the Holy Spirit (John 20:22).*

3. *Saul, later called Paul (Acts 9:1)*

4. *Ezekiel (37:5)*

5. *Adam, the first man, of course (Genesis 2:7)*

6. Joshua (10:40). We have to assume that this refers to people, not to absolutely everything that breathed.

7. Frost (Job 37:10)

8. Psalms (150:6)

9. Habakkuk (2:19)

10. "Father, into thy hands I commend my spirit" (Luke 23:46).

11. Job, who lamented that his wife found his breath "offensive" (or "strange," depending on the translation you're reading) (Job 19:17)

12. The two witnesses, who had been killed by the beast from the abyss (Revelation 11:11)

13. The man of lawlessness, who will appear at the end times (2 Thessalonians 2:8)

14. "Gave up the ghost" (Genesis 25:8; 35:18, and many other places)

15. The Song of Solomon (7:8)

16. Isaiah (30:33), who was describing the fire of Tophet, an Old Testament name for the place of destruction

17. Cried out in a loud voice (Mark 15:37)

MORE THAN MERE SURGERY: THE RITE OF CIRCUMCISION

If circumcision were "just surgery," it wouldn't belong in this book. But for ancient Israel, it was far more important than the physical act. It was a sign of the Hebrews' covenant with God (and, for Jews, it still is). In the New Testament, circumcision was a divisive issue because some Christian believers insisted that all new converts must be circumcised. However, as Paul says in Romans 2:29, true circumcision is not an outward act but a change of the heart. Test your familiarity with the practice of circumcision and its place in the biblical narrative.

1. At what age were Hebrew boys to be circumcised?
2. At what advanced age was the patriarch Abraham circumcised?
3. Who circumcised her own son and placed the foreskin at her husband's feet?
4. When the Old Testament refers to "the uncircumcised," which nation were they usually referring to?
5. Which prophet said, "Circumcise yourselves to the Lord, and take away the foreskins of your heart"?

6. What Christian martyr told the Jews that they were "uncircumcised in heart and ears"?
7. Which apostle boasted of his Jewish heritage by claiming he was "circumcised on the eighth day"?
8. With what aged man did God institute the practice of circumcision?
9. Which king committed suicide to avoid being abused by "the uncircumcised"?
10. Were the Jews allowed to perform circumcision on a Sabbath?
11. Who told Christians that circumcision (and the covenant it represented) was an inward matter, not an outward?
12. Which apostle fraternized with non-Jews until pressured to separate from them by the "circumcision group"?
13. According to Paul, what is much more important to the believer than circumcision?
14. What son of Abraham was circumcised at age 13?
15. Who was the first person to be circumcised when eight days old, as God's commandment had decreed?
16. What group of men were attacked while they were still recovering from circumcision?
17. Who described himself as having "uncircumcised lips"?
18. What Jewish feast required that any man partaking of it must be circumcised?
19. Which leader circumcised the Hebrew men after they settled in the land of Canaan?
20. Which strongman offended his parents by seeking out a wife among the uncircumcised Philistines?
21. By what name do we know the child who was named Zechariah until after his circumcision?
22. Who made a gift of 200 Philistine foreskins to his future father-in-law?
23. What book of the Old Testament refers to a "Hill of Foreskins"?
24. Which Old Testament book refers to uncircumcised fruit trees?
25. Who told the people of Israel, "Circumcise therefore the foreskin of your heart, and be no more stiffnecked"?
26. Which prophet lamented that the people of Israel had "uncircumcised ears"?
27. Who considered himself the "apostle to the uncircumcised"?
28. Which Epistle mentions a spiritual circumcision, "the circumcision made without hands"?

29. What Greek companion of Paul aroused controversy because he was uncircumcised?
30. Which prophet warned that a day was coming when God would punish the circumcised as well as the uncircumcised?
31. In which city was a famous Christian council that decided the issue of whether Christian converts had to undergo the Jewish rite of circumcision?
32. What half-Jewish, half-Greek follower of Paul was circumcised by Paul?
33. Which prophet predicted a time when the uncircumcised would never again set foot in Jerusalem?

MORE THAN MERE SURGERY: THE RITE OF CIRCUMCISION (ANSWERS)

1. Eight days (Genesis 17:12)

2. Ninety-nine (Genesis 17:24)

3. Moses' wife Zipporah (Exodus 4:25)

4. The Philistines, but also to non-Jewish people in general

5. Jeremiah (4:4)

6. Stephen (Acts 7:51)

7. Paul (Philippians 3:5)

8. Abraham (Genesis 17)

9. Saul (1 Samuel 31:4), who was about to be captured by the Philistines

10. Yes (John 7:22)

11. Paul (Romans 2:29)

12. Peter, who bowed to pressure from the Jewish Christians and was rebuked by Paul for doing so (Galatians 2:11-14)

13. Faith (Galatians 5:6)

14. Ishmael (Genesis 17:25)

15. Abraham's son Isaac (Genesis 21:4)

16. The clan of Shechem, who had submitted to circumcision under pressure from Jacob's sons. The sons attacked the Shechemites while they were still recovering (Genesis 34).

17. Moses (Exodus 6:12)

18. The Passover (Exodus 12:44-48)

19. Joshua (5:2)

20. *Samson (Judges 14:3)*

21. *John the Baptist (Luke 1:59)*

22. *David (1 Samuel 18:25). Saul had required this for David to marry Saul's daughter Michal, hoping that David would be killed in trying to acquire the foreskins.*

23. *Joshua (5:3). The name of the hill (in some Bible translations) is Gibeath Haaraloth.*

24. *Leviticus (19:23)*

25. *Moses (Deuteronomy 10:16)*

26. *Jeremiah (6:10)*

27. *Paul (Galatians 2)*

28. *Colossians (2:11)*

29. *Titus (Galatians 2:3)*

30. *Jeremiah (9:25)*

31. *Jerusalem (Acts 15)*

32. *Timothy (Acts 16:3)*

33. *Isaiah (52:1)*

 ## CLEANLINESS REALLY IS NEXT TO GODLINESS

Clean and *unclean* are words that crop up often in the Bible, particularly in the Old Testament, with its code of kosher foods and other restrictions on the details of life. But the Bible's view of "cleanliness" goes far beyond rules about food. In fact, some of what is taught about cleanness and uncleanness has nothing whatever to do with physical matters.

1. To whom did Jesus give power to cast out unclean spirits?
2. How many of each clean beast did Noah take into the ark?
3. Which Old Testament book contains the "kosher code"?
4. After a woman had given birth to a son, how many days was she ritually unclean?
5. How many days after giving birth to a daughter?
6. When Jesus said to his disciples, "You are not all clean," who was the unclean one?
7. Which apostle received a strange vision of a huge sheet filled with unclean animals?
8. According to the law of Moses, what is needed to cleanse out the blood of a murdered man?

9. According to Paul, what is the opposite of uncleanness?
10. According to Jesus, when an unclean spirit leaves a man, where does it go?
11. What, according to the New Testament, cleanses us from all sin?
12. According to the law of Moses, what could a man do with a wife in whom he had found some uncleanness?
13. What godly king cleansed Jerusalem by burning the bones of false priests on the altars?
14. Which apostle said, "I know, and am persuaded by the Lord Jesus, that there is nothing unclean of itself"?
15. What pagan army commander did the prophet Elisha cleanse from leprosy?
16. Who cleansed 10 lepers but received a thank-you from only one of them?
17. According to the Psalms, what plant is used for cleansing a person?
18. What sea creatures were unclean (and therefore forbidden as food)?
19. Which prophet lamented that he was a man of unclean lips, living among an unclean people?
20. Which prophet predicted that the Israelites would eat unclean things in Assyrian exile?
21. What did the prophet Amos mean by the phrase "cleanness of teeth"?
22. Who did Jesus criticize for being obsessive about cleaning their dishes but not their own souls?
23. Who took the body of the crucified Jesus and wrapped it in a clean linen cloth?
24. In the book of Revelation, what city is the habitation of every kind of unclean thing?
25. Whose armies are dressed in clean white linen robes?
26. Where did Jesus send the unclean spirits who had possessed a man?
27. Who had a vision of unclean spirits shaped like frogs, coming out of the mouth of a dragon?
28. What type of persons were forced to walk around in public crying out, "Unclean! Unclean!"
29. Which prophet was commissioned by the Lord to teach Israel the difference between clean and unclean?
30. Which prophet predicted a fountain in Jerusalem that would cleanse people from their sins?

CLEANLINESS REALLY IS NEXT TO GODLINESS (ANSWERS)

1. *The 12 disciples (Matthew 10:1)*

2. *Seven. He took two each of the unclean beasts (Genesis 7:2).*

3. *Leviticus (11:1-23), which lists the animals that may (and may not) be eaten*

4. *Seven days (Leviticus 12:2)*

5. *Fourteen days (Leviticus 12:5)*

6. *Judas Iscariot (John 13:11)*

7. *Peter, who was being told by God that the clean (Jews) and unclean (Gentiles) are both accepted by God (Acts 10)*

8. *The blood of the one who murdered him (Numbers 35:33)*

9. *Holiness (1 Thessalonians 4:7: "For God hath not called us unto uncleanness, but unto holiness.")*

10. *Into "dry places" (or "desert places" in some translations) (Matthew 12:43)*

11. *The blood of Jesus (1 John 1:7)*

12. *Divorce her (Deuteronomy 24:1)*

13. *Josiah (2 Chronicles 34:5)*

14. *Paul, who was commenting on dietary restrictions (Romans 14:14)*

15. *Naaman the Syrian (2 Kings 5)*

16. *Jesus (Luke 17:14)*

17. *Hyssop (Psalm 51:7)*

18. *Anything without fins or scales (thus ruling out shellfish) (Leviticus 11:12)*

19. *Isaiah, after his vision of the Lord in the Temple (Isaiah 6:5)*

20. *Hosea (9:3)*

21. *Famine—that is, the teeth are clean because nothing has been eaten (Amos 4:6)*

22. *The scribes and Pharisees (Matthew 23:25)*

23. *Joseph of Arimathea (Matthew 27:59)*

24. *Babylon (Revelation 18:2)*

25. *The Lord's (Revelation 19:14)*

26. *Into a herd of pigs (Mark 5:13)*

27. *John (Revelation 16:13)*

28. *Lepers (Leviticus 13:45)*

29. *Ezekiel (44:23)*

30. *Zechariah (13:1)*

HANDS, BUT WITH MEANING AND POWER

Touch is very important to human beings, not just because humans desire affection, but because touching also is full of symbolism and meaning. A handshake is never *just* a handshake, a hug is never *just* a hug, and so on. In the Bible are many instances of what is called laying on of *hands*—not merely touching, but trying to communicate something deeper, often the passing of power or authority from one person to another. In fact, mysterious as it sounds, it appears that in many cases, power *did* pass on to the person being touched.

1. What sort of people were brought to Jesus so he could lay hands on them and pray for them?
2. Which apostle laid his hands on a man in Malta and healed him?
3. Who laid his hands on the two sons of Joseph and blessed them?
4. In the laws of sacrifices, why would the priests lay their hands on the heads of the animals?
5. Once a year, the high priest laid his hands on a goat before driving it away into the wilderness. What term was used for the goat?
6. Who often laid his hands on people before healing them?
7. What sort of person did the Israelites stone after laying hands on him?
8. In which Gospel does Jesus tell his disciples that they will have power to lay hands on people and heal them?
9. Which of the 12 tribes of Israel was involved in the ritual of laying on of hands?
10. In Acts 8, what did people receive when apostles Peter and John laid hands on them?
11. Who received a spiritual gift when Christian elders laid their hands on him?
12. What Israelite leader was consecrated when Moses laid hands on him?
13. What character tried to buy the apostles' power to pass on the Spirit by laying on hands?
14. What is the only example of "prayer cloths" in the Bible?
15. What two Christian missionaries were ordained with the laying on of hands?
16. What spiritual gifts did the men of Ephesus receive when Paul laid hands on them?
17. Whom did Paul advise to "not be hasty in the laying on of hands"?

HANDS, BUT WITH MEANING AND POWER (ANSWERS)

1. Children (Matthew 19:13). His disciples scolded the parents for this, but Jesus scolded the disciples.

2. Paul (Acts 28:7)

3. Their grandfather, Jacob (Genesis 48:8)

4. They were consecrating them—that is, marking them as being dedicated to the Lord. Also, touching the sacrificial animals symbolized that the people's sins were being passed on to the animal.

5. The scapegoat, symbolizing that Israel's sins were being carried away (Leviticus 16:21). As in the previous question, touching the beast was a means of transferring (symbolically) the people's sins to it.

6. Jesus (Mark 6:5; Luke 4:40)

7. A blasphemer (Leviticus 24:14)

8. Mark (16:18). As Acts shows, the apostles did indeed have such power.

9. The Levites, who were consecrated to the Lord for their work in the priesthood (Numbers 8:10)

10. The Holy Spirit (Acts 8:17)

11. Timothy (1 Timothy 4:14; 2 Timothy 1:6)

12. Joshua (Numbers 27:18)

13. Simon the sorcerer (Acts 8:18-19). His name is the root of the word simony, referring to using bribery to obtain a position in the church.

14. Acts 19:11-12 reports that cloths touched by Paul's hands were used to cure sickness and drive out evil spirits.

15. Saul (Paul, that is) and Barnabas (Acts 13:3)

16. Speaking in tongues and prophesying (Acts 19:6)

17. Timothy (1 Timothy 5:22)

THE BLIND LEADING THE BLIND

In Bible times, medicine wasn't exactly in an advanced stage, so lots of people suffered blindness, particularly if they lived to be old. However, though there were plenty of folks in the Bible who suffered from physical blindness, the Book more often refers to *spiritual* blindness, the inability (or refusal) to see the truth. People were sometimes healed of physical blindness, but far rarer was the curing of spiritual blindness.

1. Who coined the phrase "the blind leading the blind"?
2. What spiritually blind persecutor was literally blind for three days before recovering his sight?
3. In one of Paul's epistles, who blinds the minds of unbelievers?
4. According to the New Testament, a man who hates his _____ is spiritually blind.
5. In Psalms, what sort of person says in his heart, "There is no God"?
6. What respected group of Jewish leaders did Jesus refer to as "blind guides"?
7. What book of the Bible refers to a church that is "wretched, pitiful, poor, blind, and naked"?
8. In which Gospel does Jesus say, "O righteous Father, the world has not known you"?
9. According to Paul, God rescued us from the _____ of darkness.
10. Which prophet was told by God that Israel was a "rebellious house, that has eyes to see, and sees not"?
11. Finish this verse from Proverbs: "The way of the _____ is as darkness."
12. What man was blindfolded and slapped around by soldiers?
13. What book of the Bible says that people lacking in self-control and kindness are "nearsighted and blind"?
14. In Acts 13, what spiritually blind man was struck with physical blindness for a time?
15. Complete this verse from Psalms: "They know not, neither do they understand; they walk in _____."

THE BLIND LEADING THE BLIND (ANSWERS)

1. *Jesus (Matthew 15:14; Luke 6:39)*

2. *Saul, later the great apostle Paul (Acts 9)*

3. *The "god of this age," meaning Satan (2 Corinthians 4:4)*

4. *Brother—meaning fellow human being (1 John 2:11)*

5. *The fool (Psalm 14:1)*

6. *The Pharisees (Matthew 23:26)*

7. *Revelation (3:17), referring to the church at Laodicea*

8.   *John (17:25)*

9.   *Dominion (Colossians 1:13)*

10. *Ezekiel (12:2)*

11. *Wicked (Proverbs 4:19)*

12. *Jesus (Luke 22:64)*

13. *2 Peter (1:9)*

14. *Elymas the sorcerer (13:8-12)*

15. *Darkness (Psalm 82:5)*

PART 11

DIVINE-HUMAN INTERFACE

"I'M WITH YOU, MAN"

Since God is spirit, not matter, how can he be "with" someone? And how can a mere human being know that God is "with" him? That is truly a mystery. The Bible presents us with several people who were assured by God himself, "I am with you."

1. Who assured his followers that "Surely I am with you always, to the very end of the age"?
2. What reluctant leader of Israel was on a mountain when God assured him that "I will be with you"?
3. Which apostle was told in a vision to continue his bold preaching, for God was with him?
4. Which king of Israel was assured by a prophet that God would be with him, but only if he kept the Lord's commands?
5. Which patriarch was told that God was with him while he lived in the Philistine lands during a famine?
6. What young prophet was told not to fear his enemies, for God was with him?
7. What military man was told by an angel that God was with him and would help him strike down the Midianites?
8. Through which prophet did God say, "When you pass through the waters, I will be with you"?
9. What man, asleep with his head on a stone pillow, was assured that God was with him?
10. Which leader was told by God that "I am with you as I was with Moses"?
11. Which prophet assured the people of Jerusalem that God was with them in their project of rebuilding the Temple?

"I'M WITH YOU, MAN" (ANSWERS)

1. *Jesus (Matthew 28:20)*

2. *Moses (Exodus 3:12)*

3. *Paul (Acts 18:10)*

4. *Jeroboam (1 Kings 11:38)*

5. *Isaac (Genesis 26:3)*

6. *Jeremiah (1:8)*

7. *Gideon (Judges 6:16)*

8. *Isaiah (43:2)*

9. *Jacob (Genesis 28:15)*

10. *Joshua (1:5; 3:7)*

11. *Haggai (1:13; 2:4)*

THE WORD: IN THE BEGINNING, AND LATER

To put it mildly, the people of Bible times took words much more seriously than we do. Blessings were believed to have real power, and so were curses. So were names, which were expected to have meaning. And just as humans' words were serious, even more serious was the word of God. When you encounter the phrase "word of the Lord" in the Bible—and it is there many, many times—brace yourself, for some serious divine-to-human communication is taking place. Just how the Lord's word is communicated is mysterious, but real enough to those who understood it.

1. What book of the Bible opens with the words "In the beginning was the Word"?
2. Who is the first man the Bible mentions as receiving the word of the Lord?
3. Which apostle wrote that the word of God is "the sword of the Spirit"?
4. What book of the Old Testament states that "every word of God is flawless"?
5. Who was ordered by the word of the Lord to take a census of Israel?
6. Which apostle was exiled to the island of Patmos because of his commitment to the word of God?
7. What book of the Old Testament makes the sad statement "the word of the Lord was rare in those days"?
8. Which king was told he had "despised the word of the Lord" by committing adultery?
9. What book of the New Testament says that Christians are born again "through the living word of God"?
10. Which prophet was commanded by the word of the Lord to live in the wilderness and be fed by ravens?

11. Which king died because he was unfaithful to the word of the Lord?
12. According to Psalm 33, what was created by the word of the Lord?
13. Which apostle proudly proclaimed he did not preach the word for profit?
14. In the Gospels, who is the first person to receive the word of God?
15. Which king was told by the word of God that he could not build a temple because he was a man of war?
16. In what famous parable does seed represent the word of God?
17. Which prophet was told to proclaim the word of the Lord to some dry bones?
18. According to Paul, what was one of the benefits of his imprisonment?
19. Which king was commanded by the word of God not to try to reunite divided Israel?
20. In Revelation 19, what sort of robe does Jesus, the Word of God, wear?
21. Who received a word from the Lord that he regretted making Saul king?
22. According to the Letter to the Hebrews, the word of God is sharper than what?
23. Which king was told by the word of God that his descendants will rule for four generations?
24. What book of the Bible mentions people who had been beheaded for their commitment to the word?
25. Which king was told by the prophet Gad that the word of the Lord had given him three options, all bad?
26. Which prophet was commanded by the word of the Lord, "Go and present yourself to Ahab"?
27. Which prophet approached King Hezekiah with "Hear the word of the Lord Almighty"?
28. What persecuted prophet received a word from the Lord that King Ahab would die in battle?
29. In Acts 8, what region (despised by the Jews) received the word of God?
30. Which prophet lamented because "the word of the Lord is offensive" to his countrymen?
31. Which church did Paul commend because its people had accepted the word as divine, not human?
32. What office was created so that the apostles could devote themselves to the word of God?

33. Who preached the word of the Lord to Sodom and Gomorrah?
34. What book of the Bible records that "the word of God continued to increase and spread"?
35. In which Gospel does Jesus say, "Blessed are those who hear the word of God and obey it"?
36. Which prophet was hiding out in a cave when the word of the Lord came to him?
37. Who was commanded to proclaim the word as people passed through the gates of Jerusalem?
38. What book of the Bible uses the phrase "the word of the Lord came to me" a grand total of 50 times?
39. Jeremiah's prophecies are called the "word of the Lord" by what later prophet?
40. Paul and Silas spoke the word of the Lord to whose family?
41. Who prophesied that men would "stagger from sea to sea," searching for the word but would not find it?
42. Who was commanded by the word of the Lord to go and preach to the pagan city of Nineveh?
43. What two prophets pinpointed to the very day the time when the word of the Lord came to them?
44. Which prophet lamented that the word of the Lord had brought him insult and reproach?
45. Where was Jesus when he proclaimed the word of the Lord?
46. In Acts 4, what caused believers to proclaim the word of God boldly?
47. What book of the Bible (besides Jonah) states that the word of the Lord had been spoken through Jonah?
48. Which prophet said, "O earth, earth, earth, hear the word of the Lord"?
49. The word came to which prophet by the Kebar River in Babylon?
50. What righteous king lamented that his people had not obeyed the word of the Lord?

THE WORD: IN THE BEGINNING, AND LATER (ANSWERS)

1. *John's Gospel. The "Word" referred to Jesus Christ, of course.*

2. *Abram (Genesis 15:1), later to have his name changed to Abraham. The Lord had, of course, communicated to men before Abram—Adam, for example, and Noah. But Abram is the first case of the Bible saying "the word of the Lord came to."*

3. *Paul (Ephesians 6:17), in his famous passage about the "armor" the Christian wears*

4. *Proverbs (30:5)*

5. *Moses (Numbers 3:16)*

6. *John (Revelation 1:9)*

7. *1 Samuel (3:1). It is no coincidence that Judges, the book that precedes 1 Samuel, makes no mention of the word of the Lord.*

8. *David (2 Samuel 12:9), confronted with his adultery with Bathsheba*

9. *1 Peter (1:23)*

10. *Elijah (1 Kings 17:2-3)*

11. *Saul (1 Chronicles 10:13)*

12. *The heavens and all the stars (33:6)*

13. *Paul (2 Corinthians 2:17). He made this statement because, sadly, some people did preach the word for profit.*

14. *John the Baptist (Luke 3:2)*

15. *David (1 Chronicles 22:8)*

16. *The parable of the sower (Luke 8:1-15)*

17. *Ezekiel (37:4), in the passage that inspired the old song "Dem bones, dem bones, dem dry bones"*

18. *Other Christians were encouraged to preach the word boldly (Philippians 1:14).*

19. *Rehoboam, Solomon's son, whose rash behavior caused Israel to split into two kingdoms (1 Kings 12:24)*

20. *A robe dipped in blood (19:13), the blood of those who had died for the faith*

21. *Samuel, who had anointed Saul, but who had also opposed the idea of Israel having a king (1 Samuel 15:10-11)*

22. *Any two-edged sword (4:12)*

23. *Jehu, king of Israel (2 Kings 15:12)*

24. *Revelation (20:4)*

25. *David (2 Samuel 24:11-14). The choices were: three years of famine, three days of plague, or three months of fleeing from enemies.*

26. *Elijah (1 Kings 18:1), a constant thorn in the side of the wicked king*

27. *Isaiah (39:5)*

28. *Micaiah (1 Kings 22), whose prophecy proved true*

29. *Samaria (8:14)*

30. *Jeremiah (6:10)*

31. *The church at Thessalonica (1 Thessalonians 2:13)*

32. Deacon (or "helper," in some translations) (Acts 6:2-6). Originally there were seven deacons, including the famous Stephen.

33. Isaiah (1:10). The names Sodom and Gomorrah here are figurative, for the two cities had been destroyed centuries earlier. Isaiah is proclaiming that his fellow Jews are as faithless as the people of Sodom and Gomorrah.

34. Acts (12:24)

35. Luke (11:28)

36. Elijah (1 Kings 19:9)

37. Jeremiah (7:2; 17:20)

38. Ezekiel

39. Daniel (9:2)

40. The jailer in Philippi, who had them in his custody until they were miraculously released by an earthquake (Acts 16:32)

41. Amos (8:12)

42. Jonah (1:1-2). You probably know what became of Jonah when he resisted this command.

43. Haggai (1:1; 2:1; 2:10; 2:20) and Zechariah (1:1;1:7; 7:1), the two great prophets after the return from exile in Babylon. These are the rare cases in the Bible where we can actually nail down specific dates when certain men prophesied.

44. Jeremiah (20:8)

45. The Lake Gennesaret, also called the Sea of Galilee (Luke 5:1). While we can assume that Jesus proclaimed the word throughout his time on earth, Luke 5:1 is the only time the Gospels actually say that he spoke the word of God.

46. They were filled with the Holy Spirit (Acts 4:31).

47. 2 Kings (14:25)

48. Jeremiah (22:29). Some translations have "land" instead of "earth."

49. Ezekiel (1:3)

50. Josiah (2 Chronicles 34:21)

"LORD, DO YOU MIND IF I ASK YOU?"

The Bible presents us with a God who is the Almighty, the Creator, the Ultimate "I AM"—and yet this awesome Being is approachable, so much so that people in the Bible are frequently questioning him, sometimes in the boldest way. In many cases (though not all), they even got their questions answered—though often not in the way they expected. See how much you know about these saints and sinners who questioned the Almighty.

1. "Am I my brother's keeper?" (Hint: Genesis)
2. "Why is my pain perpetual, and my wound incurable?" (Hint: a prophet)
3. "Shall I go and smite these Philistines?" (Hint: a king)
4. "Why dost thou show me iniquity, and cause me to behold grievance?" (Hint: a prophet)
5. "Lord, wilt thou slay also a righteous nation?" (Hint: a king)
6. "Shall not the judge of all the earth do right?" (Hint: a patriarch)
7. "Who am I, that I should go unto Pharaoh?"
8. "Ah, Lord God, wilt thou make a full end of the remnant of Israel?" (Hint: a prophet)
9. "Behold, I am vile; what shall I answer thee?" (Hint: a righteous man)
10. "Lord God, whereby shall I know that I inherit it?" (Hint: a patriarch)
11. "Why is it that thou hast sent me?" (Hint: a leader and miracle worker)
12. "Hast thou also brought evil upon the widow with whom I sojourn, by slaying her son?" (Hint: a prophet)
13. "What wilt thou give me, seeing I go childless?" (Hint: a patriarch)
14. "Shall one man sin and wilt thou be wroth with all the congregation?" (Hint: a leader and his brother)
15. "Who is able to judge this thy so great a people?" (Hint: a king)
16. "When I come unto the children of Israel, and shall say unto them, The God of your fathers hath sent me unto you; and they shall say to me, What is his name? what shall I say unto them?" (Hint: a leader)
17. "Shall I pursue after this troop? shall I overtake them?" (Hint: a king)
18. "Why is this come to pass, that there should today be one tribe lacking in Israel?" (Hint: a nation)

19. "What shall I do unto this people? They are almost ready to stone me." (Hint: a leader)
20. "Wherefore hast thou at all brought this people over Jordan, to deliver us into the hand of the Amorites, to destroy us?" (Hint: a leader)

"LORD, DO YOU MIND IF I ASK YOU?" (ANSWERS)

1. Cain (Genesis 4:9)

2. Jeremiah (15:18)

3. David (1 Samuel 23:1-2)

4. Habakkuk (1:1-3)

5. Abimelech (Genesis 20:4)

6. Abraham (Genesis 18:25)

7. Moses (Exodus 3:10-11)

8. Ezekiel (11:13)

9. Job (40:3-4)

10. Abram (Genesis 15:7-8)

11. Moses (Exodus 5:22)

12. Elijah (1 Kings 17:20)

13. Abram (Genesis 15:2)

14. Moses and Aaron (Numbers 16:22)

15. Solomon (1 Kings 3:5-9)

16. Moses (Exodus 3:13)

17. David (1 Samuel 30:3-8)

18. The Israelites (Judges 21:2-3)

19. Moses (Exodus 17:3-4)

20. Joshua (7:7)

GOD THE QUESTIONER

As seen elsewhere in this book, God the Almighty is accommodating enough to human weakness (and boldness, and foolhardiness) to allow us to question him. On other occasions, however, the Almighty himself is the questioner—which, if you think about it, seems appropriate, since the Creator has every right to call his creatures on the carpet.

1. "How long will this people provoke me?" (Hint: a leader)
2. "Whom shall I send, and who will go for us?" (Hint: a prophet)
3. "Have I any pleasure at all that the wicked should die?" (Hint: a prophet)
4. "Doest thou well to be angry?" (Hint: a reluctant prophet)
5. "Who told thee that thou wast naked?"
6. "Why is thy countenance fallen? If thou doest well, shalt thou not be accepted?" (Hint: a farmer)
7. "How long wilt thou mourn for Saul, seeing I have rejected him from reigning over Israel?" (Hint: a judge and prophet)
8. "I am the Lord, the God of all flesh: is there anything too hard for me?" (Hint: a prophet)
9. "Son of man, can these bones live?" (Hint: a prophet)
10. "Who is this that darkeneth counsel by words without knowledge?" (Hint: a righteous man)
11. "Who hath made man's mouth?" (Hint: a leader)
12. "What is this that thou hast done?" (Hint: a woman)
13. "Shall the clay say to him that fashioneth it, What makest thou?" (Hint: a foreign king)
14. "Shall seven years of famine come unto thee in thy land? Or wilt thou flee three months before thine enemies?" (Hint: a king)
15. "Shall I not spare Nineveh, that great city?" (Hint: a prophet)
16. "Hast thou an arm like God? Or canst thou thunder with a voice like him?" (Hint: a righteous man)
17. "Why then is this people of Jerusalem slidden back by a perpetual backsliding?" (Hint: a prophet)
18. "Have not I commanded thee? Be strong and of good courage; be not afraid." (Hint: a conqueror)
19. "Is anything too hard for the Lord?" (Hint: a patriarch)
20. "Hast thou killed, and also taken possession?" (Hint: a king)

GOD THE QUESTIONER (ANSWERS)

1. *Moses (Numbers 14:11)*
2. *Isaiah (6:8)*
3. *Ezekiel (18:23)*
4. *Jonah (4:9)*
5. *Adam (Genesis 3:11)*
6. *Cain (Genesis 4:6-7)*
7. *Samuel (1 Samuel 16:1)*
8. *Jeremiah (32:27)*
9. *Ezekiel (37:3)*
10. *Job (38:2)*
11. *Moses (Exodus 4:11)*
12. *Eve (Genesis 3:13)*
13. *Cyrus (Isaiah 45:9)*
14. *David (2 Samuel 24:13)*
15. *Jonah (4:11)*
16. *Job (40:9)*
17. *Jeremiah (8:5)*
18. *Joshua (1:9)*
19. *Abraham (Genesis 18:14)*
20. *Ahab (1 Kings 21:19)*

DREAM A LITTLE DREAM

In our scientific age, when the "experts" have explained away (so they think) the mysteriousness of dreams, people are still fascinated and troubled by dreams. All of us have had dreams that frightened us, puzzled us, perhaps at times even inspired us, and we can't help but wonder if the so-called experts have a limited view of our dream world. Is it really possible that God could communicate to us in our dreams? The people of ancient times certainly thought so, and the

Bible makes it clear that God does indeed speak—on occasion, anyway—through dreams.

1. Which apostle had a dream of a man begging him to come and preach the gospel?
2. According to one Old Testament prophet, there will come a day when young men will see visions and old men will dream dreams. Which prophet?
3. Who repeats the words of this prophet in an early Christian sermon?
4. Joseph, Mary's husband, was warned in dreams to do four things. What?
5. In Nebuchadnezzar's famous tree dream, who is symbolized by the majestic tree that is cut down?
6. Daniel had a dream of four beasts rising out of the sea. What did they look like?
7. In Nebuchadnezzar's dream of the statue, what four metals are mentioned as composing the statue?
8. One of Gideon's soldiers dreamed of Midianite tents being overturned by an unlikely object. What was it?
9. When God came to the young Solomon in a dream and asked him what he desired, what did Solomon ask for?
10. What three Egyptian officials did Joseph interpret dreams for?
11. God protected Jacob by sending a dream of warning that Jacob should not be pursued or harmed. Who received this dream?
12. Who irritated his brothers by telling them of his dreams?
13. Who slept on a stone pillow at Bethel and had a dream of a stairway to heaven?
14. Who told Pilate that a worrisome dream made it clear that Pilate was to have nothing to do with Jesus?

DREAM A LITTLE DREAM (ANSWERS)

1. *Paul (Acts 16:9)*

2. *Joel (2:28)*

3. *Peter, at Pentecost (Acts 2:17)*

4. *Go ahead and marry Mary, name her son Jesus, flee to Egypt, and return from Egypt (Matthew 1–2).*

5. *Nebuchadnezzar (Daniel 4:5-17)*

6. *A lion, a bear, a leopard, and a monster with iron teeth (Daniel 7)*

7. *Gold, silver, brass, and iron (Daniel 2:31-35)*

8. *A loaf of barley bread (Judges 7:13)*

9. *An understanding heart and good judgment (1 Kings 3:5-10)*

10. *The pharaoh, his baker, and his butler (Genesis 40–41)*

11. *Laban, Jacob's father-in-law (Genesis 31:29)*

12. *Joseph (Genesis 37:2-11)*

13. *Jacob (Genesis 28:10-15)*

14. *His wife (Matthew 27:19)*

👉 GOOD FOR THE SOUL: CONFESSION

You've heard it for years: Confession is good for the soul. Although those exact words aren't in the Bible, certainly the idea is. Here is one area where ancient wisdom and today's pop culture meet in harmony, for every TV show and movie is bound to contain a scene where relationships are restored because a wrongdoer confesses his sins to others. But, as you'll see in the questions below, biblical confession and TV confession usually differed in one critical way: the person in the Bible usually intended to change his ways.

1. Who confessed his denial of Jesus?
2. Which king confessed his adulterous affair after being confronted by the prophet Nathan?
3. What wicked king of Judah confessed his sins when he was taken into captivity in Assyria?
4. What sneaky Israelite confessed that he had stolen goods from fallen Jericho?
5. Who confessed his own sin and Israel's after seeing a vision of God on his throne?
6. Who confessed to God that he had done wrong in taking a census of Israel?
7. Which scribe bowed in front of the Temple and confessed the sins of Israel while the people around him wept bitterly?
8. What young man confessed his riotous living to his forgiving father?
9. Who confessed to building the gold calf?

10. Who confessed his sexual immorality with his daughter-in-law, Tamar?
11. Who made an insincere confession to Aaron and Moses?
12. Who confessed his remorse over betraying his master?
13. Who confessed Israel's sins after he heard the walls of Jerusalem were in ruins?
14. Who was visited by the angel Gabriel while he was confessing his sins?
15. Who confessed that he had been self-righteous?
16. Who confessed his sin to an angel that only his donkey had seen?
17. Who was pardoned by David after confessing his sin and begging for mercy?
18. Who confessed to Samuel that he had disobeyed God by not destroying all the spoils of war?

GOOD FOR THE SOUL: CONFESSION (ANSWERS)

1. Peter (Matthew 26:75)

2. David (2 Samuel 12:13)

3. Manasseh (2 Chronicles 33:11-13)

4. Achan (Joshua 7:20)

5. Isaiah (6:5)

6. David (2 Samuel 24:10)

7. Ezra (10:1)

8. The Prodigal Son (Luke 15:18)

9. Moses (Exodus 32:31)

10. Judah (Genesis 38:26)

11. Pharaoh (Exodus 10:16)

12. Judas (Matthew 27:4)

13. Nehemiah (1:6)

14. Daniel (9:20)

15. Job (42:6)

16. Balaam (Numbers 22:34)

17. Shimei (2 Samuel 19:20)

18. Saul (1 Samuel 15:24)

"TEACH US TO PRAY"

Prayer seems to be universal. Throughout history, and everywhere on the globe, human beings pray to Someone or Something. The typical human prayer can be pretty selfish ("I want a shiny new Lexus") or can be a cry of desperation ("Please don't let my husband die from cancer"), and the Bible presents us with these types of prayers and many others—sometimes just joyous, spontaneous outpourings of praise and thanks to God. See how much you know about this VIS (Very Important Subject) in the Bible.

1. Who is the first person in the Bible who prayed?
2. Who prayed while in the belly of a great fish?
3. According to Jesus' Sermon on the Mount, what type of people should we pray for?
4. What blinded strongman prayed to the Lord for vengeance on the cruel Philistines?
5. Which woman prayed silently with her lips moving, so that she appeared to be drunk?
6. In what book of the New Testament is incense depicted as a symbol of believers' prayers?
7. According to the Letter of James, what should church elders do in addition to praying for a sick person?
8. What barren woman conceived after her husband prayed for her?
9. Who prayed to be saved from the wrath of his peeved twin brother?
10. Which king is quoted as saying, "Pray to the Lord to take the frogs away from me and my people"?
11. Which king offered up a long prayer of dedication in the new Temple in Jerusalem?
12. What distraught prophet prayed for the Lord to take his life?
13. What book of the Bible mentions prayer the most times?
14. According to Isaiah, why does the Lord not heed certain prayers?
15. What dying king prayed for wellness so that the Lord extended his life another 15 years?
16. According to Paul, how often are we supposed to pray?
17. Which prophet prayed that enemy soldiers would be struck with blindness?
18. In the Letter of James, which Old Testament prophet is held up as a good role model for praying?

19. According to the book of Acts, what time of day was prayer time in the Temple?
20. Which martyr prayed, as his last words, "Lord Jesus, receive my spirit"?
21. What Roman military man was renowned for his prayers and his works of charity?
22. What sin of Israel so displeased God that the people asked Samuel to pray for them?
23. Who was noted for withdrawing to pray in lonely places?
24. According to Jesus, what group of hypocrites were noted for making lengthy prayers in public?
25. What pitiful man claimed that his prayers had always been pure?
26. Who is the chief author of the Psalms, the great prayer book of the Bible?
27. Which king prayed for Jerusalem to be delivered from the cruel conqueror Sennacherib of Assyria?
28. Which prophet was told by God not to pray for the people of Judah?
29. Which Old Testament book laments that God has covered himself with a cloud, so that no prayer can penetrate?
30. What pagan king issued a decree that people were not to pray to God, but to the king?
31. Which apostle stopped on a beach to pray with some friends?
32. Who was visited by the angel Gabriel while in prayer?
33. Who was praying on a rooftop when he received a weird vision of a sheet carrying unclean animals?
34. In the early church, what activity often accompanied prayer?
35. Whom did God spare after his brother prayed for him?
36. Which king prayed for the Lord to end the plague he had brought upon Israel?
37. According to Jesus, what kinds of people pray in the streets?
38. Which two Gospels contain the Lord's Prayer?
39. What evil man asked Peter and John to pray that he wouldn't be punished?
40. Which apostle received a vision while he was praying in the Temple at Jerusalem?
41. Where was Paul when his companions prayed for daylight to come?
42. Where was Jesus when he prayed that he would not have to be executed?

43. What elderly woman spent her days fasting and praying in the Temple?
44. In Jesus' parable of the hypocrite's prayer, what two type of men were praying in the Temple?
45. When Jesus ran the money changers out of the Temple, he claimed they had changed "the house of prayer" into what?
46. According to Paul, what sort of person should wear a head covering while praying?
47. What type of people were brought to Jesus so he could pray for them?
48. According to Paul, who helps us when we don't know how to pray?
49. Where was Jesus praying when the Holy Spirit descended upon him?
50. According to Paul, when a person speaks in tongues, what should he pray for?

"TEACH US TO PRAY" (ANSWERS)

1. Abraham (Genesis 20:17)

2. The prophet Jonah, of course (Jonah 2:1)

3. People who persecute us (Matthew 5:44)

4. Samson (Judges 16:28). The prayer was answered.

5. Hannah, the mother of Samuel (1 Samuel 1)

6. Revelation (5:8; 8:4)

7. Anoint him with oil (James 5:14)

8. Rebekah, the wife of Isaac (Genesis 25:21)

9. Jacob, who feared the wrath of Esau, whom he had cheated out of their father's blessing (Genesis 32:11)

10. Pharaoh, who was speaking to Moses after God had sent the plague of frogs on Egypt (Exodus 8:8)

11. Solomon (1 Kings 8). This is probably one of the most-read prayers in the Bible.

12. Elijah, on the run from the wrath of wicked Queen Jezebel (1 Kings 19:4)

13. Psalms—which is appropriate, since many of the Psalms are in fact prayers

14. Because "your hands are full of blood" (Isaiah 1:15)

15. Hezekiah (Isaiah 38:2-5)

16. *Continually (1 Thessalonians 5:17)*

17. *Elisha (2 Kings 6:18)*

18. *Elijah (James 5:17)*

19. *Three in the afternoon (Acts 3:1)*

20. *Stephen (Acts 7:59)*

21. *Cornelius the centurion (Acts 10)*

22. *They asked for a king to rule over them (1 Samuel 12:17-19).*

23. *Jesus (Luke 5:16)*

24. *The teachers of the Law (Mark 12:40)*

25. *Job (16:17)*

26. *David. Of the 150 Psalms, 73 are attributed to him.*

27. *Hezekiah (2 Kings 19:14-19)*

28. *Jeremiah (7:16; 14:11)*

29. *Lamentations (3:44)*

30. *Darius, king of Persia (Daniel 6)*

31. *Paul (Acts 21:5)*

32. *Daniel (Daniel 9:21)*

33. *Peter (Acts 10)*

34. *Fasting*

35. *Aaron, who was saved by the prayer of Moses. Aaron had angered God by building the gold calf idol the Israelites worshipped while Moses was on Sinai (Deuteronomy 9:20).*

36. *David. He had caused the plague by taking a census of Israel (2 Samuel 24).*

37. *Hypocrites (Matthew 6:5)*

38. *Matthew (6:9) and Luke (11:2)*

39. *Simon the magician of Samaria, who had tried to buy the power of the Holy Spirit from the apostles (Acts 8:9-24)*

40. *Paul (Acts 22:17-18). In the vision, God warned Paul to leave Jerusalem immediately.*

41. *On a storm-tossed ship in the middle of the Adriatic Sea (Acts 27:27-30)*

42. *In the garden of Gethsemane (Matthew 26:36)*

43. *The prophetess Anna, who was 84 years old when she saw the infant Jesus (Luke 2:37)*

44. *A Pharisee (the hypocrite) and a tax collector (the repentant sinner) (Luke 18:10)*

45. *"A den of robbers" (Luke 19:46)*

46. *Women. Men, on the other hand, are not to cover their heads during prayer (1 Corinthians 11).*

47. *Little children (Matthew 19:13)*

48. *The Holy Spirit (Romans 8:26)*

49. *The river Jordan, at the time of his baptism (Luke 3:21-22)*

50. *That he will be able to interpret what he has just uttered (1 Corinthians 14:13)*

👉 VOICES: DIVINE AND HUMAN

As we read the Bible and its stories of human beings who heard the voice of God or the voice of an angel, we find ourselves asking: Just how did this person *know* it was a divine voice? We aren't told. Somehow they just *knew*. The Bible has quite a few of these divine voice stories and a number of stories involving human voices as well.

1. When Moses was in the Tabernacle, where did God's voice come from?
2. Which New Testament character was the "voice crying in the wilderness"?
3. What blind father recognized Jacob's voice but was deceived by his glove-covered hands?
4. Who heard a voice that said, "Write down what you see"?
5. Where did God speak to Moses in a voice like thunder?
6. What barren woman moved her lips in prayer but made no sound?
7. According to Deuteronomy, where did the Israelites hear God's voice come from?
8. Who told Saul that obeying God's voice was more important than sacrificing animals?
9. Which Gospel mentions the voice of Rachel weeping for her children?
10. Who heard the voice of an angel ordering that a large tree be chopped down?
11. What book of the Bible says that the divine voice sounds like a waterfall?
12. Who said, "Is that your voice, David my son"?
13. To which church did Jesus say, "If any man hear my voice, and open the door, I will come in to him"?
14. Which apostle addressed the Pentecost crowd in a loud voice?
15. Who cried out at the top of her voice when she saw Samuel raised from the dead?

16. At what event did a voice from heaven say, "This is my beloved Son, in whom I am well pleased"?
17. Which boy was sleeping near the Ark of the Covenant when he heard God's voice calling to him?
18. Where was Jesus when the divine voice said, "This is my beloved Son. Listen to him"?
19. Who heard the voice of those who had been killed for proclaiming God's word?
20. Who heard God's voice after running away from Queen Jezebel?
21. Who screamed in a loud voice, asking Jesus not to punish him?
22. Which king was told by Isaiah that the king of Assyria had raised his voice up against God?
23. What was the problem of the 10 men who called to Jesus in a loud voice, begging him for mercy?
24. Who heard the "still, small voice" of God?
25. What criminal did the people of Jerusalem cry out for in a loud voice?
26. Who heard God speaking out of a whirlwind?
27. What kind of bird did John hear crying in a loud voice, "Woe, woe to the inhabiters of the earth"?
28. According to Psalm 19, what has a voice that goes out to all the world?
29. Who said that the bridegroom's friend is happy when he hears the bridegroom's voice?
30. According to Psalms, what trees are broken by the power of God's voice?
31. Who heard a voice telling of the fall of Babylon?
32. Which Gospel mentions the dead hearing the voice of the Son of God?
33. What, according to Proverbs, lifts its voice up in the streets?
34. What city in Revelation was seen as a place that would never again hear the voices of brides and grooms?
35. According to Jesus, whose voice do the sheep know?
36. What book of the Bible mentions the sweet voices of lovers in the garden?
37. In Revelation, where did the voice proclaiming the new heaven and earth come from?
38. Who heard God's voice in the Temple in the year that King Uzziah died?
39. Who came forth when Jesus called to him in a loud voice?

40. Which prophet predicted that Rachel's voice would be heard, wailing for her dead children?
41. Which Gospel mentions the voice of God speaking during Jesus' farewell address to his disciples?
42. Which prophet mentions Jerusalem with the voice of a ghost?
43. Who heard the voice of Jesus many months after Jesus' ascension to heaven?
44. Which Epistle mentions an archangel's voice in connection with the resurrection of believers?
45. Which prophet's voice did the returned Jewish exiles obey?
46. Which prophet mentions a voice crying in the wilderness?
47. Who heard the divine voice telling him to eat unclean animals?
48. Which king heard God's voice just as he was boasting about how great Babylon was?
49. Who heard the voice of God as he watched four mysterious creatures flying under a crystal dome?
50. Who recognized Peter's voice after he was miraculously delivered from prison?
51. According to Isaiah, what noble person will not lift up his voice in the streets?
52. According to Paul, what language did the divine voice use on the Damascus road?
53. Which king called to Daniel in an anguished voice?
54. Which Epistle mentions the voice of Balaam's donkey?

VOICES: DIVINE AND HUMAN (ANSWERS)

1. *Above the Ark of the Covenant (Numbers 7:89)*

3. *John the Baptist (Mark 1:3)*

3. *Isaac (Genesis 27:22)*

4. *John (Revelation 1:10)*

5. *Mount Sinai (Exodus 19:19)*

6. *Hannah (1 Samuel 1:13)*

7. *The fire (Deuteronomy 5:24)*

8. *Samuel (1 Samuel 15:22)*

9. *Matthew (2:18)*

10. *Daniel (4:14)*

11. *Revelation (1:15)*
12. *Saul (1 Samuel 26:17)*
13. *Laodicea (Revelation 3:20)*
14. *Peter (Acts 2:14)*
15. *The witch of Endor (1 Samuel 28:12)*
16. *Jesus' baptism (Matthew 3:17)*
17. *Samuel (1 Samuel 3:3-14)*
18. *On the Mount of Transfiguration (Matthew 17:5)*
19. *John (Revelation 6:10)*
20. *Elijah (1 Kings 19:13)*
21. *The demon that possessed the Gerasene demoniac (Mark 5:7)*
22. *Hezekiah (2 Kings 19:22)*
23. *Leprosy (Luke 17:13)*
24. *Elijah (1 Kings 19:12)*
25. *Barabbas (Luke 23:18)*
26. *Job (38:1)*
27. *An eagle (Revelation 8:13)*
28. *The heavens (Psalm 19:4)*
29. *John the Baptist (John 3:29)*
30. *The cedars of Lebanon (Psalm 29:5)*
31. *John (Revelation 18:2)*
32. *John (5:25)*
33. *Wisdom (Proverbs 1:20)*
34. *Babylon (Revelation 18:23)*
35. *The shepherd's (John 10:4)*
36. *Song of Solomon (2:14; 8:13)*
37. *The throne (Revelation 21:3)*
38. *Isaiah (6:8)*
39. *Lazarus (John 11:43)*
40. *Jeremiah (31:15)*
41. *John (12:28-30)*
42. *Isaiah (29:4)*
43. *Paul (Acts 9:4)*
44. *1 Thessalonians (4:16)*
45. *Haggai's (1:12)*

46. *Isaiah (40:3)*
47. *Peter (Acts 10:13-15)*
48. *Nebuchadnezzar (Daniel 4:31)*
49. *Ezekiel (1:24)*
50. *Rhoda (Acts 12:13-14)*
51. *The Lord's servant (Isaiah 42:2)*
52. *Hebrew (or, in some translations, Aramaic) (Acts 26:14)*
53. *Darius (Daniel 6:20)*
54. *2 Peter (2:16)*

 ## SIGN, SIGN, EVERYWHERE A SIGN

Say the word *sign,* and people think of road signs, store signs, etc. But in the Bible, a "sign" generally meant some showing of the divine power, an indication that "God was here."

1. What food was a sign of the deliverance from Egypt?
2. What was given as a sign that God would not flood the earth again?
3. What gift was given to Christians as a sign to unbelievers?
4. What day was a sign of completion and rest?
5. According to Jesus, which prophet's sign would be given to the unbelieving Jews?
6. Who received a wet fleece as a sign of God's approval?
7. Who prophesied a virgin conceiving a child as a sign of God's presence?
8. Who saw a "slow" sundial as a sign that Hezekiah would recover from his illness?
9. Who set up 12 stones as a sign of God's parting of the Jordan?
10. What nation suffered 10 plagues that were signs of God's power?
11. What was given as a sign that the shepherds had found the baby Jesus?
12. Which king saw an altar broken as a sign that God was speaking through a prophet?
13. Which prophet advised building a signal fire as a sign of the coming invasion of Babylon?

SIGN, SIGN, EVERYWHERE A SIGN (ANSWERS)

1. *Unleavened bread (Exodus 13:7-9)*

2. *A rainbow (Genesis 9:13-17)*

3. *Tongues (1 Corinthians 14:22)*

4. *The Sabbath (Exodus 31:13)*

5. *Jonah's (Matthew 16:4)*

6. *Gideon (Judges 6:36-38)*

7. *Isaiah (7:14)*

8. *Isaiah (2 Kings 20:8-11)*

9. *Joshua (4:6)*

10. *Egypt (Exodus 10:2)*

11. *The swaddling clothes and the manger (Luke 2:12)*

12. *Jeroboam (1 Kings 13:5)*

13. *Jeremiah (6:1)*

IN A VISION

What exactly is the difference between a vision and a dream? The Bible isn't always clear about this, but generally speaking, dreams occur while we sleep, visions while we are fully awake. At any rate, some of the great men of the Bible experienced visions, often changing their lives in a truly dramatic way.

1. Who had a vision of the Ancient of Days seated upon a throne?
2. Who looked up steadfastly into heaven and saw Jesus on the right hand of God?
3. Who knew a man who had been caught up into the "third heaven"?
4. What seer described himself as "in the Spirit" when he received his visions?
5. What did Isaiah see filling the Temple when he beheld God sitting on his throne?
6. Who saw the back of God, since he could not bear to see him face-to-face?

7. Who, besides Isaiah, saw the Lord sitting upon his throne?
8. What seer of weird visions beheld a throne like a sapphire?
9. Who saw a heavenly ladder with the Lord standing above it?
10. Who, along with Moses, saw God during the wilderness wanderings?

IN A VISION (ANSWERS)

1. Daniel (7:9)

2. Stephen (Acts 7:55)

3. Paul (2 Corinthians 12:2)

4. John, author of Revelation (Revelation 4:2)

5. The train of God's robe (Isaiah 6:1)

6. Moses (Exodus 33:23)

7. The prophet Micaiah (2 Chronicles 18:18)

8. Ezekiel (1:26)

9. Jacob (Genesis 28:12-13)

10. Aaron, Nadab, Abihu, and 70 of the Israelite elders (Exodus 24:9-10)

 ## SOMETHING THERE TO REMIND ME

Because we humans are (by nature) both forgetful and ungrateful, we need things to remind us of the times when God has looked after us. The Bible records many cases of festivals and other reminders of God's goodness. See how well you remember the reminders.

1. What feast was a reminder of the Israelites' deliverance from Egypt?
2. What ritual was to be a reminder of Christ's sacrifice of his body and blood?
3. What day of the week is a reminder of God's completed creation?
4. What was the manna put into the Ark of the Covenant a reminder of?
5. What festival was to be a memorial of the Jews' salvation from the wicked Persian Haman?

6. What feast was to be a reminder of the simple homes the Israelites had in Egypt?
7. What weather phenomenon was given as a reminder that the world would never again be destroyed by a flood?
8. Who made bronze censers (incense burners) to remind the people of Israel that no one except Aaron's descendants should serve as priests?
9. What woman did Jesus say would have her story remembered for doing a kindness to him?
10. Who set up 12 stones to remind the people of God's power in bringing them across the Jordan?

SOMETHING THERE TO REMIND ME (ANSWERS)

1. Passover (Exodus 12:11-14)

2. The Lord's Supper (Luke 22:19)

3. The Sabbath (Deuteronomy 5:15)

4. God's supernatural provision of food in the desert (Exodus 16:32)

5. Purim (Esther 9:28)

6. The Feast of Tabernacles (Leviticus 23:39-43)

7. The rainbow (Genesis 9:13-16)

8. Eleazar (Numbers 16:39-40)

9. The woman who anointed his feet at Bethany (Matthew 26:6-13)

10. Joshua (4:7)

PART 12

SACRED THINGS AND PLACES

THE REAL LOST ARK

Millions of people who had never read the Old Testament packed movie theaters in 1980 to see a slam-bang adventure movie about the quest to find the Ark of the Covenant, the wooden chest that was at the center of ancient Israel's worship rituals. Although the movie *Raiders of the Lost Ark* used the Bible as an excuse to turn loose some creepy special effects in the final scene, it conveyed (in Hollywood fashion) some of the mystery that surrounds the sacred Ark in the Bible. More than any other single object in the Bible, it symbolized the place where God "met" with his people.

1. Which Old Testament book describes the appearance of the Ark?
2. What was the wooden chest covered with?
3. Why was the Ark carried on poles?
4. The solid gold lid of the Ark was known as what?
5. What were the two "cherubim" on the lid of the Ark?
6. In what form would God appear over the Ark of the Covenant?
7. Which of the 12 tribes of Israel was responsible for care of the Ark?
8. Of what type of wood was the Ark made?
9. The Ark was involved in the miraculous crossing of what river?
10. What city's walls fell down after Israel marched around the city carrying the Ark?
11. What was the Tabernacle?
12. What saintly young man was not far from the Ark when he heard God calling to him in the night?
13. What pagan people (usually called "the uncircumcised") captured the Ark and set it in the temple of Dagon?
14. What damage did the Ark cause in the temple of Dagon?
15. When the Philistines returned the Ark to Israel, what guilt offering did they include with it?
16. For what irreverent act was Uzzah struck down?
17. What notable leader had the Ark brought to its permanent home, Jerusalem?
18. Which king, with lavish ceremony, installed the Ark in the new Temple at Jerusalem?
19. The inner part of the Temple where the Ark rested was called the what?
20. Which prophet predicted a future age in which men would no longer remember the Ark?
21. What became of the Ark?

22. According to the Apocrypha, which prophet hid the Ark away in a cave to preserve it?
23. According to the Letter to the Hebrews, what three objects were placed inside the Ark?
24. What book of the New Testament describes the Ark in the Temple accompanied by lightning, thunder, hail, and earthquakes?

THE REAL LOST ARK (ANSWERS)

1. *Exodus (see chapter 25)*

2. *Gold (what else?) (Exodus 25:11)*

3. *Human beings were not allowed to touch it (Numbers 4:15).*

4. *The "mercy seat" in most translations, though some other versions have "atonement cover" or such (Exodus 25:17-20)*

5. *Angels, probably, with wings instead of arms, their wings touching each other over the top of the Ark (Exodus 25:20). The figures seen in* Raiders of the Lost Ark *fit the Bible's description.*

6. *A cloud (Leviticus 16:2)*

7. *Levi, that is, the Levites (Deuteronomy 10:8). Both Moses and his brother, Aaron, the first high priest, were Levites.*

8. *Acacia wood (Exodus 25:10)*

9. *The Jordan (Joshua 3)*

10. *Jericho (Joshua 6)*

11. *The large tent, sometimes called the Tent of Meeting, that enclosed the Ark before the Temple was built (Exodus 26)*

12. *Samuel (1 Samuel 3:1-14)*

13. *The Philistines (1 Samuel 5:1-2)*

14. *The statue of Dagon (who is supposed to have been a sort of "merman"—half-man, half-fish) was found on the ground facedown, with his head and hands broken off (1 Samuel 5:3-4).*

15. *Five gold rats and five gold "tumors" (1 Samuel 6:4)*

16. *He touched the Ark in order to steady it, thus disobeying the rule about human hands touching the Ark (2 Samuel 6:6-7).*

17. *King David (2 Samuel 6). The Ark's presence had much to do with Jerusalem being Israel's capital.*

18. *Solomon (1 Kings 8)*

19. *Holy of Holies, or (in some translations) the Most Holy Place (Exodus 26:34)*

20. *Jeremiah (3:16). Obviously that age has not arrived yet.*

21. *No one knows. Presumably it was taken by the Babylonians when they captured Jerusalem in 587 BC. The mysteriousness of its whereabouts was, of course, the premise of the movie* Raiders of the Lost Ark.

22. *Jeremiah, according to 2 Maccabees 2:4-8*

23. *A jar of manna, Aaron's staff, and the broken tables of the Ten Commandments (Hebrews 9:4)*

24. *Revelation (11:19)*

"THE LORD IS IN HIS HOLY TEMPLE"

One thing distinguished the God of Israel from the other gods of the ancient world: He was never to be depicted in a statue or any other physical object. God is an invisible spirit, not localized in any idol or building. Even though God can be worshipped anywhere, the people of Israel had a special reverence for his Temple in Jerusalem, thinking of God as being "there" even though they knew he was present throughout all creation. Aside from that sacred place, numerous temples devoted to pagan gods are mentioned in the Bible, some of them the scenes of some colorful (and horrible) events. See how much you know about the Temple in Jerusalem, and also about the various other temples mentioned in the Bible.

1. What gruesome object did the Philistines fasten in the temple of their god Dagon?
2. Which goddess had a temple in Ephesus?
3. In Revelation, why did John not see a temple in the New Jerusalem?
4. Whose temple did Abimelech burn while the people of Shechem were hiding inside?
5. Who received a vision of the Jerusalem Temple while he was in exile in Babylon?
6. According to Paul, who is called to be the temple of God?
7. What Assyrian king was assassinated by his sons while he was worshipping in his pagan temple?
8. Who was told in a vision to measure the Temple in Jerusalem?

9. Who carried away furnishings from the Jerusalem Temple and put them in the temple at Babylon?
10. What was Jesus talking about when he spoke of destroying the temple and raising it up in three days?
11. What holy object was taken by the Philistines into the temple of Dagon, causing Dagon's image to fall down?
12. Who built the first Temple in Jerusalem?
13. Who built a temple for Baal in Samaria?
14. After Saul's death, where did the Philistines carry his armor?
15. Who asked Elisha's forgiveness for worshipping in the temple of the god Rimmon?
16. Which king issued an order allowing the Jews to rebuild the Temple in Jerusalem?
17. Who was taken to the highest point of the Jerusalem Temple?
18. Which king tricked the followers of Baal by gathering them in Baal's temple and then slaughtering them?
19. Who had an Assyrian-style altar made for the Jerusalem Temple?
20. Whom did Solomon hire to take charge of building the Temple?

"THE LORD IS IN HIS HOLY TEMPLE" (ANSWERS)

1. The head of Saul, Israel's king (1 Chronicles 10:10)

2. Diana (or Artemis) (Acts 19:27-28)

3. God and the Lamb are the temple (Revelation 21:22)

4. The temple of the god Berith (Judges 9:46-49)

5. Ezekiel (40–42)

6. All believers (1 Corinthians 6:19)

7. Sennacherib (2 Kings 19:37)

8. John (Revelation 11:1-2)

9. Nebuchadnezzar (2 Chronicles 36:7)

10. His body (John 2:19-21)

11. The Ark of the Covenant (1 Samuel 5:2-4)

12. Solomon (1 Kings 6)

13. Ahab (1 Kings 16:32)

14. The temple of Ashtoreth (1 Samuel 31:10)

15. Naaman the Syrian (2 Kings 5:18)

16. *Darius (Ezra 6:1-12)*
17. *Jesus (Matthew 4:5)*
18. *Jehu of Israel (2 Kings 10:18-27)*
19. *King Ahaz (2 Kings 16:10-17)*
20. *Huram (or Hiram) of Tyre (1 Kings 7:13-14)*

 ## JERUSALEM THE GOLDEN

No city in the world has been spoken about, written about, sung about, and argued about so much as Jerusalem. No other place in the Bible is mentioned so often (more than 700 times) or with such emotion. Even today, the ancient city—considered holy not only by Christians and Jews but by Muslims as well—evokes strong emotions, as evidenced (alas!) by the frequent violence there. Test your knowledge of the Holy City, the city called "Jerusalem the Golden" in a classic hymn.

1. Who made Jerusalem the capital of Israel?
2. What was the original name of the city?
3. What other name is commonly used in the Bible for Jerusalem?
4. Who lamented, "O Jerusalem, Jerusalem, which killest the prophets, and stonest them that are sent unto thee"?
5. What is the first book of the Bible to mention Jerusalem? (No, it isn't Genesis.)
6. What feast did Jesus go to Jerusalem to celebrate?
7. At what feast were devout men from many nations of the world gathered in Jerusalem?
8. Who was the first king of Jerusalem? (No, it wasn't David—much, much earlier, in fact.)
9. Which Old Testament book tells of rebuilding Jerusalem after the Babylonian exile?
10. Who had a dazzling vision of the New Jerusalem, the heavenly city?
11. What Egyptian pharaoh attacked Jerusalem and carried off the Temple treasures?
12. What does the name *Jerusalem* mean? (Hint: a name very inappropriate for this strife-torn city.)
13. Who, today, refer to Jerusalem as Al-Kuds al-Sharif?

14. Which king bribed Ben-Hadad, the king of Syria, by giving him all the Temple and palace treasures of Jerusalem?
15. Who claimed that no prophet could die outside Jerusalem?
16. What Assyrian king threatened Jerusalem but had his army destroyed by the Lord?
17. Who built the original walls of Jerusalem?
18. What female ruler came to Jerusalem with a camel caravan carrying luxurious gifts to Solomon?
19. What well-known Babylonian king's army broke down the walls of Jerusalem?
20. Which king's name is most closely associated with Jerusalem?
21. Which of the 12 tribes of Israel included the city of Jerusalem in its territory?
22. Which king ruled in Jerusalem when Jesus was born?
23. Who went with his family to Jerusalem when he was 12 years old?
24. In Jesus' parable of the Good Samaritan, where was the unfortunate traveler from Jerusalem headed?
25. What woman did Jesus tell that, in times to come, God would not be worshipped at Jerusalem but everywhere?
26. Why was the apostle Paul arrested in Jerusalem?
27. Which king built an aqueduct to bring water into Jerusalem?
28. What was the subject of the apostles' council at Jerusalem?
29. What valley of Jerusalem was associated with gory child sacrifice?
30. Who started a riot in Jerusalem by pitting the Pharisees against the Sadducees?
31. Who was taken to the Jerusalem Temple as an infant?
32. Which of the four Gospels refers to Jerusalem as "the Holy City" (a name commonly used in the Old Testament)?
33. Whose family went every year to Jerusalem to celebrate the Passover?
34. Who led the Jewish group from Babylon to rebuild the Temple in Jerusalem?
35. What notable building is not found in the New Jerusalem?
36. Who took Jesus to the pinnacle of the Temple in Jerusalem?
37. What massive trees were used to make the beams and pillars in the Jerusalem Temple?
38. Who prophesied judgment on the people of Jerusalem because they burned incense to idols on their roofs?
39. Who pitched a tent in Jerusalem to house the Ark of the Covenant?

40. Which king set up golden bull idols at Dan and Bethel so that his people would not go to Jerusalem to worship?
41. What Babylonian king caused famine in Jerusalem?
42. Who held a long feast when the Jerusalem Temple was dedicated?
43. Which apostles healed the crippled man at the Beautiful Gate in Jerusalem?
44. What criminal did the people of Jerusalem cry out to be released?
45. What tribe of Israel sacked Jerusalem and burned it?
46. Which king fortified Jerusalem with catapults for throwing stones?
47. What Assyrian field commander tried to intimidate King Hezekiah by speaking anti-Israel propaganda to the people of Jerusalem?
48. Which prophet went naked as a way of wailing over the fate of Jerusalem?
49. What church took up a large love offering for the needy believers in Jerusalem?
50. What evil queen was executed near Jerusalem's Horse Gate?
51. What kind of bird did Jesus compare to his love for Jerusalem?
52. Which prophet told the people of Jerusalem to cut off their hair as a sign the Lord had rejected them?
53. Where did Jesus weep over Jerusalem?
54. What pool in Jerusalem was the place where Jesus cured a man born blind?
55. In John's vision of the New Jerusalem, how many gates does the city have, and what are they made of?
56. What kind of leaves were thrown down in front of Jesus on his entry into Jerusalem?
57. Who brought costly stones for the foundation of the Temple in Jerusalem?
58. Which two apostles were put into prison in Jerusalem for preaching the gospel?
59. What world conqueror carried away furnishings from the Jerusalem Temple and put them in the temple at Babylon?
60. What river flows through Jerusalem?
61. What book of the Bible mentions people who had worn purple pawing through the garbage of Jerusalem?
62. How many angels will be at the gates of the New Jerusalem?
63. Which apostle referred to heaven as the "Jerusalem which is above"?
64. What Jerusalem tower collapsed, killing 18 men?
65. What pool in Jerusalem was a healing place when an angel came by and stirred up its waters?

66. Who knelt toward Jerusalem and prayed looking out of his eastern window in Babylon?

JERUSALEM THE GOLDEN (ANSWERS)

1. David, who moved the capital there from Hebron (2 Samuel 5:9)

2. Jebus, home of the Jebusites, who were finally driven out by David (2 Samuel 5)

3. Zion, which is the name of one of the hills of Jerusalem. The name occurs many times in the Bible as a synonym for the whole city.

4. Jesus (Luke 13:34)

5. Joshua (10:1)

6. The Passover (John 2:13)

7. Pentecost (Acts 2)

8. We don't know. The first one mentioned in the Bible is Adonizedek, who contended with the conquering Joshua (Joshua 10:1).

9. Nehemiah

10. John, author of Revelation

11. Shishak (1 Kings 14:26)

12. "Peace," in Hebrew

13. Muslims. In Arabic, the name means "the sanctuary."

14. Asa (1 Kings 15)

15. Jesus (Luke 13:33)

16. Sennacherib (2 Kings 18–19)

17. Solomon (1 Kings 3:1)

18. The queen of Sheba (1 Kings 10:2)

19. Nebuchadnezzar (2 Kings 25:1)

20. David. Jerusalem is referred to as "the City of David" dozens of times in the Old Testament.

21. Benjamin, originally, although the city's close association with David made Jerusalem the key city of the tribe of Judah. (See Judges 1:21.)

22. Herod (Matthew 2:1)

23. Jesus (Luke 2:42)

24. Jericho (Luke 10:30)

25. The woman at the well (John 4)

26. For bringing a Gentile (Trophimus the Ephesian) into the Temple area, which was restricted only to Jews (Acts 21:27-29)

27. Hezekiah (2 Kings 20:20)

28. The council at Jerusalem met to determine whether Gentiles had to be circumcised and obey the whole law of Moses in order to be Christians (Acts 15).

29. The valley of Hinnom (2 Kings 23:10). It had been the place where some Jews sacrificed their children to the heathen god Molech, a practice denounced by the Hebrew prophets.

30. Paul, at his trial before the Sanhedrin (Acts 23). Paul started the riot by mentioning the resurrection, which the Pharisees believed in and the Sadducees denied.

31. Jesus (Luke 2:22)

32. Matthew (4:9; 27:53), which is appropriate, since Matthew's is the most Jewish of the four Gospels.

33. Jesus' (Luke 2:41)

34. Zerubbabel (Ezra 5)

35. The Temple (Revelation 21). There is no Temple because God himself is in the city.

36. The devil (Matthew 4:5-7)

37. The cedars of Lebanon (1 Kings 5:6)

38. Jeremiah (19:13)

39. David (1 Chronicles 15:1)

40. King Jeroboam (1 Kings 12:26-31)

41. Nebuchadnezzar (2 Kings 25:1-3)

42. Solomon (1 Kings 8:65)

43. Peter and John (Acts 3:2)

44. Barabbas (Luke 23:18), who was imprisoned at the same time as Jesus

45. Judah (Judges 1:8). This occurred at the time when Jerusalem was considered to be within the tribe of Benjamin's territory.

46. Uzziah (2 Chronicles 26:14-15)

47. Rabshakeh (2 Kings 18:17-37)

48. The prophet Micah (1:8)

49. Antioch (Acts 11:30)

50. Athaliah, Ahab's daughter (2 Chronicles 23:15)

51. A hen gathering her chicks (Matthew 23:37)

52. Jeremiah (7:29)

53. The Mount of Olives (Luke 19:41)

54. The pool of Siloam (John 9:7-11)

55. *Twelve, made of pearl (as in "pearly gates") (Revelation 21)*
56. *Palm leaves (as in "Palm Sunday") (John 12:13)*
57. *Solomon (1 Kings 5:17)*
58. *Peter and John (Acts 4:3)*
59. *Nebuchadnezzar (2 Chronicles 36:7)*
60. *None does. Jerusalem is a rarity among world cities in that it does not lie on a river. Jerusalem's water supply has always presented problems.*
61. *Lamentations (4:5). The "purple" refers to expensive clothing—meaning, the rich were reduced to scavenging through garbage to find food.*
62. *Twelve (Revelation 21:12)*
63. *Paul (Galatians 4:26)*
64. *The tower of Siloam (Luke 13:4)*
65. *The pool of Bethesda (John 5)*
66. *Daniel (6:10)*

 ## ONE DAY OUT OF SEVEN: THE SABBATH

We take our seven-day week for granted, forgetting that it was the Hebrews who gave the world the concept of a seven-day week with one day of rest. Test your knowledge of the Sabbath day.

1. Who instituted the Sabbath day rest?
2. Which of the Ten Commandments says that the Sabbath day must be kept holy?
3. What was the penalty in Israel for working on the Sabbath?
4. What kind of work was the man described in Numbers 15:32-36 doing on the Sabbath that led him to be put to death?
5. When does the Sabbath officially begin?
6. What Jewish leader was deeply offended when he saw people engaging in trade on the Sabbath in Jerusalem?
7. According to Matthew's Gospel, what Sabbath healing caused the Pharisees to plot to kill Jesus?
8. Whom did Jesus heal in a synagogue on the Sabbath?
9. What miraculous food did God allow the Israelites to gather for only six days?
10. Which Old Testament books were read in the synagogues on the Sabbath?

11. What was the normal offering made on the Sabbath day?
12. Which psalm is called "a song for the Sabbath day"?
13. Who criticized Jesus for healing on the Sabbath?
14. What led the early Christians to start observing the first day of the week as holy instead of the seventh day?

ONE DAY OUT OF SEVEN: THE SABBATH (ANSWERS)

1. God did, by resting on the seventh day after six days of labor (Genesis 2:2-3). Interestingly enough, the word sabbath itself does not occur in the book of Genesis.

2. The fourth (Exodus 20:8-11)

3. Death (Exodus 31:14). Actually, we know of only one person who was actually put to death for this offense.

4. Gathering sticks. This occurred while the Israelites were in the wilderness.

5. On Friday evening (sundown), ending at Saturday evening

6. Nehemiah (13:15)

7. The healing of the man with the withered hand (Matthew 12:10-14)

8. The Gospels include accounts of at least two people that Jesus healed in a synagogue on a Sabbath: a crippled woman (Luke 13:10-17), and a man with a shriveled hand (Matthew 12:9-14; Mark 3:1-5; Luke 6:6-11).

9. The manna in the wilderness (Exodus 16). On the sixth day they were supposed to gather enough to see them through the seventh day.

10. The books of Moses (the first five books) (Acts 15:21)

11. Two lambs (Numbers 28:9-10)

12. Psalm 92. Interestingly, it does not mention the Sabbath.

13. The Pharisees, who apparently regarded healing as work, which was forbidden on the Sabbath (Luke 13:14)

14. The fact that Jesus' resurrection had been on the first day of the week (Acts 2:1; 1 Corinthians 16:1-2).

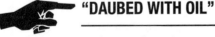 ## "DAUBED WITH OIL"

You'll run across the word *anoint* many times in the Bible, and in the simplest physical sense, it means to daub or pour oil on a person or thing. But the real meaning of anoint goes way beyond that, for the ritual signified that the person or thing had been dedicated to the service of God. You might almost say that the anointing was as if God had "marked his territory." The idea had a powerful influence throughout the centuries. Kings were (and still are) anointed with oil at their coronations, and throughout history the ruler was often referred to as "the Lord's anointed." See how much you know about the people and objects that were "marked for God."

1. What common (and extremely important) New Testament word means "anointed"?
2. What holy man was anointed by an immoral woman?
3. What substance was usually used for anointing in Israel?
4. Who, according to James, should anoint the sick believer with oil?
5. Whom did Moses anoint with the blood of a ram?
6. Who anointed a stone and dedicated it to God?
7. What revered judge anointed Saul?
8. Which priest anointed Solomon king?
9. Who was anointed by the Holy Spirit?
10. What Persian king was considered to be God's anointed one?
11. What Old Testament word means "anointed"?
12. Which apostle told the early Christians that all believers were anointed by the Holy Spirit?
13. Who anointed the Tabernacle with oil?
14. Which leader anointed David as king?
15. What person was, prior to his fall, anointed by God?
16. Where did the men of Judah gather to anoint David as their king?
17. Which New Testament letter says believers are "anointed by the Holy One"?

"DAUBED WITH OIL" (ANSWERS)

1. *Christ. "Jesus Christ" literally means "Jesus the anointed one."*

2. *Jesus (Luke 7:38)*

3. *Olive oil*

4. *The church elders (James 5:14)*

5. *Aaron and his sons (Leviticus 8:23)*

6. *Jacob (Genesis 28:18)*

7. *Samuel (1 Samuel 9:16)*

8. *Zadok (1 Kings 1:39)*

9. *Jesus (Matthew 3:16)*

10. *Cyrus (Isaiah 45:1)*

11. *Messiah*

12. *Paul (2 Corinthians 1:21)*

13. *Moses (Exodus 40:9)*

14. *Samuel (1 Samuel 16:12)*

15. *Lucifer (Ezekiel 28:14—some translations have "the king of Tyre," not Lucifer)*

16. *Hebron (2 Samuel 2:4)*

17. *1 John (2:20)*

WAYWARD WORDS: BLASPHEMY

Deliberately insulting, slandering, or dishonoring God is referred to as blasphemy, and the Bible takes it very seriously. Humans have a habit of saying cruel, malicious things about each other—and, even worse, about the God who made them.

1. Which of the Ten Commandments prohibits blasphemy?
2. In Revelation, who "opened his mouth in blasphemy against God"?
3. According to Jesus, what form of blasphemy cannot be forgiven?
4. Which apostle admitted he had been a blasphemer in his pre-Christian days?
5. In Leviticus, what punishment is given to a blasphemer?
6. What official tore his robe because he believed Jesus was a blasphemer?
7. What Christian martyr was accused of blaspheming God and the law of Moses?
8. Who was denounced as a blasphemer because he claimed the power to forgive sins?
9. Who had tried to get Jewish Christians to blaspheme by renouncing their faith?
10. In Acts 19, Paul was accused of blaspheming against what pagan goddess?

11. In which Gospel do the Jews wish to stone Jesus for claiming to be God's Son?

12. In 2 Peter, what people "blaspheme in matters they do not understand"?

WAYWARD WORDS: BLASPHEMY (ANSWERS)

1. *The third, not taking the name of God in vain (Exodus 20:7)*

2. *The Beast (Revelation 13:1)*

3. *Blaspheming against the Holy Spirit (Matthew 12:31-32)*

4. *Paul (1 Timothy 1:13). He regarded his former persecution of Christians as a form of blasphemy.*

5. *Death by stoning (Leviticus 24:16-23)*

6. *The Jewish high priest (Matthew 26:65). Tearing the robe was a sign of his intense rage.*

7. *Stephen (Acts 6:11). As in Leviticus 24, he was given the legal punishment for blasphemy, stoning.*

8. *Jesus (Mark 2:7)*

9. *Paul, in his pre-Christian life (Acts 26:11)*

10. *Artemis*

11. *John (10:33-36)*

12. *False teachers (2 Peter 2:12)*

PART 13

GOD IN NATURE

BROTHER SUN, SISTER MOON, AND OTHER HEAVENLY BODIES

Ancient man was fascinated by the sun, the moon, the stars, and the planets. And so are we, investing huge sums of time and money sending men and robots to explore these faraway locales. But while we're trying to get "up close and personal" with the heavenly bodies, ancient man really did think of them as "heavenly," regarding them as gods and worshipping them. The people of ancient Israel were commanded by God *not* to worship the things in the skies—after all, fascinating as these things are, they are creations of God, not gods themselves. But even so, the lights of heaven did fascinate the Israelites, just as they fascinate us today.

1. What city has no need of the light of the sun?
2. On what day of creation did God make the sun and moon?
3. What event was going on when the sun was darkened and the curtain in the Temple was torn in two?
4. What miraculous food melted in the heat of the sun?
5. Who warned Israel against worshipping the sun, moon, and stars?
6. Who commanded the sun and moon to stand still while the Israelites defeated the Amorites in battle?
7. What happened when an angel poured out the fourth bowl of wrath on the sun?
8. Who peeved his 11 jealous brothers by telling them of his dream of 11 stars bowing down to him?
9. What praise-filled book proclaims, "Praise ye him, sun and moon: praise him, all ye stars of light"?
10. What woman lamented the sun darkening her skin? (Remember, this was long before people were conscious of melanoma and premature aging.)
11. According to Genesis, why was the moon created?
12. What denoted the beginning of the month for the Israelites?
13. What was the name of the bizarre star that caused the earth's waters to become undrinkable?
14. Which Old Testament book proclaims that God is a "sun and shield"?
15. Which prophet predicted the coming of the "sun of righteousness," who has been identified with Christ?
16. What items in Jerusalem proved that some of the Israelites worshipped the sun?

17. Which prophet stood in the Temple court and saw people bowing to worship the sun?
18. What righteous king on his sickbed watched the sun go miraculously backward?
19. Which prophet fainted from the heat of the sun, until God made a shady vine for him?
20. Who were the wise men speaking to when they said, "We have seen his star in the east, and are come to worship him"?
21. Where was Jesus when his face shone like the sun?
22. What is the only book of the Bible to mention constellations by name?
23. Who was in such a violent storm at sea that for days he didn't see the sun or stars?
24. Which prophet condemned people worshipping a god in the form of a star?
25. Who was told by God that his descendants would be as numerous as the stars?
26. Who predicted that at the end of time, the stars would fall from the heavens?
27. What color did the moon become when the sixth seal (in Revelation) was broken open?
28. What wicked king of Judah built altars for the worship of Baal and the stars?
29. Which apostle claimed he had been struck down at midday by a light brighter than the sun?

BROTHER SUN, SISTER MOON, AND OTHER HEAVENLY BODIES (ANSWERS)

1. The New Jerusalem, heaven (Revelation 22:5)

2. The fourth day (Genesis 1:14-19). Interestingly, light was made on the second day, before the sun and moon.

3. Jesus had died on the cross (Luke 23:45).

4. The manna the Israelites ate in the wilderness (Exodus 16:21)

5. Moses (Deuteronomy 4:19). The warning was needed, since most of the ancient cultures did indeed worship the heavenly bodies.

6. Joshua (10:12-13)

7. The sun scorched people, who then cursed God (Revelation 16:8-9).

8. Joseph, Jacob's son (Genesis 37:9)

9. Psalms (148:3)

10. The bride in the Song of Solomon (1:6)

11. To denote the passing of weeks and seasons (Genesis 1:14)

12. The new moon, which is often mentioned in the Old Testament as being a special day

13. Wormwood, a name denoting bitterness (Revelation 8:10-11)

14. Psalms (84:11). This is poetic and is not intended to literally identify God with the sun.

15. Malachi (4:2)

16. Horses (probably horse statues) and chariots dedicated to the sun (2 Kings 23:11)

17. Ezekiel (8:16)

18. Hezekiah (Isaiah 38:7-8)

19. Jonah (4:8)

20. Herod (Matthew 2:2)

21. On the Mount of Transfiguration, with Moses and Elijah (Matthew 17:2)

22. Job, which mentions Orion (9:9), the Pleiades (38:31), the Bear (9:9), and others

23. The apostle Paul (Acts 27:20)

24. Amos (5:26), who may have been referring to a star-shaped idol

25. Abraham (Genesis 22:17)

26. Jesus (Mark 13:25)

27. Bloodred (Revelation 6:12)

28. Manasseh (2 Kings 21:3-5)

29. The apostle Paul (Acts 26:13)

WHEN "WIND" IS REALLY *WIND*

Something that perplexes Bible translators is this: Both in Hebrew and Greek, the words for "wind" and "spirit" (and also "breath") are the same. (It's *ruach* in Hebrew, *pneuma* in Greek. You can see the Greek root in the English words *pneumonia* and *pneumatic*.) Apparently, people in the ancient world realized that wind, like a spirit, is mysterious and unpredictable, as Jesus observed in John 3:8.

Generally, the translator has to figure out from the context whether to use *wind* or *spirit*, and in most cases it is clear enough. At any rate, the questions below deal with actual wind.

1. Which prophet experienced a furious wind that split the hills and shattered the rocks?
2. Where were the disciples when they heard a noise that sounded like a mighty wind filling the house they had gathered in?
3. Who had a dream of seven heads of grain being scorched by a hot east wind?
4. What loathsome creatures did God drive into Egypt with an east wind?
5. Which prophet was told to cut off his hair and scatter a third of it in the wind?
6. How long did the wind that parted the Red Sea blow?
7. According to James, what sort of person is like a wave tossed by the wind?
8. Which Old Testament book speaks of life as a "chasing after the wind"?
9. Whose children were destroyed when a strong wind struck the house they were banqueting in?
10. According to the book of Job, what directional wind will inevitably strike down the wicked?
11. Which Epistle compares false teachers to rainless clouds blown about by the wind?
12. According to Psalms, what sort of people are like chaff that the wind blows away?
13. Whom did God address from a whirlwind?
14. According to Jesus, what sort of man sees his house fall when the winds beat against it?
15. What was blown out of Egypt by a strong west wind?
16. Who had a dream about a statue that crumbled into dust that was driven away by the wind?
17. Which prophet spoke of people who sow a wind and reap a whirlwind?
18. What runaway boarded a ship that the Lord struck with a strong wind?
19. Which prophet suffered from a hot east wind after his shade plant was eaten by a worm?
20. Who lost faith and began to flounder when he noticed the strong wind on a lake?
21. Who was saved from being a full-time sailor when God sent a wind to dry up the flood waters?
22. What food did God bring to the Israelites by using a wind?

23. According to the book of Job, which directional wind punishes the land with its heat?
24. According to Revelation, what sort of creatures held back the winds from blowing on the earth?
25. Which prophet had a vision of the four winds lashing the surface of the oceans?
26. In which book of the Bible does a woman call on the north wind and south wind to blow on her garden?
27. According to Proverbs, what kind of woman is as hard to restrain as the wind itself?

WHEN "WIND" IS REALLY WIND (ANSWERS)

1. *Elijah (1 Kings 19:11)*

2. *Jerusalem (Acts 2:2)*

3. *Pharaoh (Genesis 41:6)*

4. *Locusts (Exodus 10:13)*

5. *Ezekiel (5:2)*

6. *All night (Exodus 14:21)*

7. *A doubter (James 1:6)*

8. *Ecclesiastes (1:14; 2:11; 4:4; etc.). This is a classic case of translators not being sure whether the Hebrew word should be translated "wind" or "spirit," as you can see in the King James Version, which has "vexation of spirit" instead of (in the modern versions) "chasing the wind" or "striving after wind."*

9. *Job's (Job 1:19)*

10. *East (Job 27:21)*

11. *Jude (1:12)*

12. *The wicked (Psalm 1:4)*

13. *Job (38:1)*

14. *The foolish man who builds on the sand (Matthew 7:26-27)*

15. *Locusts (Exodus 10:19)*

16. *Nebuchadnezzar (Daniel 2:35)*

17. *Hosea (8:7)*

18. *Jonah (1:4)*

19. *Jonah (4:8)*

20. *Peter (Matthew 14:30)*

21. *Noah (Genesis 8:1)*
22. *Quails (Numbers 11:31)*
23. *South (Job 37:17)*
24. *Four angels (Revelation 7:1)*
25. *Daniel (7:2)*
26. *Song of Solomon (4:16)*
27. *A nagging wife (Proverbs 27:16)*

THOSE MYSTERIOUS CLOUDS

In our scientifically minded era, we know that clouds are just big accumulations of water vapor suspended in the air, but they still fascinate us with their strange and changing shapes. They fascinated the people of the Bible as well, not just the normal rain clouds of the atmosphere, but also the supernatural clouds in which God made his presence known.

1. At what critical spot did the pillar of cloud separate the Egyptians from the Israelites?
2. What sign did God set in the clouds to indicate that he would never again flood the world?
3. Did the pillar of cloud in the wilderness lead the Israelites by day or by night?
4. Which prophet's servant saw a little cloud "like a man's hand"?
5. Which Epistle talks about a "cloud of witnesses"?
6. What two long-dead men were with Jesus when a shining cloud covered them?
7. Which Epistle mentions believers being caught up in the clouds to meet the Lord?
8. According to Jesus, what person will appear coming in glory on the clouds of heaven?
9. In Revelation, what two martyred men are raised by God and then taken to heaven in a cloud?
10. On what mountain did God appear in the form of a cloud?
11. What object of the Israelites was notable for having the cloud of God's glory upon it?
12. Which king, seeing the cloud in the Temple, said that God had chosen to live in clouds and darkness?

13. What portable object did the cloud of God's glory appear over?
14. Which Epistle compares false teachers to clouds that bring no rain?
15. At what event did a cloud hide Jesus from the apostles' sight?
16. According to Zephaniah, what special day will be a day of clouds and blackness?

THOSE MYSTERIOUS CLOUDS (ANSWERS)

1. By the Red Sea (Exodus 14:20)

2. The rainbow (Genesis 9:13)

3. By day (Exodus 13:21-22)

4. Elijah (1 Kings 18:44)

5. Hebrews (12:1)

6. Moses and Elijah (Matthew 17:5). This was the famous event known as the Transfiguration.

7. 1 Thessalonians (4:17)

8. The Son of Man (Matthew 24:30)

9. The two witnesses (Revelation 11:12)

10. Sinai (Exodus 19:9)

11. The Tabernacle (Exodus 40:34)

12. Solomon (1 Kings 8:10-11)

13. The Ark of the Covenant (Leviticus 16:2)

14. Jude (1:12)

15. The Ascension (Acts 1:9)

16. The Day of the Lord (Zephaniah 1:15)

SALT OF THE EARTH

We take salt for granted these days—in fact, so easily available is it that many folks have to reduce their salt intake. This was not a problem in Bible times, when salt was a valuable commodity, as it was for most of human history. This very common but very essential substance figures in some of the great sayings of the Bible and is also one of the most mysterious occurrences of the Old Testament (see question 1).

1. Who was turned into a pillar of salt?
2. At what stage of life were people rubbed down with salt?
3. Who purified Jericho's water supply by throwing salt into it?
4. What lake is called the Salt Sea in Genesis 14:3?
5. By what other name is the Salt Sea (Dead Sea) known in the Old Testament?
6. Who told Christians to let their speech always be "seasoned with salt"?
7. What book of the Old Testament commands salting the meat offered as sacrifices?
8. Who annihilated the city of Shechem and then sowed its soil with salt?
9. Who asked the question "Can that which is unsavory be eaten without salt"?
10. In which Gospel does Jesus say, "Everyone shall be salted with fire"?
11. "Ye are the salt of the earth" is from the Sermon on the Mount in which Gospel?

SALT OF THE EARTH (ANSWERS)

1. *Lot's wife (Genesis 19:26), who was punished for looking back on the destroyed city of Sodom*

2. *As newborn infants (Ezekiel 16:4), apparently to purify them, though the verse only alludes to the practice and offers no further explanation*

3. *Elisha (2 Kings 2:19-22)*

4. *The Dead Sea. The reason the Dead Sea is dead is its high salt content; nothing can live in it.*

5. *The Sea of the Arabah (Deuteronomy 3:17)*

6. *Paul (Colossians 4:6)*

7. *Leviticus (2:13)*

8. *Abimelech (Judges 9:45), who apparently wanted to make the land unfruitful forever*

9. *Job (6:6)*

10. *Mark (9:49)*

11. *Matthew (5:13)*

PART 14

HOLY COMPANY

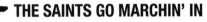 **THE SAINTS GO MARCHIN' IN**

For a Catholic or Orthodox Christian, you know that a "saint" is a person believed to be in heaven already. But the Bible has a broader view of things: A saint is anyone on earth or in heaven who is committed to God. Some are "big names" in Scripture, but many of the saints mentioned in the Bible are nameless—good people who somehow, mysteriously and faithfully, lived a righteous life in an extremely unrighteous world.

1. What future apostle had a reputation as a persecutor of saints?
2. In what book of the Bible would you find "Precious in the sight of the Lord is the death of his saints"?
3. In Daniel, what mysterious heavenly figure pronounced judgment in favor of the saints?
4. In Revelation, what fragrant substance symbolizes the prayers of the saints?
5. Which Epistle was addressed to "the saints throughout Achaia"?
6. Which Epistle mentions that there were saints even in Caesar's household?
7. In Revelation, what fabric stands for the righteous deeds of the saints?
8. According to Romans 8, who intercedes for the saints?
9. What book of the Bible laments that the wicked have given the flesh of saints to the beasts of the earth?
10. What Old Testament woman proclaimed that God guards the feet of his saints?
11. In which book of the Bible does a beast with iron teeth and bronze claws war against the saints?
12. In Psalm 85, what does God promise to his saints?
13. Who admitted he had thrown many saints in prison?
14. In which Epistle does Paul state that the saints will "judge the world"?
15. Which Epistle refers to widows washing the feet of saints?
16. Paul was collecting money for the poor saints in what place?
17. What book of the Bible states that the Lord's saints lack nothing?
18. According to Paul, what group of people should keep silent in any gathering of the saints?
19. In Revelation, who made war on the saints?
20. Which Epistle is addressed to the saints, bishops, and deacons?

21. What woman did Paul request the Roman Christians to receive "in a manner worthy of the saints"?
22. Which Epistle speaks of the "mystery that has been hidden for ages," now revealed to the saints?
23. What very short Epistle was addressed to one who had "refreshed the hearts of the saints"?
24. In Revelation, what woman is "drunk with the blood of the saints"?
25. What book of the Bible refers to the saints as the "glorious ones" that delight the Lord?
26. Who prayed that the saints could grasp "how wide and long and high and deep is the love of Christ"?

THE SAINTS GO MARCHIN' IN (ANSWERS)

1. Saul, later more famous as Paul (Acts 9:13)

2. Psalms (116:15)

3. The Ancient of Days (Daniel 7:22)

4. Incense (Revelation 5:8)

5. 2 Corinthians. Achaia was the province that included the city of Corinth.

6. Philippians (4:22)

7. Clean linen (19:8)

8. The Holy Spirit (8:27)

9. Psalms (79:2)

10. Hannah, mother of Samuel (1 Samuel 2:9)

11. Daniel (7:19-22)

12. Peace (85:8)

13. Paul (Acts 26:10)

14. 1 Corinthians (6:2)

15. 1 Timothy (5:10)

16. Jerusalem (Romans 15:25-27)

17. Psalms (34:9)

18. Women (1 Corinthians 14:33-35). This passage has generated a lot of controversy and led to accusations of Paul being antiwoman.

19. The Beast (13:7)

20. Philippians. Some translations have "overseers" instead of "bishops."

21. *Phoebe (Romans 16:2)*
22. *Colossians (1:26)*
23. *Philemon (see verse 7)*
24. *The "scarlet woman," Babylon, symbolizing the world's immorality and corruption (Revelation 17:6)*
25. *Psalms (16:3)*
26. *Paul (Ephesians 3:18)*

MEN OF GOD, BY CALLING

How many men in the Bible are called "men of God"? Surprisingly, very few. Test your knowledge of the select handful who received that name.

1. Who is the first man in the Bible to be called "man of God"?
2. What strongman's birth was foretold by a man of God "with a face like an angel"?
3. Which of Paul's young followers did he refer to as a "man of God"?
4. Who referred to Jesus as a man of God?
5. What aged priest received a visit from a man of God, who prophesied doom for the priest's greedy, lecherous sons?
6. What man of God told King Rehoboam of Judah not to make war on the other tribes of Israel?
7. What fiery prophet of the Lord was called "man of God"?
8. Who was the only king of Israel referred to as "man of God"?
9. According to Paul, what did God give us so that "the man of God may be perfect"?
10. What future king sought out Samuel, "the man of God," in order to find out where his lost donkeys were?
11. Which king received a bad case of arthritis when a man of God prophesied against him?
12. Which king spared the tomb of a man of God when he was desecrating tombs at a pagan shrine?
13. Which prophet received 40 camel-loads of luxury goods from the dying king of Syria?

14. What mighty prophet of the Old Testament told the king of Israel's military men, "If I be a man of God, let fire come down from heaven, and consume thee and thy fifty men"?

15. What man of God healed a pagan king of leprosy by dipping him seven times in the Jordan River?

MEN OF GOD, BY CALLING (ANSWERS)

1. *Moses (Deuteronomy 33:1)*

2. *Samson's (Judges 13:6)*

3. *Timothy (1 Timothy 6:11)*

4. *No one. Surprisingly, Jesus is never called this.*

5. *Eli, Samuel's mentor, and father of the corrupt Hophni and Phinehas (1 Samuel 2:27-36)*

6. *The prophet Shemaiah (1 Kings 12:22)*

7. *Elijah (1 Kings 17:18)*

8. *David, of course (2 Chronicles 8:14)*

9. *The Scriptures (2 Timothy 3:16-17)*

10. *Saul (1 Samuel 9:6)*

11. *Jeroboam, who was offering incense on a pagan altar when the prophet came. When Jeroboam stretched out his hand and said, "Arrest him!" the king's hand withered (1 Kings 13:1-4).*

12. *Josiah, whose birth and deeds had been foretold by this very man of God (2 Kings 23:16-18)*

13. *Elisha, who received the gifts from the king Ben-hadad, who wanted the prophet to foretell whether he would die or not (2 Kings 8:7-9)*

14. *Elijah, who was being pursued by wicked King Ahaziah's soldiers (2 Kings 1:10)*

15. *Elisha, who cured the Syrian army commander Naaman (2 Kings 5)*

 THE HOLY APOSTLES

Speaking of mysteries, here is a big one: How did 12 working-class men in ancient Palestine (an insignificant corner of the mighty Roman Empire) manage to spread a faith that in time reached every corner of the globe? It's pretty amazing, really—four fishermen, a tax collector, a political agitator, and the others, a motley crew, yet through the mysterious workings of God these companions of Jesus have had their names enshrined in churches and a million other locales. As seen in the New Testament, they are a pretty human group, yet through their weaknesses and failings, some divine light still manages to shine through. See how much you know about the famous Twelve—and the other New Testament folks who are referred to as "apostles."

1. Who was not one of the original 12 apostles, though he probably labored harder for the gospel than anyone else?
2. Who succeeded Judas Iscariot as an apostle?
3. Which apostle was a tax collector from Capernaum?
4. According to tradition, which apostle was a missionary to India?
5. Which apostle was probably crucified in Rome, head downward?
6. Who was the only one of the 12 apostles not from Galilee?
7. According to tradition, how did Simon the Zealot die?
8. Who was called the "beloved" disciple?
9. Who, according to tradition, preached in Assyria and Persia and died a martyr in Persia?
10. Who was the first apostle to be martyred?
11. According to church tradition, which apostle was crucified in Egypt?
12. Which apostle, originally a disciple of John the Baptist, was supposed to have been crucified on an X-shaped cross?
13. Which of the apostles were fishermen?
14. Of all the apostles, who is the only one who is believed to have died a natural death?
15. Who is thought to have provided the background information for the Gospel of Mark?
16. Who, according to tradition, preached in Phrygia?
17. What hardworking companion of Paul's was called an apostle?
18. In Romans 16, whom does Paul refer to as apostles?
19. Who is supposed to have been a missionary to Armenia?
20. Who preached at Pentecost?
21. Who is thought to have suffered martyrdom in Ethiopia?
22. Who was banished to the island of Patmos?
23. According to tradition, which apostle was killed by flaying (skinning)?
24. Who is thought to have been pushed from a summit of the Temple, then beaten to death?

25. By what other name was Matthew known?
26. Who is supposed to have been executed by being sawn in pieces?
27. Who is famous for doubting that Jesus really had risen from the dead?
28. What was Peter's original name?
29. Who were the sons of Zebedee?
30. Who was the apostle to the Gentiles?
31. What was Paul's original name?
32. Who brought Peter to Jesus?
33. Who had Jesus as a guest at a meal with many tax collectors?
34. Who, according to Catholic tradition, was the first pope?
35. Who requested special places for themselves in Jesus' Kingdom?
36. Who is identified with Nathanael of Cana, mentioned in John 1:45?
37. Who brought Nathanael to Jesus?
38. Who said to Jesus, "My Lord and my God"?
39. Which disciple asked Jesus to show them the Father?
40. Who were the "sons of thunder"?
41. Who was with Jesus at the Transfiguration?
42. Who was the only apostle we know for sure was married?
43. In which Gospel is John not mentioned by name?
44. Who spoke for all the apostles at Caesarea Philippi?
45. Who, in John's Gospel, is the "son of perdition"?
46. Who criticized the woman who anointed Jesus?
47. Who was absent when the risen Jesus appeared to the apostles?
48. Which disciple brought Greeks to Jesus?
49. Which apostle had Silas as a traveling companion on his second journey?
50. Which apostles were present at the raising of Jairus's daughter?
51. Which apostle was a natural Roman citizen?
52. Who healed the crippled man at the Beautiful Gate?
53. Who healed a paralytic named Aeneas in Lydda?
54. Who was baptized by a man named Ananias?
55. What was Barnabas's original name?
56. Whom did the Sanhedrin put in jail for disturbing the peace?
57. Who raised a young man named Eutychus from the dead?
58. Whom did Paul oppose when he met him in Antioch?
59. Who asked Jesus why he intended to show himself to the disciples but not to the world?
60. To whom did Jesus say, "Feed my lambs"?
61. Who preached to the intellectuals of Athens?

62. Who had a vision of a sheet filled with unclean animals?
63. Whom did Jesus say he would make into fishers of men?
64. Who told Jesus he had seen a man driving out demons in Jesus' name?
65. Which disciples did Jesus ask to keep watch while he prayed in Gethsemane?
66. Who expressed dismay over how to feed the 5,000?
67. Who had a dispute with a Greek silversmith named Demetrius?
68. Who brought the boy with loaves and fishes to Jesus?
69. Who was reluctant to have Jesus wash his feet?
70. Which apostle was bitten by a viper on the island of Malta?
71. Which brother of Jesus does Paul call an apostle?
72. Which young friend of Paul's, a coauthor of 1 Thessalonians, was an apostle?
73. Which apostle, a traveling companion of Paul's, was sometimes called Silvanus?
74. According to tradition, which apostle lived to a ripe old age after miraculously surviving being boiled in oil?

THE HOLY APOSTLES (ANSWERS)

1. Paul

2. Matthias (Acts 1:23-26)

3. Matthew

4. Thomas

5. Peter

6. Judas Iscariot

7. Crucifixion

8. John

9. Jude

10. James (Acts 12:1-2)

11. James the Less

12. Andrew

13. Peter, Andrew, James, John

14. John

15. Peter

16. *Philip*

17. *Barnabas (Acts 13:1-3; 14:4)*

18. *Andronicus and Junias*

19. *Bartholomew*

20. *Peter (Acts 2)*

21. *Matthias*

22. *John*

23. *Bartholomew*

24. *James the Less*

25. *Levi*

26. *Simon the Zealot*

27. *Thomas (John 21:25)*

28. *Simon*

29. *James and John*

30. *Paul*

31. *Saul*

32. *Andrew*

33. *Matthew (Luke 5:29)*

34. *Peter*

35. *James and John (Mark 10:39)*

36. *Bartholomew*

37. *Philip (John 1:43-46)*

38. *Thomas (John 20:28)*

39. *Philip (John 14:8)*

40. *James and John (Mark 3:17)*

41. *Peter, James, and John (Mark 9:2)*

42. *Peter (Mark 1:30)*

43. *John*

44. *Peter (Mark 8:27-33)*

45. *Judas Iscariot (John 17:12)*

46. *Judas Iscariot (John 12:3-5)*

47. *Thomas (John 20:24)*

48. *Philip and Andrew (John 12:20-28)*

49. *Paul (Acts 15–18)*

50. *Peter, John, and James (Mark 5:37)*

51. *Paul (Acts 23:27)*
52. *Peter and John (Acts 3:1-10)*
53. *Peter (Acts 9:32-35)*
54. *Paul (Acts 9:10-18)*
55. *Joseph (Acts 4:36)*
56. *Peter and John (Acts 4:1-4)*
57. *Paul (Acts 20:7-12)*
58. *Peter (Galatians 2:11-21)*
59. *Jude (John 14:22)*
60. *Peter (John 21:15-19)*
61. *Paul (Acts 17:16-34)*
62. *Peter (Acts 10:9-16)*
63. *Peter and Andrew (Mark 1:17)*
64. *John (Mark 9:38)*
65. *Peter, James, and John (Mark 14:32-34)*
66. *Philip (John 6:7)*
67. *Paul (Acts 19:23-41)*
68. *Andrew (John 6:8-9)*
69. *Peter (John 13:6-9)*
70. *Paul (Acts 28:1-6)*
71. *James (Galatians 1:19)*
72. *Timothy (1 Thessalonians 1:1; 2:6)*
73. *Silas (1 Thessalonians 1:1; 2:7)*
74. *John*

CALL IN A PRIEST

In religions throughout the world, a priest is a kind of go-between, a mediator between a god and the people. Ancient Israel had its priests, as did the many pagan nations nearby. Because the priests were responsible for offering up sacrifices to God (or some god), the people often thought of them as very special people, somehow "close" to the divine. Some of the priests were good and righteous, whereas others were downright scandalous in their behavior. They were a mixed bag, definitely, and among them were some of the more interesting and colorful people in the Bible. See how much you know about this motley mix.

1. What three books of the Bible are named after priests?
2. What Hebrew married the daughter of an Egyptian priest?
3. What was the penalty in Israel for disobeying a priest?
4. Which priest was made mute because he did not believe the prophecy given by an angel?
5. What oil was supposed to be used to anoint Israel's priests?
6. Which priest made the world's first piggy bank by placing a chest with a hole in it near the altar of the Temple?
7. What righteous king fired all the priests that had been appointed to serve pagan gods?
8. Which priest in the Bible is mentioned as having no mother or father?
9. What kind of head covering did the priest wear?
10. What book of the Bible mentions the priests of Israel more than any other?
11. Which priests—two of Aaron's sons—were killed because they offered "strange" or unauthorized fire to the Lord?
12. Which priest was the first head of the Levites?
13. Which priest gave David the ritual bread when David fled from Saul?
14. Which priest of Midian taught Moses how to administer justice among the Hebrews?
15. Which priest in the Old Testament was also a king?
16. Who was priest during Joshua's conquest of Canaan?
17. Which priest had the boy Jehoash proclaimed king, causing the death of wicked Queen Athaliah?
18. Which priest scolded a distressed woman because he thought she was drunk at the Tabernacle?

19. What was engraved on the 12 stones in the high priest's breast-plate?
20. What two gluttonous priests were notorious for keeping the sacrificial meat for themselves?
21. What reform priest was killed by the orders of King Joash, a pupil of his father?
22. Which priest had a son named Ichabod, a name meaning "the glory has departed"?
23. What five men were called to be the first priests of Israel?
24. Which king ordered the execution of Ahimelech and other priests because they had conspired with David?
25. Who was the only priest to escape when Saul slaughtered the 85 priests of Nob?
26. Which priest found the Book of the Law in the Temple during Josiah's reign?
27. When Adonijah tried to grab the throne of Israel, which priest took his side?
28. What high priest had John and Peter arrested after the two disciples had healed a lame man?
29. Which priest was told by Jeremiah that he would be taken to Babylon as a prisoner?
30. Which king of Israel sinned by appointing priests that had not been chosen by God?
31. In the time of the judges, what man was brassy enough to set up one of his sons as priest, though he had no authority to do so?
32. Which priest led a reform movement in Judah, so that the people tore down their Baal temple and idols?
33. Which priest of Baal was killed in Jerusalem when a reform movement threw out all the idols?
34. What was the name of the two stones worn in the high priest's breastplate and used to determine God's will?
35. Which king ordered the priest Uriah to make a copy of a pagan altar he had seen in Damascus?
36. What two men were high priests during David's reign?
37. Which priest received the boy Samuel as a servant?
38. When Jerusalem fell to the Babylonians, which priest was taken prisoner to Babylon?
39. Which king reversed the reform policies of Jehoiada the priest immediately after Jehoiada died?
40. What fat priest of Israel died when he heard the Ark had been captured?

41. Which priest scolded King Uzziah for daring to offer incense to God?
42. Which leader after the exile traced his ancestry back to the high priest Aaron?
43. What kinds of objects were around the hem of the priest's robe?
44. During Nehemiah's ministry, which priest dedicated the newly rebuilt walls of Jerusalem?
45. Who is the first priest mentioned in the Bible?
46. What book of the Bible mentions a "priest forever, after the order of Melchizedek"?
47. Which priest served as a witness when Isaiah gave his son the bizarre name Maher-Shalal-Hash-Baz?
48. What evil priest had Jeremiah beaten and placed in chains?
49. Which priest was banished by Solomon, fulfilling a prophecy that Eli's descendants would be stripped of the priesthood?
50. Which priest received a letter criticizing him for not putting an iron collar on Jeremiah's neck?
51. Which priest, a prisoner in Babylon, was also a prophet?
52. What is the only parable of Jesus to have a priest as a character?
53. Which prophet locked horns with the wicked priest Amaziah at Bethel?
54. What miracle of Jesus led the priests to conspire to have him executed?
55. Which prophet was sent to encourage the rebuilding of the Temple under the priest Joshua?
56. Who had a vision of the high priest Joshua standing beside Satan?
57. What was the affliction of the man who was healed by Jesus, then sent to the priest?
58. In which priest's home did the enemies of Jesus meet to plot against him?
59. Which disciple angrily cut off the ear of the high priest's servant when Jesus was arrested?
60. What book of the New Testament says that God has made his people to be a kingdom of priests?
61. What crime did the high priest charge Jesus with?
62. Which priest was the father of John the Baptist?
63. Which priest was the "king of peace"?
64. According to Ezekiel, what was the one kind of woman a priest could not marry?
65. Which priest announced that Jesus should die because it was appropriate for one man to die for the people?

66. Which priest was told by the prophet Amos that his wife would become a prostitute?
67. According to John's Gospel, which priest was the first to examine the arrested Jesus?
68. Which priest anointed Solomon as king?
69. What man asked the high priest for letters so he could arrest Christians in the synagogues of Damascus?
70. What two apostles were met by a priest of Zeus, who tried to offer sacrifices to them?
71. Which priest had seven sons who were casting out demons in the name of Jesus?
72. What high priest ordered his men to slap Paul, which caused Paul to call him a "whitewashed wall"?
73. According to the Epistle to the Hebrews, who is the present high priest of Israel?
74. According to the Epistle to the Hebrews, which Old Testament priest is Jesus like?
75. Which kinsman of Moses was a priest of Midian?
76. Which priest was responsible for taking the first census of Israel?
77. Which New Testament Epistle mentions the priesthood more than any other?
78. What tribe of Israel did all the priests spring from?
79. Which New Testament Epistle tells Christians that they are all priests?
80. Which priest examined Jesus before the council?

CALL IN A PRIEST (ANSWERS)

1. Ezra, Jeremiah, and Ezekiel

2. Joseph (Genesis 41:45)

3. Death (Deuteronomy 17:12)

4. Zechariah (Luke 1:20)

5. Olive oil (Exodus 30:24)

6. Jehoiada (2 Kings 12:9)

7. Josiah (2 Kings 23:5)

8. Melchizedek (Hebrews 7:3)

9. A turban (Exodus 28:39)

10. *Leviticus*
11. *Nadab and Abihu (Numbers 3:4)*
12. *Eleazar, Aaron's son (Numbers 3:32)*
13. *Ahimelech (1 Samuel 21:1-6)*
14. *Jethro, also called Reuel (Exodus 18:13-27)*
15. *Melchizedek (Genesis 14:18)*
16. *Eleazar (Joshua 17:4)*
17. *Jehoiada (2 Kings 11:9-16)*
18. *Eli, who scolded Hannah, future mother of Samuel (1 Samuel 1:13-14)*
19. *The names of the tribes of Israel (Exodus 28:21)*
20. *Hophni and Phinehas (1 Samuel 2:17)*
21. *Zechariah (2 Chronicles 24:21)*
22. *Phinehas (1 Samuel 4:21)*
23. *Aaron and his sons Nadab, Abihu, Eleazar, and Ithamar (Exodus 28:1)*
24. *Saul (1 Samuel 22:18)*
25. *Abiathar (1 Samuel 22:20)*
26. *Hilkiah (2 Kings 22:8)*
27. *Abiathar (1 Kings 1:7)*
28. *Annas (Acts 4:6)*
29. *Passhur (Jeremiah 20:6)*
30. *Jeroboam (1 Kings 13:33)*
31. *Micah (Judges 17:5)*
32. *Jehoiada (2 Kings 11:17-20)*
33. *Mattan (2 Kings 11:18)*
34. *Urim and Thummim (Exodus 28:30)*
35. *Ahaz (2 Kings 16:11)*
36. *Abiathar and Zadok (2 Samuel 20:26)*
37. *Eli (1 Samuel 2:11)*
38. *Seraiah (2 Kings 25:18)*
39. *Joash (2 Chronicles 24:17)*
40. *Eli (1 Samuel 4:18)*
41. *Azariah (2 Chronicles 26:18)*
42. *Ezra (7:5)*
43. *Bells and pomegranates (Exodus 28:33-34)*
44. *Eliashib (Nehemiah 3:1)*

45. *Melchizedek (Genesis 14:18)*
46. *Psalms (110:4)*
47. *Uriah (Isaiah 8:2)*
48. *Passhur (Jeremiah 20:1)*
49. *Abiathar (1 Kings 2:27)*
50. *Zephaniah (Jeremiah 29:26)*
51. *Ezekiel*
52. *The Good Samaritan (Luke 10:31)*
53. *Amos (7:10-17)*
54. *The raising of Lazarus (John 11:47)*
55. *Haggai*
56. *Zechariah (3:1)*
57. *Leprosy (Matthew 8:4)*
58. *Caiaphas's (Matthew 26:3)*
59. *Peter (Matthew 26:51)*
60. *Revelation (1:6)*
61. *Blasphemy (Matthew 26:65)*
62. *Zechariah (Luke 1:5)*
63. *Melchizedek (Hebrews 7:2)*
64. *A divorcée (Ezekiel 44:22)*
65. *Caiaphas (John 11:49)*
66. *Amaziah (Amos 7:17)*
67. *Annas (John 18:13)*
68. *Zadok (1 Kings 1:45)*
69. *Saul of Tarsus (Acts 9:2), later known as the apostle Paul*
70. *Paul and Barnabas (Acts 14:13)*
71. *Sceva (Acts 19:14)*
72. *Ananias (Acts 23:3)*
73. *Jesus (Hebrews 3:1)*
74. *Melchizedek (Hebrews 5:6)*
75. *Jethro, also called Reuel (Exodus 3:1), who was Moses' father-in-law*
76. *Eleazar (Numbers 26:1-2)*
77. *Hebrews*
78. *Levi*

79. *1 Peter (2:9)*

80. *Caiaphas (Matthew 26:62)*

A WHOLE PACK O' PROPHETS

The Bible's prophets were not primarily predictors of the future
(though they did play that role at times). Mostly they were those who
spoke on behalf of the Lord. In fact, the Hebrew word for prophet was
nabi, meaning something like "mouthpiece" or "spokesman." True
prophets didn't preach their own message; instead, they preached
because they felt compelled to speak out on God's behalf. Prophets
attacked individual and social sins, warned of punishment to come,
and even gave comfort to the people in times of distress. Some of the
more colorful people in the Bible were the prophets, some of whom
were real "characters."

1. Which prophet is quoted in the New Testament more often than
    any other? (Hint: He is famous for his vision of God in the
    Temple.)
2. What court prophet confronted King David with his adultery?
3. What young prophet had a vision of a statue composed of differ-
    ent metals?
4. Which prophet, put into a hole in the ground for being too
    outspoken, was often called the "weeping prophet"?
5. Which king of Israel was, early in his career, associated with a
    group of prophets?
6. What wilderness man confronted the prophets of Baal in a famous
    contest?
7. Which prophet, famous for his vision of the dry bones, was with
    the exiles in Babylon?
8. What bald prophet was the performer of many miracles and the
    successor to another great prophet?
9. Which kinsman of Jesus ate locusts, preached repentance, and
    baptized penitents in the Jordan?
10. What Christian prophesied a famine in the land?
11. Which New Testament character prophesied the destruction of
    Jerusalem?
12. What woman was sent for when the long-neglected Book of the
    Law was found during Josiah's reign?

13. What four young women, daughters of a Christian evangelist, were considered prophetesses?
14. What elderly woman recognized the infant Jesus as being the Messiah?
15. What man, who anointed the first two kings of Israel, was considered both a judge and a prophet?
16. Which Old Testament patriarch was revealed as a prophet to King Abimelech?
17. What Egyptian-raised Hebrew leader predicted the coming of a prophet like himself?
18. Which prophet took David to task for numbering the people of Israel?
19. Which prophet predicted that Jeroboam would be king over 10 tribes of Israel?
20. What reluctant prophet was thrown overboard in a storm?
21. What man of Tekoa was a simple laborer who had the audacity to confront the king's priest at his shrine?
22. What men prophesied against Nineveh?
23. Which prophet was famous for his marriage to a prostitute?
24. Which prophet predicted the outpouring of God's Spirit upon all people?
25. What man wrote a brief book against Edom?
26. What sister of a Hebrew leader, who for a time was afflicted with leprosy, was herself a prophetess?
27. What woman, the only female judge of Israel, was also considered a prophetess?
28. Which apostle of Jesus recorded his visions of the world's end times?
29. What man, who traveled to Antioch with Paul, Silas, and Barnabas, was considered a prophet?
30. Which prophet, who spoke of the coming of someone like the prophet Elijah, also spoke of the need to purify Temple worship after the return from exile in Babylon?
31. What man of Moresheth, who spoke of the need to walk humbly with God, was a contemporary of Isaiah?
32. Which prophet, who posed much of his book in the form of questions and answers, concluded that "the just shall live by faith"?
33. Active during Josiah's reign, which prophet spoke about judgment and the coming "Day of the Lord"?
34. What unlucky prophet delivered an unfavorable message to King Ahab?

35. What false prophet wore a yoke, which Jeremiah broke?
36. What traveling companion of Paul was considered a prophet?
37. Active at the time of the rebuilding of the Temple in Jerusalem, which prophet is associated with Zechariah?
38. Which prophet, who lived in Jerusalem after the Babylonian exile, had visions of a flying scroll and a gold lampstand?
39. What man is spoken of as being his brother's prophet? (He is also famous for having constructed a golden calf.)
40. What false prophet wore iron horns and told King Ahab he would be victorious in battle?
41. Which prophet told King Rehoboam that Judah would be abandoned to the forces of the Egyptian king?
42. Which prophet, who lived in the reign of King Asa in Judah, was the son of the prophet Oded?
43. What false prophet was a sorcerer and an attendant of the proconsul Sergius Paulus?
44. Which prophetess is mentioned as an intimidator of Nehemiah?
45. What evil prophetess is referred to in Revelation by the name of an Old Testament queen?

A WHOLE PACK O' PROPHETS (ANSWERS)

1. *Isaiah*

2. *Nathan (2 Samuel; 1 Kings)*

3. *Daniel*

4. *Jeremiah*

5. *Saul (1 Samuel 10:1-13)*

6. *Elijah (1 Kings 18; 2 Kings 2)*

7. *Ezekiel*

8. *Elisha (2 Kings)*

9. *John the Baptist*

10. *Agabus (Acts 11:27-28; 21:10-11)*

11. *Jesus*

12. *Huldah (2 Kings 22)*

13. *The daughters of Philip (Acts 21:8-9)*

14. *Anna (Luke 2:36-38)*

15. *Samuel*
16. *Abraham (Genesis 20:1-7)*
17. *Moses (Deuteronomy 18:15)*
18. *Gad (2 Samuel 24:10-14)*
19. *Ahijah (1 Kings 11:29-40)*
20. *Jonah*
21. *Amos*
22. *Nahum and Jonah*
23. *Hosea*
24. *Joel*
25. *Obadiah*
26. *Miriam (Exodus 15:20)*
27. *Deborah (Judges 4:4)*
28. *John*
29. *Judas Barsabbas (Acts 15:22, 32)*
30. *Malachi*
31. *Micah*
32. *Habakkuk*
33. *Zephaniah*
34. *Micaiah son of Imlah (1 Kings 22:8-28)*
35. *Hananiah (Jeremiah 28)*
36. *Silas (Acts 15:32)*
37. *Haggai*
38. *Zechariah*
39. *Aaron (Exodus 7:1)*
40. *Zedekiah (1 Kings 22:1-12)*
41. *Shemaiah (2 Chronicles 15:5-8)*
42. *Azariah (2 Chronicles 13:1-8)*
43. *Bar-Jesus (Acts 13:6-11)*
44. *Noadiah (Nehemiah 6:14)*
45. *Jezebel (Revelation 2:20)*

👉 PRENATALLY CHOSEN BY GOD

Does the Bible teach predestination? In some Christian circles, you don't want to raise that question unless you've got time for a long and heated discussion. Over the centuries, believers have debated the topic at length. One thing that isn't debatable is that the Bible tells us plainly that certain special people were chosen by God, even before their births, for some divine purpose. Some of these people were genuine saints, but some of them were—well, some of them will surprise you, because God in his mysterious ways can work through very imperfect human beings.

1. What kinsman of Christ was ordained to be his forerunner?
2. What child, who later ministered with the priest Eli, was ordained before birth to serve God?
3. Which apostle was foreordained to minister to the Gentiles?
4. What strongman was ordained before birth to deliver Israel from the Philistines?
5. What Greek conqueror's reign is usually considered to be predicted in the book of Daniel?
6. Which prophet was ordained before birth to be God's messenger?
7. Which king of Judah had his birth and reign foretold to King Jeroboam?
8. What psalm, usually assumed to have been written by David, talks about God knowing him before his birth?
9. Who foretold Jesus' birth and ministry to Mary?

PRENATALLY CHOSEN BY GOD (ANSWERS)

1. *John the Baptist (Luke 1:13-17)*

2. *Samuel (1 Samuel 1:11-20)*

3. *Paul (Galatians 1:15)*

4. *Samson (Judges 13:2-5)*

5. *Alexander the Great (Daniel 11:2-4)*

6. *Jeremiah (1:5)*

7. *Josiah (1 Kings 13:2)*

8. *Psalm 139*

9. *The angel Gabriel (Luke 1:26-38)*

PART 15

WALKING IN FAITH

WE AREN'T THE WORLD

In Genesis 1, God uses the word *good* several times to describe his newly created world. Alas, the world didn't *stay* good, thanks to Adam and Eve's disobedience (not to mention all the mischief done by Satan and his demons). So, as you browse through the Bible, you get the distinct impression that "the world"—marred by human sin and the work of Satan—is a not-so-nice place. In fact, the saints are very *un*worldly people, taking their marching orders from God, not from sinful human beings. You can't read far in the New Testament without realizing that "the world" is very much opposed to God and his people. The theme song of believers might be "We Aren't the World."

1. Who stated that "we brought nothing into the world, and we can take nothing out of it"?
2. The devil tempted Jesus by taking him to a high mountain and showing him all the _____ of the world.
3. Complete this saying of Jesus: "If the world _____ you, keep in mind that it _____ me first."
4. John the Baptist announced that Jesus was "the _____ of God, who takes away the sins of the world."
5. According to Revelation, who is it that leads the whole world astray?
6. In his Sermon on the Mount, Jesus refers to people of faith as the _____ of the world.
7. Which apostle wrote that believers are "strangers and aliens" in this world?
8. Which of the Gospels says that "the true light that enlightens every man was coming into the world"?
9. According to 1 John, what sort of person "overcomes the world"?
10. Paul stated that believers "have not received the _____ of the world but the _____ who is from God."
11. John stated that though "the world and its desires pass away," a certain type of person lives forever. What type?
12. Who stated that "friendship with the world is hatred toward God"?
13. What people is the Letter to the Hebrews referring to when it says "the world was not worthy of them"?

14. According to Galatians, unsaved people are enslaved to the basic _____ of the world.
15. Which Epistle states that "greater is he that is in you than he who is in the world"?

WE AREN'T THE WORLD (ANSWERS)

1. *Paul (1 Timothy 6:7)*

2. *Kingdoms (Matthew 4:8). Jesus resisted the temptation.*

3. *Hates, hated (John 15:18)*

4. *Lamb (John 1:29)*

5. *Satan, of course (Revelation 12:9)*

6. *Light (Matthew 5:14)*

7. *Peter (1 Peter 2:11)*

8. *John (1:9)*

9. *Anyone who believes that Jesus is the Son of God (1 John 5:5)*

10. *Spirit (1 Corinthians 2:12)*

11. *One who does the will of God (1 John 2:17)*

12. *James (4:4)*

13. *People of faith (Hebrews 11:38)*

14. *Principles (Galatians 4:3)*

15. *1 John (4:4)*

 ## BORN AGAIN, START ANEW

Thanks to advertising, we are all too familiar with the phrase "new and improved." Actually, the idea is very old, rooted in the Bible, where people are constantly advised to improve themselves spiritually. But improvement isn't enough, frankly, so we need something more radical: to be "born again," as Jesus himself phrased it. The first time he used that phrase, it puzzled the man who heard it, and it still puzzles people today. If you've ever seen how someone's life has been miraculously changed by God, it seems even more mysterious and amazing.

1. To whom did Jesus say the words "You must be born again"?
2. Which prophet quoted the Lord as saying, "Though your sins be as scarlet, they shall be white as snow"?
3. Complete this verse from Paul: "If any man be in Christ, he is a new _____."
4. In which book of the Bible does Christ say, "Behold, I make all things new"?
5. According to 1 John, how do we know we have "passed from death to life"?
6. Who prophesied a future when God would write his law on humans' hearts?
7. Who told people to "bring forth fruit in keeping with repentance"?
8. Complete this verse: "Be not conformed to this world, but be _____ by the renewing of your mind."
9. According to Jesus, we have to become like what in order to enter heaven?
10. Who prophesied a time when God would give a "new heart" and "new spirit" to people?
11. Which Epistle says that believers have born "not of perishable seed, but imperishable"?
12. What former persecutor of believers said that "I have been crucified with Christ"?
13. What tax collector of Jericho was one of the most dramatic "born again" stories in the Bible?
14. Which apostle urged people to be converted "so that times of refreshing may come from the Lord"?
15. Complete this verse: "As in Adam all die, even so in _____ shall all be made alive."
16. In which book of the Bible would you find these words: "Those whom I love I rebuke and discipline. So be earnest, and repent"?
17. According to James, if we humble ourselves before God, he will do what?
18. Who claimed that he came to call not the righteous, but sinners?
19. Which prophet promised that God would "abundantly pardon" sinners?
20. What is the only book of the Bible to use the actual term "new birth"?

BORN AGAIN, START ANEW (ANSWERS)

1. Nicodemus (John 3:3-7), in one of the more often quoted passages in the Bible

2. Isaiah (1:18)

3. Creature (or, in some versions, creation) (2 Corinthians 5:17)

4. Revelation (21:5)

5. If we love the brothers—that is, fellow believers (1 John 3:14)

6. Jeremiah (31:33)

7. Jesus (Matthew 3:8; Luke 3:8)

8. Transformed (Romans 12:2)

9. Little children (Matthew 18:3; 19:14)

10. Ezekiel (18:31; 36:26)

11. 1 Peter (1:23)

12. Paul (Galatians 2:20)

13. Zacchaeus (Luke 19:8). After he repented, he promised to pay back fourfold anyone he had cheated.

14. Peter (Acts 3:19)

15. Christ (1 Corinthians 15:22)

16. Revelation (3:19)

17. He will lift us up (James 4:10).

18. Jesus (Matthew 9:13)

19. Isaiah (55:7)

20. 1 Peter (1:3)

SLIP SLIDING AWAY

You might say that the Bible is the Book of Ingratitude, one story after another showing how people forget all the good things God has done for them. This shouldn't surprise us, because we ourselves are chronically ungrateful to people (such as our parents) who have been kind and generous. Time and time again, people in the Bible resolve to do better—then backslide once more. The great mystery is not human ingratitude and backsliding but the fact that God is always willing to forgive.

1. According to Joshua, what fate awaits those who forsake God and pursue other gods?
2. What book of the Bible laments that the people of Israel "remembered not the Lord their God," who had delivered them from enemies on every side?
3. Which prophet recorded God as saying, "Return to me, and I will return to you"?
4. Which prophet lamented that the ox and donkey knew their master, but the people of Israel did not know theirs?
5. Which Epistle states that a person who turns a sinner from his ways will "hide a multitude of sins"?
6. Which prophet records God as saying, "Return, backsliding Israel"?
7. What book of the Bible compares a backsliding fool to a vomiting dog?
8. Who lamented that Demas had forsaken him, "loving this present world"?
9. Which of Jesus' parables is concerned with people who embrace the faith but then turn from it?
10. What group of Christians did Paul lament had been "bewitched" away from the faith?
11. In which book of the Bible does Christ scold a group of believers who "left their first love" of the faith?
12. According to Paul, the love of _____ caused many people to wander from the faith.
13. In a famous saying of Jesus, whose wife was a symbol of people who "looked back" longingly on their sinful pasts?
14. Complete the verse from 1 Timothy: "Some have already turned aside after _____."

SLIP SLIDING AWAY (ANSWERS)

1. They will be "consumed" (Joshua 24:20).

2. Judges (8:34)

3. Malachi (3:7)

4. Isaiah (1:3)

5. James (5:19-20)

6. Jeremiah (3:12). The words are in Jeremiah, but the sentiment is found throughout the whole Bible.

7. *Proverbs (26:11), which states that a fool returns to his folly the same way a dog returns to his vomit. Ugly, yes, but the words do stick in the mind, don't they?*

8. *Paul (2 Timothy 4:10). Apparently Demas had been a fellow Christian who lost his faith.*

9. *The parable of the sower, in which some of the "seeds" (people) look promising but fail to mature (Mark 4:7-19)*

10. *The Galatians (1:6)—in the memorable phrase "O foolish Galatians!"*

11. *Revelation (2:4)*

12. *Money—in the passage with the famous phrase "the love of money is the root of all evil" (1 Timothy 6:10)*

13. *Lot's wife (Luke 17:32). In Genesis 19:26, Lot's wife is turned into a pillar of salt when she looks back on the burning city of Sodom.*

14. *Satan (1 Timothy 5:15)*

 ## "CHILDREN OF GOD" BY ADOPTION

In "street theology"—that is, what the general public believes about God—all human beings are "children of God." That seems like a nice sentiment, but it isn't based on the Bible. According to the Book, God is *Creator* of all people, yes, but not everyone's *Father*—except by adoption. We *become* the children of God by doing what good children do: love and obey our parents, or, in this case, the heavenly Parent.

1. According to Jesus, who shall be called the "children of God"?
2. Who gave Pharaoh the divine message that Israel was God's "first-born son"?
3. According to Romans, if we are led by the _____ of God, we are sons of God.
4. What term of endearment do believers use to call upon the heavenly Father?
5. Through which prophet did God say, "Out of Egypt I called my son"?
6. Which Epistle says that we know we are God's children because he disciplines us?
7. Complete this verse from Galatians: "You are all the children of God by faith in _____ _____."

8. In 1 John, what group of people is contrasted with the children of God?
9. In which book of the Bible does God say, "He that overcomes shall inherit all things"?
10. According to Jesus, what people shall shine like the sun in the Kingdom of their Father?

"CHILDREN OF GOD" BY ADOPTION (ANSWERS)

1. The peacemakers (Matthew 5:9)

2. Moses (Exodus 4:22)

3. Spirit (Romans 8:14; Galatians 4:6)

4. Abba, the Aramaic term meaning something close to "dear Father" or "Papa" (Romans 8:15)

5. Hosea (11:1). "Son" here refers to the people of Israel. In the New Testament, this verse is applied to Jesus (Matthew 2:15).

6. Hebrews (12:6)

7. Christ Jesus (Galatians 3:26)

8. Children of the devil, naturally (1 John 3:10)

9. Revelation (21:7)

10. The righteous (Matthew 13:43)

 ## PERFECT, OR PRACTICALLY PERFECT

Back in the 1980s, a movie with the title *Perfect* was released. It dealt with *physical* perfection, but its characters were some of the shallowest people ever depicted on the silver screen. By contrast, the "perfection" spoken of in the Bible has nothing whatsoever to do with our physical appeal. Although achieving physical perfection may be a great mystery, achieving spiritual perfection is an even greater one.

1. Whose pagan wives turned him away from God so that "his heart was not perfect with the Lord his God"?
2. Who said, "Be ye therefore perfect, even as your Father which is in heaven is perfect"?

3. What pitiful man, sorely tested by Satan, was "perfect and upright"?
4. Which Old Testament man was "perfect in his generations" and one who "walked with God"?
5. Who was able to preach boldly after Aquila and Priscilla taught him "the way of God more perfectly"?
6. To whom did Jesus say, "If thou wilt be perfect, go and sell that thou hast, and give to the poor"?
7. Which prophet said, "Thou wilt keep him in perfect peace, whose mind is stayed on thee"?
8. Which king's heart was "perfect with the Lord all his days"?
9. Who warned Christians against thinking that they could be perfect by their own efforts alone?
10. Who predicted he would be "perfected" on the third day?
11. What Book of the Law commands people to use "perfect" weights and measures so they will deal honestly?
12. Who wept and begged the Lord to remember that he had served him with a perfect heart?
13. Whom did God tell that Job was a perfect and upright man?
14. What city was called "the perfection of beauty, the joy of the whole earth"?

PERFECT, OR PRACTICALLY PERFECT (ANSWERS)

1. *King Solomon (1 Kings 11:4)*

2. *Jesus (Matthew 5:48)*

3. *Job (1:1)*

4. *Noah (6:9)*

5. *Apollos (Acts 18:26)*

6. *The rich young ruler (Matthew 19:21)*

7. *Isaiah (26:3)*

8. *Asa's (1 Kings 15:14)*

9. *Paul (Galatians 3:3)*

10. *Jesus (Luke 13:32). Apparently his meaning was this: with his resurrection on the third day, his work would be completed.*

11. *Deuteronomy (25:15)*

12. *King Hezekiah (2 Kings 20:3)*

13. *Satan (Job 1:8)*

14. *Jerusalem (Lamentations 2:15)*

"RELIGION" OR FAITH?

The Bible talks a lot more about "faith" than about "religion," and (as Jesus made so clear) it is quite possible to be "religious" and still not be the kind of person with whom God is pleased. So, in the few places where our English Bibles mention religion, it isn't necessarily implied that religion is a good thing—unless, of course, we "walk the walk" as well as "talk the talk."

1. In what famous city did Paul tell the people, "I see that in every way you are very religious"?
2. What group was Paul referring to when he mentioned he had belonged to "the strictest sect of our religion"?
3. What book of the Bible states that a truly religious person will be able to control his tongue?
4. In which Epistle does Paul say that people should prove their religion by taking care of their own family members?
5. Which Epistle refers to priests performing their "religious duties" day after day, repeating sacrifices over and over?
6. According to James, what people should we look after if we are genuinely religious?

"RELIGION" OR FAITH? (ANSWERS)

1. *Athens, the great (and very pagan) city in Greece. Paul definitely didn't mean it as a compliment when he called the Athenians "religious," for they were worshippers of false gods (Acts 17:22).*

2. *The Pharisees (Acts 26:5)*

3. *James (1:26)*

4. *1 Timothy (5:4)*

5. *Hebrews (10:11)*

6. *Widows and orphans (James 1:27)*

UNFORGIVEN (AND FORGIVEN)

"To err is human, to forgive divine"—so said the poet Alexander Pope, though many people think those words came from the Bible. In fact, Pope's words do nicely sum up the Bible's teaching about forgiveness. People are expected to forgive, just as God does. Unfortunately, in the Bible (as in our own lives) there are more examples of *not* forgiving than forgiving.

1. What young man confessed his riotous living to his forgiving father? (Hint: parable)
2. According to Jesus, how many times are we supposed to forgive someone?
3. What is the one sin that cannot be forgiven?
4. Who asked the prophet Elisha's forgiveness for worshipping in the temple of the god Rimmon?
5. Who was the first man recorded as forgiving those who wronged him?
6. To whom did Jesus say "Your sins are forgiven"?
7. Who was Jesus' immediate predecessor in preaching the forgiveness of sins?
8. In which Gospel does Jesus say from the cross, "Father, forgive them, they know not what they do"?
9. According to the Letter to the Hebrews, what is required if sins are to be forgiven?
10. What book of the Old Testament is concerned with offering animal sacrifices for the forgiveness of sins?
11. According to Deuteronomy, what sin cannot be forgiven?
12. Who begged David's forgiveness for her husband's boorish behavior?
13. What book of the Bible mentions forgiveness the most times?
14. What abused prophet prayed that God would not forgive his enemies' many plots against him?
15. What happens to people who will not forgive their enemies?
16. According to Jesus, what was poured out for the forgiveness of men's sins?
17. According to Mark's Gospel, what activity should we cease from until we have forgiven our brothers?
18. What woman loved much because she had been forgiven much?

UNFORGIVEN (AND FORGIVEN) (ANSWERS)

1. The Prodigal Son (Luke 15:18)

2. Seventy times seven (Matthew 18:21-22). Peter had assumed (wrongly) that seven times was adequate.

3. Blasphemy against the Holy Spirit (Matthew 12:31)

4. Naaman, the Syrian soldier whom Elisha healed of leprosy (2 Kings 5:18)

5. Joseph, who had been so badly treated by his brothers (Genesis 50:17)

6. The paralytic man whom he healed (Matthew 9:2)

7. His kinsman, John the Baptist (Mark 1:4)

8. Luke (23:34)

9. The shedding of blood (Hebrews 9:22)

10. Leviticus

11. Leading others into idolatry (Deuteronomy 29:16-20)

12. Abigail, the wife of surly Nabal. After Nabal died, Abigail became one of David's many wives (1 Samuel 25:28).

13. Psalms, the Bible's prayer book, mentions it more than 10 times.

14. Jeremiah (18:23)

15. They will not be forgiven by God (Matthew 6:15).

16. His blood (Matthew 26:28)

17. Praying (Mark 11:25)

18. The immoral woman who anointed Jesus' feet with precious ointment (Luke 7:36-46)

HOPE SPRINGS ETERNAL

Strictly speaking, the Bible is an optimistic book. It has a happy ending, with the Lord and his people triumphant over evil and all pain and sorrow banished. True, hell is part of the picture too, but it's clear that hell can be avoided. For those who cling to God, there is heaven, and this anticipation of heaven casts a glow over the present life, making the grayest days sunny.

1. According to Proverbs, hope deferred makes the heart _____.
2. Which prophet looked forward to a time when "the wolf shall dwell with the lamb, and the leopard shall lie down with the kid"?

3. Who stated, "If in this life only we have hope in Christ, we are of all men most miserable"?
4. Complete this verse from Hebrews: "Now _____ is the substance of things hoped for, the evidence of things not seen."
5. Which prophet said, "You will keep him in perfect peace him whose mind is stayed on you, because he trusts in you"?
6. Complete this verse from Proverbs: "The hope of the righteous shall be _____, but the _____ of the wicked shall perish."
7. Which Epistle refers to the "living hope" of believers?
8. Who lamented that his days had come to an end without hope?
9. In what book of the Bible would you find these words: "Why are you downcast, O my soul? Put your hope in God"?
10. According to Paul, the three greatest things of all are _____, hope, and _____.

HOPE SPRINGS ETERNAL (ANSWERS)

1. Sick (Proverbs 13:12)

2. Isaiah (11:6). "Kid" referred to a young goat, of course.

3. Paul, who strongly emphasized the hope of heaven after death (1 Corinthians 15:19)

4. Faith (Hebrews 11:1)

5. Isaiah (26:3)

6. Gladness, expectation (Proverbs 10:28)

7. 1 Peter (1:3)

8. Job (7:6)

9. Psalms (42:5; 43:5)

10. Faith, love (or charity) (1 Corinthians 13:13)

☞ LET THERE BE LIGHT

"Light" in the Bible more often refers to something spiritual than physical. The Bible says God is light, and those who walk in the light are on God's side, whereas Satan and the wicked are on the side of darkness. Physical light is a mysterious thing—physicists still aren't sure whether to describe it as waves or particles—and even more mysterious is spiritual light, which is a powerful force in the universe.

1. Who told his followers they were the "light of the world"?
2. Which wisdom book says that wisdom excels folly just as light excels darkness?
3. Which Gospel refers to the "true light that enlightens every man"?
4. What city has no need of the sun's or moon's light?
5. Who told people to put on the "armor of light" and lay aside the works of darkness?
6. According to Jesus, what organ is the "light of the body"?
7. Complete this verse from 2 Corinthians: "The _____ of this world has blinded the minds of unbelievers to keep them from seeing the light"?
8. What book of the Bible refers to God as the "Father of lights"?
9. Complete this verse from Psalms: "The Lord is my light and my _____; whom shall I fear?"
10. What man did Jesus refer to as a "burning and a shining light"?
11. To what people was Paul sent to "open their eyes and turn them from darkness to light"?
12. Whom did Jesus say would "shine like the sun in the kingdom of their Father"?
13. Who can disguise himself as an angel of light?
14. Who said, "I am the light of the world"?
15. Which Epistle says that believers are a "royal priesthood" called to live in God's "marvelous light"?
16. Complete this verse from Psalm 119: "Your _____ is a lamp unto my feet and a light unto my path."
17. What expectant father foretold that his son would "shine on those living in darkness"?
18. In Handel's *Messiah,* the words "the people that walked in darkness have seen a great light" are from which prophet?
19. On what day of creation does God make light?
20. Complete this verse from John: "The light shines in the darkness, but the darkness has never _____ it."
21. Which Epistle says that in a crooked and perverse world, believers should "shine like stars"?
22. What pagan nation experienced three full days of darkness?
23. Which Epistle says that the immortal God "dwells in unapproachable light"?
24. Which king spoke of the Lord as "the light of morning at sunrise"?

25. Which Gospel says that light came into the world, but people preferred the darkness?
26. According to Paul, at what time would light shine upon all things now hidden in darkness?
27. Complete this verse from Proverbs: "The light of the _____ shines brightly, but the lamp of the _____ is snuffed out."
28. Which apostle warned against being "unequally yoked" with unbelievers, since light and darkness can have no fellowship?
29. Complete this verse from Psalms: "From Zion, perfect in beauty, God ____ forth."
30. Which Epistle refers to the "fruit of the light"?
31. According to 1 Kings, which of the 12 tribes of Israel was kept as a "lamp" before the Lord?

LET THERE BE LIGHT (ANSWERS)

1. *Jesus, of course (Matthew 5:14-16)*

2. *Ecclesiastes (2:13)*

3. *John (1:9). The "light" is Christ, of course.*

4. *The new Jerusalem—that is, heaven (Revelation 21:23)*

5. *Paul (Romans 13:12)*

6. *The eye (Luke 11:34), and people are still puzzling over just what he meant.*

7. *God—"god of this world" referring to Satan (2 Corinthians 4:4)*

8. *James (1:17)*

9. *Salvation (Psalm 27:1)*

10. *John the Baptist (John 5:35)*

11. *The Gentiles, that is, non-Jews (Acts 26:18)*

12. *The righteous (Matthew 13:43)*

13. *Satan (2 Corinthians 11:14)*

14. *Jesus (John 8:12)*

15. *1 Peter (2:9)*

16. *Word (Psalm 119:105)*

17. *Zechariah, the father of John the Baptist (Luke 1:79)*

18. *Isaiah (9:1-2). The words have been understood as a prophecy of Jesus (Matthew 4:16).*

19. The first day (Genesis 1:3). In fact, light is the first thing created. This is interesting because the sun and moon come later.

20. Understood—or, overcome (John 1:5). The Greek word can mean either, which is why some versions have "mastered," a word that contains both meanings.

21. Philippians (2:15)

22. Egypt (Exodus 10:23), experiencing one of the 10 plagues

23. 1 Timothy (6:16)

24. David (2 Samuel 23:4)

25. John (3:19)

26. Jesus' second coming (1 Corinthians 4:5)

27. Righteous, wicked (Proverbs 13:9)

28. Paul (2 Corinthians 6:14)

29. Shines (Psalm 50:2)

30. Ephesians (5:9)

31. Judah, the tribe from which King David and (centuries later) Jesus came

SHALOM, AKA PEACE

We typically use the word *peace* to mean simply "no war." The Bible's words—*shalom* in Hebrew, *eirene* in Greek—are richer than that, carrying the idea of well-being, wholeness; people existing in harmony and not vexing each other. Needless to say, that type of peace is pretty elusive in this fallen world, but the Bible holds out the possibility that anyone can have peace inwardly if not outwardly. That kind of peace can only be had when the person takes a deep breath and says, "First of all, God is in control."

1. In Jesus' Beatitudes, what reward is there for the peacemakers?
2. Complete this quotation from Paul: "The God of peace will soon crush _____ under your feet."
3. In the Old Testament law, the sacrifices called "peace offerings" were also called what?
4. What man in Genesis was promised he would die in peace, and at a ripe old age?
5. Who spoke the famous words, "Glory to God in the highest, and peace on earth"?

6. Complete this quotation of Jesus: "My peace I give you, not as the _____ gives."
7. What book of the Bible states that "better is a dinner of vegetables than a fattened calf and hatred with it"?
8. Complete this verse from Psalms: "Mark the blameless man and behold the _____, for the reward of that man is peace."
9. According to Isaiah, God says that there is no peace for what sort of person?
10. Complete this verse from Hebrews: "Follow peace with all men, and _____, without which no man shall see the Lord."
11. Who prophesied a peaceful time when men would turn their swords into plowshares and their spears into pruning hooks?
12. What did Jesus cause to happen with the words, "Peace, be still"?
13. In Isaiah's prophecy of a time of peace, what animal will lie down with the lamb?
14. According to Paul's Letter to the Romans, to set one's mind on the _____ gives life and peace.
15. Complete this Proverb: "When a man's ways please the Lord, he makes even his _____ be at peace with him."
16. The famous blessing that ends "the Lord lift up his countenance upon you and give you peace" was first spoken by whom?
17. Who claimed that he came not to bring peace to earth but division?
18. Complete this saying of Jesus: "I have told you these things that in me you may have peace. In this world you will have tribulation, but be of good cheer. I have _____ the world."
19. To whom did the risen Jesus address the words "Peace be with you"?
20. Who prophesied the coming of someone who would be called "the Prince of Peace"?
21. Which Epistle lists peace among the fruit of the Spirit?
22. Complete this much-quoted verse from Philippians: "The peace of God, which passes all _____, shall keep your hearts and minds through Christ Jesus."
23. What old man blessed the baby Jesus and then asked God to let him "depart in peace"?
24. Complete this familiar verse from Isaiah: "You will keep him in perfect peace whose mind is stayed on you, because he _____ in you."
25. Which king from the book of Genesis in referred to in the New Testament as the "king of peace"?

26. According to the Letter of James, people who sow in peace will reap a harvest of _____.

27. According to the Old Testament, under which king did Israel live in safety, "every man under his vine and his fig tree"?

SHALOM, AKA PEACE (ANSWERS)

1. They will be called children of God (Matthew 5:9).

2. Satan (Romans 16:20)

3. Fellowship offerings, mentioned many times in Leviticus and Numbers

4. Abraham (Genesis 15:15)

5. The angels who appeared to the shepherds (Luke 2:14)

6. World (John 14:27)

7. Proverbs (15:17)

8. Upright (Psalm 37:37)

9. The wicked (Isaiah 48:22)

10. Holiness (Hebrews 12:14)

11. Isaiah (2:4). Interestingly, the prophet Joel foretold a time when just the opposite would happen.

12. He calmed a storm that was threatening him and his disciples (Mark 4:35-41).

13. The wolf (Isaiah 9:6), which in normal times would eat the lamb, of course

14. Spirit (Romans 8:6)

15. Enemies (Proverbs 16:7)

16. Aaron, Israel's first high priest (Numbers 6:26)

17. Jesus (Matthew 10:34; Luke 12:51)

18. Overcome (John 16:33)

19. His disciples (Luke 24:36)

20. Isaiah (9:6). Christians believe that Jesus is this Prince of Peace.

21. Galatians (5:22)

22. Understanding (Philippians 4:7)

23. Simeon, who had been promised he would not die until he had seen the Messiah (Luke 2:29)

24. Trust (Isaiah 26:3)

25. Melchizedek (Hebrews 7:2)

26. *Righteousness (James 3:18)*
27. *Solomon (1 Kings 4:25)*

👉 FREE INDEED!

When the Bible was being written, *free* had a very specific meaning: It meant "not a slave." In ancient times, societies rested on the backs of slave labor, so being "free" was a fine thing, but most slaves could look forward to freedom only by dying. The Bible holds out another kind of freedom, however—a spiritual freedom, available even to overworked slaves. In the Bible's view of things, a slave could be, in some mysterious way, freer than his masters.

1. Who said, "You will know the truth, and the truth will set you free"?
2. According to Paul, believers have been set free from sin and become slaves of what?
3. In the Old Testament, every fiftieth year, when all slaves were to be freed, was known as what?
4. Complete this saying of Jesus: "If the _____ sets you free, you will be free indeed."
5. What people were promised they would be freed by God's "outstretched arm and with mighty acts of judgment"?
6. According to Paul, where the _____ of the Lord is, there is freedom.
7. Which New Testament Epistle was addressed to the owner of a runaway slave?
8. According to the Old Testament law, what was the maximum number of years an Israelite could hold a fellow Israelite as a slave?
9. Complete this verse from Psalms: "I will walk about in freedom, for I have sought out your _____."
10. Who said that any slave who became a believer was "the Lord's freedman"?
11. According to Hebrews, what normal human fear enslaves all people except believers?
12. Which Old Testament prophet foretold the coming of one who would "bind up the brokenhearted and proclaim freedom for the captives"?

13. Complete this saying of Paul's: "Why should my freedom be judged by another man's _____?"

14. Which epistle of Paul's warns believers not to submit to a "yoke of slavery" to rules and regulations?

FREE INDEED! (ANSWERS)

1. *Jesus (John 8:32)*

2. *Righteousness (Romans 6:18)*

3. *Jubilee (Leviticus 25:10-15)*

4. *Son—that is, Christ (John 8:36)*

5. *The Israelite slaves in Egypt (Exodus 6:6)*

6. *Spirit (2 Corinthians 3:17)*

7. *Philemon, written by Paul*

8. *Six (Deuteronomy 15:12)*

9. *Precepts, or teachings (Psalm 119:45)*

10. *Paul (1 Corinthians 7:21). He also stated the opposite: Any free man who became a believer was the slave of Christ.*

11. *Fear of death (Hebrews 2:15)*

12. *Isaiah (61:1)*

13. *Conscience (1 Corinthians 10:29)*

14. *Galatians (5:1)*

A KINGDOM GREATER THAN THIS WORLD

In Jesus' day, some people hoped that he had come to free Israel from domination by the Romans and set up an earthly kingdom. However, Jesus made clear that the "Kingdom of Heaven" was nothing like the worldly kingdoms with their pomp, oppression, and status-seeking. The Kingdom of Heaven lay in the future—but was also a present reality for some, even those living under the thumb of wicked political powers (which includes most of the human beings who have ever lived). This spiritual kingdom was of great concern to the first Christians. Here is your chance to see how "Kingdom savvy" you are.

1. What person did Jesus tell, "My kingdom is not of this world"?
2. According to Jesus, "If I drive out _____ by the finger of God, then the kingdom of God has come to you."
3. Who was Jesus speaking of when he said, "The kingdom of God belongs to such as these"?
4. The familiar phrase "kingdom come" is from what famous passage of Scripture?
5. In the Beatitudes, Jesus referred to the _____ in spirit when he said, "Theirs is the kingdom of heaven."
6. In John's Gospel, what does Jesus say is necessary for someone to see the Kingdom of God?
7. What book of the Bible says that "the Lord has established his throne in heaven, and his kingdom rules over all"?
8. What is more likely to happen than a rich man entering the Kingdom of God?
9. Complete this verse from Matthew: "Blessed are those who are _____ for righteousness' sake, for theirs is the kingdom of heaven."
10. In Revelation, who is the "King of kings and Lord of lords"?
11. According to Paul, _____ and _____ cannot inherit the Kingdom of God.
12. What mighty king of Babylon lost his sanity for a time, then acknowledged that God alone was King of a lasting Kingdom?
13. According to Jesus, what patriarchs from the book of Genesis will be dining in the Kingdom of Heaven?
14. Which of the 12 disciples was given the "keys of the kingdom of heaven"?
15. In the Gospels, what rich man was "waiting for the kingdom of God"?
16. Jesus' followers were told that in order to enter the Kingdom of God, their righteousness would have to exceed whose?
17. What two groups of sinful people did Jesus say were entering the Kingdom of God?
18. In which Gospel does Jesus say, "The kingdom of God is within you"?
19. In Acts, what two men preached that "we must go through many hardships to enter the kingdom of God"?
20. In one of Jesus' parables, the Kingdom of Heaven is compared to a _____ hidden in a field.
21. What people did Jesus accuse of "shutting the kingdom of heaven in men's faces"?

22. Who asked Jesus the question, "Who is the greatest in the kingdom of heaven"?

23. In one of Jesus' parables, the Kingdom of Heaven is compared to the tiny seed of what plant?

24. What angel announced that Jesus' Kingdom would have no end?

25. According to Paul, what final enemy shall be destroyed before the Kingdom is fulfilled?

26. In John's Gospel, who referred to Jesus as the "King of Israel"?

27. What dying man said to Jesus, "Lord, remember me when you come into your kingdom"?

28. What group of men came to find the "King of the Jews"?

29. What was Jesus doing when people called out, "Blessed be the King that comes in the name of the Lord"?

30. Where was there a sign that read, "Jesus of Nazareth, King of the Jews"?

31. Which Epistle says that in the future, every knee shall bow and every tongue confess that Christ is Lord?

32. Complete this saying of Jesus: "Not everyone who says to me, '_____, _____,' will enter the kingdom of heaven, but only he who does the will of my Father."

33. What common kitchen item did Jesus compare to the Kingdom of Heaven in a parable?

34. According to Paul, the Kingdom of God is not a matter of talk but of _____.

35. What precious gem did Jesus compare the Kingdom to?

36. What kinsman of Jesus lived in the wilderness and preached the message, "Repent, for the kingdom of heaven is near"?

A KINGDOM GREATER THAN THIS WORLD (ANSWERS)

1. *Pilate, the Roman governor (John 18:36)*

2. *Demons (Mark 11:20)*

3. *Little children (Luke 18:16-17)*

4. *The Lord's Prayer (Matthew 6:9-13)*

5. *Poor (Matthew 5:3)*

6. *Being born again (John 3:3)*

7. *Psalms (103:19)*

8. *A camel going through the eye of a needle (Luke 18:24-25)*

9. Persecuted (Matthew 5:10)

10. The Lamb—that is, Christ (Revelation 17:14; 19:16)

11. Flesh and blood (1 Corinthians 15:50)

12. Nebuchadnezzar (Daniel 4:34)

13. Abraham, Isaac, and Jacob (Matthew 8:11)

14. Simon Peter (Matthew 16:19)

15. Joseph of Arimathea (Luke 23:51)

16. The Pharisees (Matthew 5:20)

17. The tax collectors and prostitutes (Matthew 21:31)

18. Luke (17:21)

19. Paul and Barnabas (Acts 14:22)

20. Treasure (Matthew 13:44)

21. The Pharisees and teachers of the Law (Matthew 23:13)

22. His disciples (Matthew 18:1)

23. Mustard (Matthew 13:31-32)

24. Gabriel, speaking to the Virgin Mary (Luke 1:33)

25. Death (1 Corinthians 15:26)

26. Nathanael (John 1:49)

27. The repentant thief on the cross (Luke 23:42)

28. The wise men, or magi (Matthew 2:2). By the way, the Bible does not say there were three of them. The number three is based on the three gifts presented to the baby Jesus.

29. Riding into Jerusalem on a donkey (Luke 19:38)

30. Hung on Jesus' cross (John 19:19)

31. Philippians (2:10-11)

32. Lord, Lord (Matthew 7:21)

33. Yeast (Matthew 13:33)

34. Power (1 Corinthians 4:20)

35. A pearl (Matthew 13:45-46)

36. John the Baptist (Matthew 3:2)

GOD'S POOR CHILDREN

Why are some people poor? Though some are that way because they're lazy (let's admit it), many are poor because of circumstances they can't control. The poor are not all saints, but the Bible generally looks favorably on them. How we treat the poor is a kind of "spiritual thermometer."

1. Which New Testament Epistle warns churches against treating rich folks better than poor folks?
2. Which Old Testament book forbids charging interest on loans to the poor?
3. Who told King David a parable of a poor man who had his one pet lamb taken away from him by a rich man?
4. What wealthy man, deeply moved by meeting Jesus, gave half his goods to the poor?
5. What festival of the Jews featured giving gifts to the poor?
6. What wise king said, "Better is a poor and a wise child than an old and foolish king"?
7. To whom did Jesus say, "If thou wilt be perfect, go and sell that thou hast, and give to the poor"?
8. Which of Jesus' disciples protested Jesus' anointing with oil, saying that the money spent on the oil could have been given to the poor?
9. The Christians in Greece took up a love offering for the poor Christians in what city?
10. Who said, "Though I bestow all my goods to feed the poor, and though I give my body to be burned, and have not charity, it profiteth me nothing"?
11. Who stated that, being a poor man, he couldn't possibly marry Saul's daughter?
12. Which judge of Israel protested that he wasn't fit to lead because he came from a poor family?
13. What commendable deed was done by a poor widow Jesus saw in the Temple?
14. Which prophet accused the people of Israel of selling the poor people for a pair of sandals?
15. What Christian woman was noted for helping the poor in the early church?
16. Matthew 5:3 has Jesus saying, "Blessed are the poor in spirit." What does he say in Luke 6:20?
17. What did Elisha miraculously supply a poor widow with?

GOD'S POOR CHILDREN (ANSWERS)

1. *James (2:2)*

2. *Exodus (22:25)*

3. *Nathan the prophet, who was condemning David's adultery with Bathsheba (2 Samuel 12)*

4. *The tax collector Zacchaeus (Luke 19:8)*

5. *Purim, which is told of in the Book of Esther*

6. *Solomon, who (according to tradition) is the author of Ecclesiastes (4:13)*

7. *The rich young ruler (Matthew 19:21)*

8. *Judas Iscariot (Matthew 26:9)*

9. *Jerusalem (Romans 15:26)*

10. *Paul (1 Corinthians 13:3)*

11. *David, who did indeed marry Saul's daughter (1 Samuel 18:23)*

12. *Gideon (Judges 6)*

13. *She put two mites (coins) in the Temple treasury, even though this was almost all she owned (Mark 12:42).*

14. *Amos (2:6)*

15. *Dorcas (Acts 9:36, 39)*

16. *"Blessed are the poor."*

17. *Large quantities of oil (2 Kings 4:1-7)*

HOLY U-TURNS: REPENTANCE

It's rare, but it happens: a sinner sees the error of his wicked ways and turns his life around. It so happens that the Bible has several such stories, which can be considered as miraculous as turning water into wine or walking on water. Regrettably, some of these weren't "permanent fixes," for in some cases the person made another U-turn back to his old habits.

1. Whose band of jealous brothers at long last were sorry they had sold him as a slave?
2. What wicked, idol-worshipping king of Israel repented—temporarily—after hearing a word of warning from the prophet Elijah?

3. What foreign king would always "harden his heart" again after temporarily recognizing the power of Israel's God?
4. What pagan city's inhabitants repented of their sins after the preaching of Jonah?
5. Which king repented after being confronted by the prophet Nathan with his adultery and murder?
6. What idolatrous king of Judah repented after being carried away in chains to Babylon?
7. What pagan prophet repented after being confronted by God's angel—and by his talking donkey?
8. What plague from the Lord caused the Israelites to repent of their grumbling against Moses?
9. What book of the Bible records the repentance of the Jewish men for having married foreign wives?
10. Which Gospel records that the traitor Judas Iscariot "changed his mind" after delivering Jesus to the authorities?
11. Which leader heard the Israelites beg for a king, then repent of it after he explained the problems in having a king?
12. What famous parable of Jesus concerns a very forgiving father and a young man who squanders his money?
13. Whose preaching in the wilderness led many people to confess their sins and be baptized in the Jordan River?
14. What greedy (and short) tax collector turned his life around when Jesus visited his home?
15. What distraught king confessed to Samuel that he had broken the Lord's commandment?
16. What did the new Christians of Ephesus burn to show they had parted from their heathen ways?
17. Who lamented that many of the cities where he worked miracles did not repent of their sins?
18. What converted magician was ordered to repent after he tried to purchase the power of the Holy Spirit?
19. What book of the Bible tells of people still refusing to repent of their evils even after several plagues have visited them?
20. Which disciple "went out and wept bitterly" after he had denied knowing Jesus?
21. What sin of David, which brought a plague on Israel, caused him to repent after much heartache?
22. Which of the Psalms, supposed to have been written by David, is the classic "repentance Psalm"?

23. Which prophet, who saw a vision of God in the Temple, lamented that he was an unclean man living among unclean men?
24. What great apostle always grieved that in his earlier days he had persecuted Christians?
25. Complete this saying of Jesus: "I came not to call the _____, but sinners to repentance."
26. According to Psalms, "The Lord is near to those who are of a _____ heart."
27. What wayward king of Judah repented (temporarily) after the Egyptians plundered Jerusalem?
28. Complete this verse from Proverbs: "He that covers his sins shall not prosper, but whoever confesses and _____ them shall have mercy."
29. Which king of Judah promoted a religious revival after hearing the preaching of the prophet Azariah?
30. In the book of Isaiah, the Lord says, "I have blotted out, like a thick _____, your offenses and your sins."
31. In Acts, which apostle urged people to repent "so that times of refreshing may come from the Lord"?
32. Complete this verse from the Letter of James: "Cleanse your hands, you sinners, and purify your _____, you double-minded."
33. Which Israelite confessed that he had disobeyed God's command by keeping some of the treasures from the sacking of Jericho?
34. Which king of Judah repented at the preaching of the prophet Micah?
35. What did the repentant woman do for Jesus while he dined in the home of a Pharisee?
36. In Acts 2, what gift did Peter promise those who repented?
37. What powerful Babylonian ruler turned to the Lord after going insane and living for a time like a beast?
38. Complete this verse from Psalms: "Depart from evil and do good; seek _____ and pursue it."
39. In what great pagan city were the people and even the livestock covered with sackcloth as a sign of repentance?
40. Complete this verse from Isaiah: "Let the wicked forsake his way and the unrighteous man his _____."
41. Which scribe bowed in front of the Temple and confessed the sins of Israel while the people around him wept bitterly?
42. Who confessed the making of the golden calf to God?
43. Who confessed his sexual immorality with his daughter-in-law, Tamar?

44. Who confessed Israel's sins after he heard the walls of Jerusalem were in ruins?
45. Who was pardoned by David after confessing his sin and begging for mercy?

HOLY U-TURNS: REPENTANCE (ANSWERS)

1. Joseph's (Genesis 42:21; 45:14-15; 50:17-18)

2. Ahab (1 Kings 21:27-29)

3. The Pharaoh at the time of Moses (Exodus 9:27; 10:16-17)

4. The people of Nineveh (Jonah 3:5-9)

5. David (2 Samuel 12:7-23)

6. Manasseh (2 Chronicles 33:10-17)

7. Balaam (Numbers 22:34)

8. The "fiery serpents" that caused many of them to die in the wilderness (Numbers 21:4-9)

9. Ezra (chapter 10)

10. Matthew (27:3-9)

11. Samuel (1 Samuel 12)

12. The Prodigal Son (Luke 15:17-21)

13. John the Baptist (Matthew 3:6)

14. Zacchaeus (Luke 19:6-8)

15. Saul (1 Samuel 15:24)

16. Their books of "magic arts" (Acts 19:19)

17. Jesus (Matthew 11:20)

18. Simon (Acts 8:9-24)

19. Revelation (9:20-21; 11:9-11)

20. Peter (Matthew 26:75)

21. He took a census of the people, against the Lord's will (2 Samuel 24:10-17).

22. Psalm 51, beginning "Have mercy upon me, O God"

23. Isaiah (6:5)

24. Paul (1 Corinthians 15:9)

25. Righteous (Luke 5:32)

26. Broken (Psalm 34:18)

27. *Rehoboam, son of Solomon (2 Chronicles 12:9-12)*

28. *Forsakes (Proverbs 28:13)*

29. *Asa (2 Chronicles 15:1-16)*

30. *Cloud (Isaiah 44:22)*

31. *Peter (Acts 3:20)*

32. *Hearts (James 4:8)*

33. *Achan (Joshua 7:20)*

34. *Hezekiah (Jeremiah 26:18-19)*

35. *Anointed his feet with some expensive ointment (Luke 7:36-39)*

36. *The Holy Spirit (Acts 2:38)*

37. *Nebuchadnezzar (Daniel 4:28-37)*

38. *Peace (Psalm 34:14)*

39. *Nineveh (Jonah 3:8-9)*

40. *Thoughts (Isaiah 55:7)*

41. *Ezra (10:1)*

42. *Moses (Exodus 32:31), who was confessing the Israelites' sin, not his own, because he had nothing to do with the calf idol*

43. *Judah (Genesis 38:26)*

44. *Nehemiah (1:6)*

45. *Shimei (2 Samuel 19:20)*

PART 16

AND SOME TASTY LEFTOVERS

 **CURSE YOU!**

Today we think of cursing as referring to profanity. This wasn't the case in Bible times, for people put a great deal of stock in curses: Words spoken against a person or thing had (so people believed) real power. A curse, like a blessing, would "stick." In some cases, the curses really did have power, for it was God himself who pronounced the curse.

1. Who cursed a fig tree for not bearing fruit?
2. Who was sent by the king of Moab to put a curse on Israel?
3. Which grandson of Noah was cursed for his father's sins?
4. What was the only animal to be cursed by God?
5. Who put a curse on Cain and made him a wanderer?
6. Which son of Josiah was cursed by God?
7. In what story did Jesus place a curse on the unrighteous?
8. According to Paul, what was put under a curse because of man's sin?
9. What nation did God say would have its towns and fields cursed because of disobedience?
10. What happened to the ground as a result of God's curse?
11. Who received a promise from God that all persons who cursed him would be cursed themselves?
12. According to Galatians, what people remain under a curse?
13. Who said that people who taught a false gospel would be cursed?
14. According to Paul, who was made a curse for our sins?
15. According to the Law, what sort of handicapped people should we not curse?
16. Who was told by his wife to curse God and die?
17. Which prophet ended his book with God's threat to come and strike the land with a curse?
18. Which Epistle says that blessing and cursing should not come out of the same mouth?
19. Who had enemies that bound themselves under a curse because they were so determined to kill him?
20. Who told God that Job would curse him to his face?
21. What book of the Bible says that kings should not be cursed, for little birds will tell on the cursing person?

CURSE YOU! (ANSWERS)

1. *Jesus (Mark 11:21)*

2. *Balaam (Numbers 22:1-6)*

3. *Canaan (Genesis 9:18-27)*

4. *The serpent in the Garden of Eden (Genesis 3:14-15)*

5. *God (Genesis 4:11)*

6. *Jehoiakim (Jeremiah 22:18; 36:30)*

7. *The story of the sheep and the goats (Matthew 25:31-41)*

8. *Nature (Romans 8:19-22)*

9. *Israel (Deuteronomy 28:15-16)*

10. *It brought forth thorns and weeds (Genesis 3:17-18)*

11. *Abraham (Genesis 12:3)*

12. *Those who attempt to remain under the Law (Galatians 3:10)*

13. *Paul (Galatians 1:8)*

14. *Christ (Galatians 3:13)*

15. *The blind and the deaf (Leviticus 19:14)*

16. *Job (2:9)*

17. *Malachi (4:6)*

18. *James (3:10)*

19. *Paul (Acts 23:12)*

20. *Satan (Job 1:11; 2:5)*

21. *Ecclesiastes (10:20)*

ABOMINABLE ABOMINATIONS

The word *abomination* occurs often in the Bible and refers to something that (in the words of my neighbor's young grandson) "makes God go *Ugh!*" Generally we find the word associated with idolatry, worshipping the created object rather than the Creator. But abomination goes beyond regular idolatry, all the way to something—*ugh!* In a few cases, there is great mystery about just what the abomination was, as you'll see below in questions 5 and 23.

1. What people considered it an abomination to eat with Hebrews?
2. Which Old Testament book declares that it is an abomination for a man to wear women's clothing (or vice versa)?
3. To which prophet did God say, "Incense is an abomination unto me"?
4. In which Gospel does Jesus say, "That which is highly esteemed among men is abomination in the sight of God"?
5. What woman was "the mother of harlots and abominations of the earth"?
6. What city will not have any abomination within it?
7. Whose wages would be considered an abomination if offered to the Lord?
8. What loathsome god was "the abomination of the Ammonites"?
9. What sort of lips are an abomination to the Lord?
10. Whose sacrifice is an abomination to the Lord?
11. What innocent occupation was considered an abomination by the Egyptians?
12. What sort of seafood is supposed to be an abomination?
13. What was the punishment for the abomination of homosexual intercourse?
14. King Ahaz of Judah committed what abomination with his own son?
15. What godly king expelled the sorcerers who were an abomination to the Lord?
16. What were the Israelites supposed to do with the idols of other nations?
17. What kind of animal is an abomination to sacrifice to the Lord?
18. Saul's military prowess made Israel an abomination to what people?
19. What kind of prostitutes, an abomination to the Lord, flourished under Solomon's son?
20. What wise king built pagan temples for his foreign wives?
21. What kind of scale is an abomination to the Lord?
22. What kind of heart is an abomination to the Lord?
23. Who predicted "the abomination of desolation" standing in the Jerusalem Temple?

ABOMINABLE ABOMINATIONS (ANSWERS)

1. *The Egyptians (Genesis 43:32)*

2. *Deuteronomy (22:5)*

3. *Isaiah (1:13)*

4. *Luke (16:15)*

5. *Babylon, the scarlet woman (Revelation 17:5)*

6. *The New Jerusalem (Revelation 21:27)*

7. *A prostitute's (Deuteronomy 23:18)*

8. *The god Milcom (or Molech, in some translations) (1 Kings 11:5)*

9. *Lying lips (Proverbs 12:22)*

10. *The sacrifice of the wicked (Proverbs 15:8)*

11. *Sheepherding (Genesis 46:34)*

12. *Anything without fins and scales (Leviticus 11:10)*

13. *Death (Leviticus 20:13)*

14. *Sacrificed him to a pagan god (2 Kings 16:3)*

15. *Josiah (2 Kings 23:24)*

16. *Burn them (Deuteronomy 7:25)*

17. *One with a blemish of any kind (Deuteronomy 17:1)*

18. *The Philistines (1 Samuel 13:4)*

19. *Male shrine prostitutes (1 Kings 14:24)*

20. *Solomon (1 Kings 11)*

21. *A dishonest one (Proverbs 11:1)*

22. *A proud heart (Proverbs 16:5)*

23. *Jesus (Matthew 24:15)*

 ## IN BETWEEN THE OLD AND NEW

One Bible mystery that has perplexed people for centuries is this: Just which books belong to the Bible? Your Bible may or may not contain the books known as the Apocrypha (a word that, by the way, means "hidden"). These were written in the centuries between the Old and New Testaments, and they are accepted as sacred Scripture by Catholics, Eastern Orthodox, and some other denominations. Protestant Christians have long been "iffy" about the Apocrypha, hesitant to regard the books as really inspired. One thing all Christians do agree on is rejecting the other intertestamental books called the pseudepigrapha (it means "false writings"), which are definitely *not* considered sacred. Below are one-sentence descriptions of these books written between the Old and New Testaments. See if you can identify each book based on its description.

1. A historical work that recounts the story of the Jewish revolt against the evil ruler Antiochus Epiphanes and his successors
2. A romantic story of a pious Jew whose son is aided by the angel Raphael
3. A tale of a brave Jewish woman who saves her city from the army of Nebuchadnezzar by murdering a Babylonian captain
4. A book of wisdom whose author is identified in the text as Sirach of Jerusalem
5. A book of wise sayings attributed to a king of Israel
6. A book of prayers and confessions, supposedly written by the friend of an Old Testament prophet
7. A tale of a virtuous woman accused of adultery and proved innocent by Daniel
8. An eloquent prayer reputed to be the work of a repentant king of Judah
9. A tale of Babylonian idol worship and some conniving priests
10. A historical work that covers some of the same history chronicled in Ezra, Nehemiah, and 2 Chronicles
11. This book consists of alleged predictions of Moses, given to Joshua just before Moses' death.
12. These are additions, not found in the Hebrew Bible, to an Old Testament book about the Persian period.
13. This addition to the book of Daniel contains an eloquent prayer, a miraculous deliverance, and a hymn of praise.
14. This work is a shortened form of a five-volume historical work by Jason of Cyrene. It contains letters to the Jews in Egypt.
15. This apocalyptic work contains bizarre visions, images of the Messiah, and references to the Roman Empire.
16. This book about a famous Judean prophet tells of his martyrdom under wicked King Manasseh.
17. These 18 poems about the coming Messiah are ascribed to a famous Hebrew poet.

18. This collection of predictions speaks about the downfall of empires and the messianic age.
19. This book of revelations purports to have been written by Enoch and Noah.
20. This book purports to be the dying speeches of Jacob's 12 sons.
21. Written by a Pharisee, this book extols the law and the Hebrew patriarchs and urges Jews not to be influenced by Greek culture.
22. These are loose translations of the Hebrew Scriptures into the Aramaic language, made after Aramaic, not Hebrew, was the common language of Palestine.
23. This collection of laws based on the laws of Moses was not completed until AD 500. It consists of the Mishnah and the Gemara and is still widely studied by Jewish scholars today.

IN BETWEEN THE OLD AND NEW (ANSWERS)

1. *1 Maccabees (Apocrypha)*

2. *Tobit (Apocrypha)*

3. *Judith (Apocrypha)*

4. *Ecclesiasticus (Apocrypha)—not to be confused with the Old Testament book Ecclesiastes*

5. *Wisdom of Solomon (Apocrypha), sometimes referred to simply as Wisdom (since it's fairly certain that Solomon was not the real author)*

6. *Baruch (Apocrypha)*

7. *Susanna (Apocrypha)*

8. *The Prayer of Manasseh (Apocrypha)*

9. *Bel and the Dragon (Apocrypha). In Roman Catholic Bibles, this story is part of the book of Daniel.*

10. *1 Esdras (Apocrypha)*

11. *The Assumption of Moses (Pseudepigrapha)*

12. *Additions to Esther (Apocrypha). Catholic Bibles contain this longer version of Esther.*

13. *Song of the Three Children (Apocrypha), part of the book of Daniel in Catholic Bibles.*

14. *2 Maccabees (Apocrypha)*

15. *2 Esdras (Apocrypha)*

16. *Ascension of Isaiah (Pseudepigrapha)*

17. *Psalms of Solomon (Pseudepigrapha)*

18. *Sybilline Oracles (Pseudepigrapha)*
19. *Book of Enoch (Pseudepigrapha)*
20. *Testament of the Twelve Patriarchs (Pseudepigrapha)*
21. *Book of Jubilees (Pseudepigrapha)*
22. *Targums*
23. *The Talmud*

40, THE ULTIMATE BIBLICAL NUMBER

Why does the number 40 occur so often in the Bible? No one is sure, so you might say it is a "mystery number." It is frequently used simply to express a long duration. Whatever the significance was for the biblical authors, it is used often enough in Scripture to supply us with the questions here.

1. Who was told by God that rain would fall for 40 days and 40 nights?
2. Who boasted that he had five times received the punishment of 40 lashes?
3. Who prophesied that the pagan city Nineveh would be destroyed in 40 days?
4. What wise king reigned in Israel for 40 years?
5. Who was 40 years old when he married Rebecca?
6. What did Noah release from the ark after 40 days?
7. With whom was God grieved for 40 years?
8. Who was the target of an assassination plot by 40 men?
9. Who was tempted by the devil for 40 days?
10. Which prophet asked, "Have ye offered unto me sacrifices and offerings in the wilderness 40 years, O house of Israel"?
11. Who pleaded with God not to destroy Sodom for the sake of 40 righteous people?
12. What Hebrew man was mourned by the Egyptians for 40 days?
13. What food did the Israelites eat for 40 years?
14. Who was in the midst of a cloud for 40 days?
15. What did Moses receive after being with the Lord 40 days?
16. Who explored the land of Canaan for 40 days?
17. Why did God make Israel wander in the wilderness for 40 years?
18. Which leader did 40,000 Israelites muster under?

19. Who subdued the Midianites so that Israel had 40 years of peace?
20. Who bragged for 40 days in front of the Israelite army?
21. Which king died at the age of 70 after reigning for 40 years?
22. Which prophet received a gift of 40 camel-loads of Syrian luxuries?
23. Which king slaughtered 40,000 Syrian foot soldiers?
24. Who reigned 40 years after beginning his reign at age seven?
25. Who complained that the governors of Israel had taxed the people 40 shekels of silver?
26. Which prophet was told to lie on his right side for 40 days?
27. Who fasted 40 days and 40 nights?
28. Which apostles healed a man who had been crippled for 40 years?
29. What hairy man was 40 years old when he married a woman named Judith?
30. Which leader died on Mount Hor after the Israelites had been out of Egypt for 40 years?
31. Who was ministered to by angels after 40 days in the wilderness?
32. Which prophet predicted that Egypt would lie desolate for 40 years?
33. Who went without food or drink for 40 days because he was in the Lord's presence?
34. Who was 40 years old when he became a spy for Moses?
35. Who gave Israel 40 years of peace from the Arameans?
36. Which Old Testament book sets the maximum number of lashes at 40?
37. Who died from a broken neck after he had been Israel's judge for 40 years?
38. What son of Saul became king at age 40?
39. Which king had 40,000 stalls for his horses?
40. What book of the Bible mentions that Jesus was seen for 40 days after his resurrection?
41. Which judge of Israel had 40 sons?
42. Who came to the rescue after Israel suffered under the Philistines for 40 years?
43. What notable Jerusalem building was 40 cubits long?
44. What man-and-woman military leadership team gave Israel 40 years of peace?

40, THE ULTIMATE BIBLICAL NUMBER (ANSWERS)

1. Noah (Genesis 7:4)
2. Paul (2 Corinthians 11:24)
3. Jonah (3:4)
4. Solomon (2 Chronicles 9:30)
5. Isaac (Genesis 25:20)
6. A raven (Genesis 8)
7. The Israelites in the wilderness (Hebrews 3:17)
8. Paul (Acts 23:21)
9. Jesus, of course (Luke 4:2)
10. Amos (5:25)
11. Abraham (Genesis 18)
12. Joseph (Genesis 50:3)
13. Manna (Exodus 16:35)
14. Moses (Exodus 24:18)
15. The Ten Commandments (Exodus 34:28)
16. The 12 Israelite spies (Numbers 13:25)
17. Because they had done evil (Numbers 32:13)
18. Joshua (Joshua 4:13)
19. Gideon (Judges 8:28)
20. Goliath (1 Samuel 17:16)
21. David (2 Samuel 5:4)
22. Elisha (2 Kings 8:9)
23. David (1 Chronicles 19:18)
24. King Joash of Judah (2 Chronicles 24:1)
25. Nehemiah (5:15)
26. Ezekiel (4:6)
27. Jesus (Matthew 4:2)
28. Peter and John (Acts 4:22)
29. Esau, Jacob's brother (Genesis 26:34)
30. Aaron (Numbers 33:38)
31. Jesus (Mark 1:13)
32. Ezekiel (29:12)

33. *Moses (Deuteronomy 9:9)*
34. *Joshua (14:7)*
35. *Othniel (Judges 3:11)*
36. *Deuteronomy (25:3)*
37. *Eli, Samuel's mentor (1 Samuel 4:18)*
38. *Ishbosheth (2 Samuel 2:10)*
39. *Solomon (1 Kings 4:26)*
40. *Acts (1:3)*
41. *Abdon (Judges 12:14)*
42. *Samson (Judges 13)*
43. *The Temple (Ezekiel 41)*
44. *Deborah and Barak (Judges 5:31)*

FORESEEING THE MESSIAH

Did the Old Testament prophets foresee the coming of Jesus the Messiah? Indeed they did. Many passages in the Old Testament are prophecies that were fulfilled by events in Jesus' life. For each event listed here, name the Old Testament book that contains the prophecy of the event.

1. The 30 pieces of silver
2. Jesus' crucifixion with two thieves
3. Casting lots for Jesus' robe
4. The Virgin Birth
5. Jesus' birth in Bethlehem
6. Jesus' resurrection
7. The piercing of Jesus' side with a spear
8. Not breaking the bones of the crucified Jesus
9. Betrayal by a close companion
10. Jesus' entry into Jerusalem on a donkey
11. Giving vinegar to the crucified Jesus
12. Jesus, Mary, and Joseph leaving Egypt and returning to Galilee
13. Speaking in parables

FORESEEING THE MESSIAH (ANSWERS)

1. *Zechariah 11:12: "So they weighed for my price thirty pieces of silver."*

2. *Isaiah 53:12: "He was numbered with the transgressors."*

3. *Psalm 22:18: "They part my garments among them, and cast lots upon my vesture."*

4. *Isaiah 7:14: "Behold, a virgin shall conceive, and bear a son."*

5. *Micah 5:2: "Thou Bethlehem Ephrathah, though thou be little among the thousands of Judah, yet out of thee shall he come forth unto me that is to be ruler in Israel; whose goings forth have been from of old, from everlasting."*

6. *Psalm 16:10: "Thou wilt not leave my soul in hell; neither wilt thou suffer thine Holy One to see corruption."*

7. *Zechariah 12:10: "They shall look upon me whom they have pierced."*

8. *Psalm 34:20: "He keepeth all his bones; not one of them is broken."*

9. *Psalm 41:9: "Yea, mine own familiar friend, in whom I trusted, which did eat of my bread, hath lifted up his heel against me."*

10. *Zechariah 9:9: "Behold, thy King cometh unto thee . . . lowly, and riding upon an ass, and upon a colt the foal of an ass."*

11. *Psalm 69:21: "In my thirst they gave me vinegar to drink."*

12. *Hosea 11:1: "I called my son out of Egypt."*

13. *Psalm 78:2: "I will open my mouth in a parable."*

 **MYTH MATTERS**

Critics of the Bible generally believe that the Bible's stories are just like the myths of Greek and Roman mythology—false stories, not history. Jews and Christians have not accepted that view, believing instead that the Bible records truth, not falsehood, and that the truth is rooted in history. The Greek word *mythos* meant nothing more than "story," with no judgment as to whether the story was fact or fiction. The few times it is used in the New Testament, it is pretty clear the Christian authors did not put much stock in the factuality of myths.

1. According to 1 Timothy 1:4, to what do myths lead?

2. In the book of Acts, the Christian missionaries Barnabas and Paul were confused with what two gods of Greek mythology?
3. Who warned Christians against "godless myths and old wives' tales"?
4. Which Epistle warns against "Jewish myths"?
5. What popular goddess of Greek mythology was at the center of the infamous riot in Acts 19?

MYTH MATTERS (ANSWERS)

1. *Controversies, rather than the truth of God*

2. *Zeus and Hermes (Acts 14:12-13). The two made it very clear that they were merely human, not gods.*

3. *Paul (1 Timothy 4:7)*

4. *Titus (1:14). The author, Paul, was not referring to the Old Testament, but to Jewish legends not found in the Bible.*

5. *Artemis (or Diana, the goddess's Roman name). It isn't surprising that this goddess is mentioned in the Bible, because she was probably the most widely honored of all the Greek divinities.*

 ## THE BIBLE ON THE BIBLE

To the first Christians, the "Bible" or "Scripture" referred to what we call the Old Testament, since the New Testament was still in the process of being written. Paul, John, Luke, Matthew, and the other New Testament authors possibly had no idea that they themselves were writing things that later generations of believers would consider to be God-inspired words. The questions below will test your knowledge of what those New Testament writers had to say about the Old Testament.

1. Which apostle claimed that the prophets, in writing of the coming Christ, were writing for later generations?
2. What group of Christians examined the Scriptures every day to see if Paul was telling the truth?
3. To what young pastor did Paul address his famous words on the divine inspiration of all Scripture?

4. According to Paul, who takes away the "veil" over the Old Testament?
5. Who told the Jews that the Scriptures had testified about him?
6. Where was Jesus when he taught two people how the prophets had predicted his death?
7. To what church did Paul say the Old Testament was written as a set of examples and warnings for the church?
8. In the parable of Lazarus and the rich man, what does Abraham say to the rich man who wants to keep his relatives out of hell?
9. To whom does the writer of Hebrews attribute Psalm 95?
10. Which apostle claimed that no Scripture had come about through the prophet's own efforts, but by God's will?
11. In which Epistle does Paul promote the public reading of Scripture?
12. To what foreign official did Philip teach the predictions of Jesus contained in the Old Testament?
13. In which Gospel does Jesus say that the Scripture cannot be broken?
14. To whom did Peter and John attribute the words of David in Psalm 2?
15. To whom did Jesus say, "Ye do err, not knowing the Scriptures" after they had posed a ridiculous riddle to him?

THE BIBLE ON THE BIBLE (ANSWERS)

1. Peter (1 Peter 1:10-12)
2. The Christians at Berea (Acts 17:11)
3. Timothy (2 Timothy 3:15-17)
4. Christ (2 Corinthians 3:14)
5. Jesus (John 5:39-40)
6. The road to Emmaus (Luke 24:25-27)
7. Corinth (1 Corinthians 10:11)
8. He tells him that the people have Moses and the prophets (Luke 16:27-29).
9. The Holy Spirit (Hebrews 3:7)
10. Peter (2 Peter 1:20)
11. 1 Timothy (4:13)
12. The Ethiopian eunuch (Acts 8:32-35)

13. *John (10:35)*
14. *The Holy Spirit (Acts 4:25)*
15. *The Sadducees (Matthew 22:29)*

👉 THE COLOR WITH NOTHING TO HIDE

In some ways, the world hasn't changed a bit since Bible times: We still see white as the color of purity and innocence. In the Bible, white was also the color of holiness, so in a sense it is "God's color," as well as the color of holy people.

1. Among the Israelites, what official's garments were made of white linen?
2. What book of the Bible contains the line, "Wash me, and I shall be whiter than snow"?
3. Who had a vision of a heavenly being with white hair and white clothing?
4. What book of the Bible advises people always to wear white clothing?
5. According to Isaiah, what color sins would God change to white?
6. Where was Jesus when his clothes became radiantly white?
7. In Revelation, what did the rider on the white horse bring to the earth?
8. What church was told to buy white clothes to cover its nakedness?
9. What book of the Bible mentions making robes white by washing them in blood?
10. Which Gospel says that the transfigured Jesus wore clothes whiter than anyone could ever wash them?
11. What curious object was in the hand of the person sitting on the white cloud in Revelation?
12. What servant of a prophet had his skin turned white as snow?
13. White hair on the skin was often considered a symptom of what loathsome disease?
14. Which prophet spoke out several times against "whitewashing"?
15. In Revelation 19, what is the name of the rider on the white horse?
16. The last white thing mentioned in the Bible is the _____ of God.

THE COLOR WITH NOTHING TO HIDE (ANSWERS)

1. *The high priest (Leviticus 16). Since he was mediator between Israel and God, he had to look (and be) pure.*

2. *Psalms (51:7). This is considered the Bible's great "repentance song."*

3. *Daniel (7:9)*

4. *Ecclesiastes (9:8)*

5. *Scarlet (Isaiah 1:18)*

6. *The Mount of Transfiguration (Matthew 17:2)*

7. *Conquest (Revelation 6:2)*

8. *Laodicea (Revelation 3:18)*

9. *Revelation (7:14). The blood of the Lamb (Christ) makes them clean.*

10. *Mark (9:3)*

11. *A sickle (Revelation 14:14)*

12. *Gehazi, Elisha's servant (2 Kings 5:27)*

13. *Leprosy (Leviticus 13:3). White wasn't always a good thing in the Bible.*

14. *Ezekiel (13:11-15; 22:28)*

15. *Faithful and True (19:11)*

16. *Throne (Revelation 20:11)*

Books in The Complete Book Popular Reference Series

The Complete Book of Bible Trivia contains more than 4500 questions and answers about the Bible.
ISBN 0-8423-0421-5

The Complete Book of Christian Heroes is an in-depth popular reference about those who have suffered for the cause of Christ throughout the world.
ISBN 0-8423-3485-8
Coming Spring 2005

The Complete Book of When and Where in the Bible and throughout History focuses on more than 1000 dates that illustrate how God has worked throughout history to do extraordinary things through ordinary people.
ISBN 0-8423-5508-1

The Complete Book of Zingers is an alphabetized collection of one-sentence sermons.
ISBN 0-8423-0467-3
Coming Spring 2005

The Complete Book of Who's Who in the Bible is your ultimate resource for learning about the people of the Bible.
ISBN 0-8423-8369-7
Coming Spring 2005

The Complete Book of Bible Basics identifies and defines the names, phrases, events, stories, and terms from the Bible and church history that are familiar to most Christians.
ISBN 1-4143-0169-3
Coming Summer 2005

In **The Complete Book of Bible Secrets and Mysteries** Stephen Lang, an expert in the Bible, serves up secrets and mysteries of the Bible in a fun, entertaining way.
ISBN 1-4143-0168-5
Coming Spring 2005

The Complete Book of Bible Trivia: Bad Guys Edition, an extension of Stephen Lang's best-selling book *The Complete Book of Bible Trivia*, focuses on facts about the "bad guys" in the Bible. *ISBN 1-4143-0379-3*
Coming Summer 2005